COMMON
FUTURES

"How do we replace the figure of homo economicus and his cut-throat world with that of the steward, caretaker to the living? *Common Futures* makes the compelling case that Cornelius Catstoriadis' notion of "self-limitation"—at the heart of his thinking about ecology, democracy, and the necessary relation between the two—is where we begin."

—Kristin Ross
author of *Communal Luxury*

"Tarinksi and Schismenos have produced a profoundly timely book that is essential reading. The crisis of unfettered ecological destruction through capitalism and the nation-state's synergistic exploitation of nature and promotion of destructive normalcy, produces a collective sense of hopelessness and fatalism. The alternative is a radical change towards direct democracy and political ecology, which the authors powerfully argue arises through horizontal and leaderless social movements. This is the perfect book for those who wish to make the radical shift from capitalism's despondent citizenry to that of the empowered, re-rooted, politicized consciousness. Highly recommended, and certain to be a classic."

—Dr. Hawzhin Azeez
founder of *The Middle Eastern Feminist*

"Tarinksi and Schismenos capture our unnervingly discordant experience of time. We are, on one level, stuck in the déjà vu of capitalism, where the presents just repeats itself and nothing changes, in fact nothing is allowed to change, despite surface appearances. But on another level, we are hurtling blindly towards global ecological catastrophe, fearing a future that approaches with frightening speed. To change this 'futureless present', something else is needed, something that is not enmeshed in the same mindset that it seeks to transcend."

—Mat Little
author of *The Disobedient Society*

"Mobilizing many voices of radical thought and events of rebellious practice of the last two centuries, Tarinksi and Schismenos outline a timely autonomist political ecology. Its readers will be challenged and inspired."

—Vassilis Lambropoulos
author of *The Rise of Eurocentrism*

"This is a timely book that seeks to break our present asunder, opening up the possible future of direct democracy and political ecology. Drawing force and inspiration from recent social movements which enact and agitate for a world beyond nationalism and alienated representation, the authors flesh out the political projects of direct self-institution, radical political ecology and social self-limitation, which promise to break with thez 'eternal present' of (non-) representative democracy, nation-states and the unsustainable economics of growth. This is a future of life, freedom and real democracy that we can create together, equally, collectively and rhizomatically from the grassroots, in order to overcome the present dead-ends of elite rule, consumerism, ecological devastation and global injustice."

—Alexandros Kioupkiolis
author of *Common and Counter-Hegemonic Politics: Re-thinking Social Change*

COMMON FUTURES

SOCIAL TRANSFORMATION AND POLITICAL ECOLOGY

Yavor Tarinski

Alexandros Schismenos

 Montréal/Chicago/London

Copyright ©2021 Black Rose Books

Thank you for purchasing this Black Rose Books publication. No part of this book may be reproduced or transmitted in any form, by any means electronic or mechanical including photocopying and recording, or by any information storage or retrieval system–without written permission from the publisher, or, in the case of photocopying or other reprographic copying, a license from the Canadian Copyright Licensing Agency, Access Copyright, with the exception of brief passages quoted by a reviewer in a newspaper or magazine. If you acquired an illicit electronic copy of this book, please consider making a donation to Black Rose Books.

Black Rose Books No. UU424

Library and Archives Canada Cataloguing in Publication

Title: Common futures : social transformation and political ecology / Yavor Tarinski, Alexandros Schismenos, eds.
Names: Tarinski, IAvor, editor. | Schismenos, Alexandros, 1978- editor.
Identifiers: Canadiana (print) 20200348248 | Canadiana (ebook) 20200348515 | ISBN 9781551647753 (hardcover) | ISBN 9781551647739 (softcover) | ISBN 9781551647777 (PDF)
Subjects: LCSH: Protest movements—History—21st century. | LCSH: Protest movements—Political aspects—History—21st century. | LCSH: Social movements—History—21st century. | LCSH: Social movements—Political aspects—History—21st century.
Classification: LCC HM883 .C66 2020 | DDC 303.48/4—dc23

C.P. 35788 Succ. Léo Pariseau
Montréal, QC H2X 0A4
CANADA
www.blackrosebooks.com

ORDERING INFORMATION

USA/INTERNATIONAL	CANADA	UK/EIRE
University of Chicago Press Chicago Distribution Center 11030 South Langley Avenue Chicago IL 60628	University of Toronto Press 5201 Dufferin Street Toronto, ON M3H 5T8	Central Books Freshwater Road Dagenham RM8 1RX
(800) 621-2736 (USA) (773) 702-7000 (International) orders@press.uchicago.edu	1-800-565-9523 utpbooks@utpress.utoronto.ca	+44 20 8525 8800 contactus@centralbooks.com

CONTENTS

Preface 7
  Dimitrios Roussopoulos

I. Introduction
Yavor Tarinski & Alexandros Schismenos
  Futureless Present 11
  Reclaiming the Future 16
  Political Ecology and Democratic Theory 17
  Social Movements 19

II. Political Ecology and Social Change
Yavor Tarinski
  Introduction 21
  Roots of the Contemporary Crisis 22
  The Fallacy of Economic Growth 26
  The Overpopulation Myth 31
  Ecology Beyond Narrow Technoscience 32
  Interconnectedness of Ecology and Democracy 35
  Democratic Traits of the Early Cities 41
  Toward Democratic and Ecological Cities 47
  Political Ecology in Practice 64

III. Theoretical Outlines of Direct Democracy
Yavor Tarinski

Democracy as a Regime of Self-Limitation 73
Political Parties: An Obstacle to Democracy 82
Nation-State, Nationalism and the Need for Roots 89
Time and Ideology 98

IV. The Temporality of Social Movements
Alexandros Schismenos

What Is To Be Done? Lenin's Question 109
The Question Before Us 113
Lessons From The Past: The Legacy of May '68 117
Lessons From Experience: The Brief Summer
of the Anti-Globalization Movement 131
The 2006-2007 Greek Student Movement 137
Rural Movements Toward Social Ecology 138
The Rebellious Event of December 2008 143
The Occupy Movement in Greece 148
The Rise of the Xenophobic Right 151
The Yellow Vests Against Capitalist Temporality 156
Modern Technology and Digital Movements 162

V. Conceptual Challenges
Alexandros Schismenos

The Paradoxes of Nationalistic Discourse 177
Representative Oligarchy and Democracy 182
The Temporality of Autonomy 193

Bibliography 209

PREFACE

Dimitrios Roussopoulos

"Man is by nature a political animal."
ARISTOTLE, POLITICS, BOOK I, 2

"If Liberty and Equality, as is thought, by some, are chiefly to be found in democracy, they will best be attained when all persons alike share in the government to the utmost."
ARISTOTLE, POLITICS, BOOK IV, 4

TWO EXCEPTIONAL young public intellectuals and activists, Yavor Tarinski and Alexandros Schismenos, invite us to consider their analyses and insights into our present circumstances and potential options for our common futures. Their contributions are well worth taking very seriously indeed.

Conventional politics are stuck, torn between the redundant doctrines of market or State capitalism and Keynesianism. As we face, across the planet, the pandemic plague, the collapse of Nature, social breakdown, and a gathering crisis of large scale migration, massive urbanisation, and permanent under-unemployment, neither of these current politics offers much. These State-driven economic politics are dismal, managerial politics which fail to articulate a vision of a better society. Thus, many people are again drifting and driven into the anti-politics of fascistic right-wing options. What then is urgently needed is a constructive, engaging vision that can welcome people into a politics which is social and cultural with a regenerating humanism rooted in community. And this is the promise of social ecology.

On top of all the major problems we are facing across the planet, since 2019–2020, and now into 2021, the plague has wrought changes in our society which are so far-reaching that it is impossible to imagine the course of history without it. Will we return to 'business as usual' or turn towards radical democratic alternatives away from the way things were? A year of futile strife, accompanied by economic difficulties and attendant social upheavals has led many people to question their relationship to the world around them. For a number of recent years, public intellectuals began to ask basic questions about human society and the prevailing human condition. These questions and concerns are also spoken about in various civil society movements and community associations in almost every region.

Questions like: What is the purpose of civic life when mutual aid and solidarity campaigns sprang up in various cities to help the elderly, the poor, the underclass, and the unemployed? Why have people come together, especially in communities, in the first place? Where is the conduct of cities or society given the ongoing conflict with the rhythm of nature? How are we on this side of a line called a border different from another on the other side?

Both Yavor Tarinski and Alexandros Schismenos address some of these concerns. As we grapple with the present and future, we have to acknowledge that the emergence and victories of the world's largest social movements are still in the process of unfolding. I am referring here to Occupy Wall Street, Idle No More, the Arab Spring, Black Lives Matters, and many others, that are really affecting the tide of history. Recall that all of these movements are of the same spirit of resistance, drawing from the same well, articulating a need for another society, a more open and democratic one. The people's cry is that power, all power, has to be localized in the interest of globalizing justice. History is in the present.

In considering what needs to be done, we must learn from the past to inform the present and beyond. We know that both Thucydides and Plato were critics of democracy, it should be noted that almost all the major thinkers of ancient Greece were. Fearing the destruction of the species, Zeus sent Hermes to bring *aidos* ('shame') and *dike* ('justice') to mortals. When Hermes asked Zeus whether these should be distributed to a select few, as was the case with the arts of medicine and other techniques to a select few, or to everyone, Zeus ordered him to give some to everybody, since cities cannot be formed if only a few share in these skills as they do in other arts. It is for this reason, that Protagoras says, that when the Athenians come together to make decisions that this requires a sense of justice that goes into political wisdom, 'they take advice from everybody, since it is held that for states to exist everyone must partake of this excellence.' Protagoras concludes, the Athenians do right to welcome political advice from anyone who is moved to give it. Nowhere does he suggest that everyone is equally skilled in civics, but everyone, he argues, has at least a little. And in dozens of orations surviving the fourth century, praise is offered to freedom of speech, liberty, equality before the laws, and the rule of law with justice. Our best understanding of the theory of democracy, however, is its practice (its praxis). In a word, the practice entailed active participation by all citizens, guaranteed by frequent rotation in office, in the belief that average men could make decisions, as evidenced by the use of the lot and taking important decisions in the assembly by majority vote. They believed in trial by jury, and they took measures to protect the polis from corruption, and their right to call all officials to account without exception regularly, and on the slightest pretext. They also believed, needless to add, in slavery and patriarchy.

We have much to learn from this praxis, nevertheless, and modern archaeology has uncovered much new evidence in how the citizen assembly actually functioned, concretely. Citizens' assemblies preceded, and in unexpected places, from those of ancient Greece to more sophisticated forms that the Greeks created.

Based on his reading of Hannah Arendt's *The Human Condition*, Maurizio Passerin d'Entreves's gives as an estimation of her importance:

> Arendt's theory of action and her revival of the ancient notion of praxis represent one of the most original contributions to twentieth-century political thought. …Moreover, by viewing action as a mode of human togetherness, Arendt is able to develop a conception of participatory democracy which stands in direct contrast to the bureaucratised and elitist forms of politics so characteristic of the modern epoch.

The roots of such insights are very much alive.

In their engagement as activists in the praxis of social ecology, Yavor Tarinski and Alexandros Schismenos draw on the resources from the Transnational

Institute of Social Ecology (TRISE), thus their politics attempt to merge theory and practice. In doing so what must be taken into account is that in Europe (where the TRISE is based), there are several radical currents that have emerged on the ground. These include urban movements for radical democratic and ecological shifts in various cities in France and Spain around the theme of 'the municipalisation of Europe.' While at the same time, the USA and its 'progressives and so-called left' are caught in a quagmire. Witness a political system caught in the lock-jaw of a Congress deeply divided, facing a society which is split between the centre-left and right-wing. To paraphrase the recently deceased actor Sean Connery, the Dems will be holding a knife in a gunfight. The one hopeful sign may be that the ideological gloves are finally off. Words like 'the Left', 'progressives', 'socialists' 'capitalism' are no longer banned in the US mass media. How and when the political soil will be seeded remains to be seen. When will the mass protests demanding change develop into a new politics?

Joe Biden received some 79 million votes, including 87 per cent of African-American voters. Trump won over 73 million voters, the majority being white. The elections brought out historic numbers, including over 10 million young voters. Once the reality of the Biden presidency becomes clear, however, then what will emerge? To be sure, there will be seemingly important alternative developments, here and on the other side of the Atlantic.

By many objective accounts, China within three to four years will become the world's largest economy. What does this mean concretely for our common futures?

In the meantime, let's keep our eyes on old Europe, which seems to show some promise of a break from the present and toward a new reconstruction on a transnational basis.

INTRODUCTION

Futureless Present

WHY HAVE we incorporated the term 'future' in the title of this book, one might ask. Well, most of all, because we live in a futureless present. This might seem quite strange to many, since most people today perceive time as unstoppably moving in a one-way direction. In such an imaginary representation, there is always a clearly defined past, present and future. But the reality is much different than that.

What is time? Let us take a look at our nearest clock. It is supposed to measure time, but in actuality it counts repetitive oscillations of the clock central mechanism. It assigns these measurements to homogenous time-intervals that are both the same as regards their duration and distinct as regards their position on a linear counting table. Clocks rather assign arbitrary coordinates to the temporal flow, just like a map assigns arbitrary coordinates to the planetary surface. They map natural temporality in terms of social processes, creating the artificial measured time that is distinct from the natural temporality itself; in natural time, every day is differently balanced with the night, depending on the season and the amount of sunlight; traditional agricultural societies organized their lives along these natural rhythms. But in the time of the clocks, every day is similarly divided and an arbitrary, unnatural division of temporal intervals has been established; the clocks are a symbol of the detachment of social temporality from natural time.

On the other hand, actual moments of time are neither the same nor linear, their content and value differ as regards each individual. Our subjective time is not the time of the clocks and nothing that happens in time is accounted for by the clocks. There are moments of boredom, that seem to never pass and moments of action where time seems to fly. The value content of time depends on the activity we indulge ourselves in. Our subjective time cannot be detached from the time assigned by the clocks, since we organize our everyday lives on a time-schedule determined by that arbitrary measurement of oscillations. And, even if we escape these constraints, our subjective time bears an inherent differentiation between our unconscious psychical temporality, a dream time that is neither ordained nor repetitive, nor directly accessible to us but rather felt in terms of emotional affects, and our conscious personal temporality, which is already a socialized temporality, a time devoted to our conscious interactions with others or with the world.

All those interactions create new forms of co-existence, presence, and activity, therefore creating new forms of social temporality. They create the common present in which we all live in, the social-historical locus of actual co-existence, which is not isolated, but also carries with it the representations of the past and the aspirations of the future. Time is not external to us, not only because we are temporal beings and our existence is temporally situated, but also because our actions create new forms of being, new processes of becoming, transform the past and gestate possible futures. Things change constantly, but they do not change in the same way, neither at the same rhythm. Social entities have different durations, social institutions and structures are supposed to endure, while individuals are finite. But the social present created by the social imaginary always carries with it a dimension of pastness, a public representation of history, which forms the basis of our identity, our self-identification with social significations and roles and also an orientation toward the future, which invests our actions with the meaning of foreseeable aspirations and inscribes them to a common and indefinite future horizon.

Yes, our daily experiences are being rushed by the capitalist clock. We feel as there is never enough time for all the things we have or desire to do. And this is true, as our daily temporalities are being densely fragmented in a highly precarious setting, where we have to rush from one task to another, in increasingly fragmented routines, if we don't want to fell at the bottom layers of society, among those most disempowered.

But there simultaneously is another feeling, that of time saturation, when looking at the world at longer temporal scale. We are not speaking here of history repeating itself, as argued by Marx when quoting Hegel.[1] Instead, what we have is a general feeling of Déjà vu. People grow older, things get worn out, the planet keeps spinning, but on social level things remain generally the same. Yes, governments still change, new reforms are being passed and alliances forged or disbanded etc. But the organizational form our societies have remains unchanged, often even when people try to imagine an alternative social model. This is the promise of stability and normality offered by the Capital-Nation-State complex—an oligarchic order, whose institutions remain unapt for alteration. The only choice people have to do more than just minor reforms or revoking of certain individuals is to revolt and initiate their own alternative institutions. But this is more difficult than it sounds.

Even before Fukuyama's proclamation for the end of the history we had two opposing sides, each claiming to be alternative to the other. But, in reality, they were the two faces of the same coin. Castoriadis described them as "Fragmented" (i.e. Western) versus "Totalitarian" (i.e. Soviet) bureaucratic capitalism,[2] thus underlying their sameness.

But it still seems as people remain unable to imagine a future that will go beyond that déjà vu. We hear of Degrowth, Commons, Circular economy, Zero Waste economy, etc. but all these supposedly radical new theories seem to stem from the very same imaginary they aim to challenge: Thinking of social change in economic terms.

Paolo Virno suggests that "[d]éjà vu arises when the past-form, applied to the present, is exchanged for a past-content, which the present will repeat with obsessive loyalty – that is to say, when a possible-present is exchanged for a real-past."[3] This is exactly what nation-states do as they strive to create a national identity by homogenizing their subjects—extracting certain interpretation of a particular event from the past and turn it into what McKenzie Wark calls past-in-general.[4] In the imaginary of the nation-state, the national identity is something that does not change over time. Minor developments, like those occurring in the language, are being recognized, but the present nation is seen as a direct continuation of the past. In this sense there is no really tangible future in the imaginary of the nation, only a futuristic setting in which its future generations will continue their national legacy.

Besides the feeling of déjà vu, provoked by the current status quo, the absence of future is also present on an existential level. Due to the danger of global warming, our existence as a specie on this planet has come under question. Not only will cities and other human settlements come under water, but also deserts will expand faster, displacing millions of people from their homes, creating massive waves of climate refugees. The worst thing is that there already are such.

The planetary conditions that make life as we know it possible are very fragile. The smallest climate change might have disastrous consequences and our societies are set on a course that is already overpassing the danger-zone. World governments and corporations seem unable, but also unwilling, to take any measure to tackle one of the most dangerous and existential crises in human history—the climate one. Despite thousands of international treaties, summits and agreements, we are still on a collision course with the planetary boundaries.

During the 21st century and amidst the digital and informational revolution, social time has been transformed in three important ways. First, there is an unprecedented sense of actual global temporality, emerging from the global interconnectivity provided by digital networks; this global temporality consists of a new sense of global synchronicity, which practically means that we can have direct access to events happening in other places of the world and a new sense of global diachronicity, which practically means that we can have direct access to the historical archives of other societies. This has presented current social movements with a new range and depth, since they can communicate their actions around the world, but also become points of reference for future actions elsewhere, that form a common history of emancipation against the official narratives of authority. But this diachronicity, based on the dominant informational technologies, may be more shallow than we think.

Second, there a new sense of acceleration and presentism, imposed from above with corrosive effects against collective memory. Big Data, used by companies and governments to plan the future based on the statistics of the recent past, is the driving force behind this phenomenon. Luciano Floridi has argued that the use of Informational Communication Technologies (ICT's) creates a "hyperhistory," which is the secondary interpretation of historical events based on Big Data. He debunks two myths related to hyperhistory. The first regards the quality of recorded data memory:

" 'Save this document' means 'replace its old version', and every digital document of any kind may aspire to such an ahistorical nature. The risk is that differences are erased, alternatives amalgamated, the past constantly rewritten, and history reduced to the perennial here and now. When most of our knowledge is in the hands of this forgetful memory, we may find ourselves imprisoned in a perpetual present."[5]

The second myth regards the quantity of recorded data memory:

"Since 2007 the world has been producing many more data than available storage. [...] In history the problem was what to save [...] The problem becomes what to erase And this leads to a slightly reassuring vicious circle: we should soon be able to ask big data what data are worth saving."[6]

This artificial perennial present threatens to reduce historical memory to a shallow, constantly, rewritten pastness, that does not lean on human experience but on data recordings and their interpretations. Along with systemic accelarationism, which forces social processes to speed up without pause for reflection, they form the core of systemic presentism, which obscures our collective memory of the past and leaves no time to envision a different future.

Third, this existential crisis introduces another temporality—one of urgency, brought up by the threat of global ecological catastrophe, toward which humanity is blindly running while striving to fulfill the unfulfillable systemic ambition of expansive growth and unlimited exploitation of nature and society. Urgency, on the one hand complements the system's accelerationism, bounding society in an exhausting agony between a rush for the future and a fear of the future, but on the other it has inspired social movements that rise against the system and the dreadful dystopian horizon of self-destruction that its policies have made all too real. We have to act as soon as possible, otherwise there might not be tomorrow. Future generations must also be taken into consideration as our (in)action today will directly affect the world they will inhabit one day.

This sense of urgency urges us to act toward radical change. Nation-states and their business associates respond by attempting to enforce the déjà vu effect of normality, reaching as far as deeming peaceful climate movements as terrorist.[7] Some argue that the political form, which will appropriately correspond to this urgency is the totalitarian one, as it allows for quick unchallengeable decisions to be taken—the so-called eco-fascists. But they seem to be lurking still within the contemporary imaginary, based on domination and exploitation. It is this mindset that led us exploit nature in the first place.

Reclaiming the Future

When we think of the future, we lean on our conception of the past, and our thinking takes place at the present. In every moment we reflect on time, we find ourselves both immersed in and detached from a temporal flow that seems to supersede us in every way. Immersed, since our envisioning of the future is never in nihilo or cum nihilo, but rather conditioned by our present situation, which, in turn, is framed by the past; detached, since our envisioning of the future places us on an imaginative a-temporal point of view, which functions as an imaginary escape from our past and present reality. However, neither this immersion nor this detachment is complete, since we are always present, always open to outside temporality, but also, we are always individuals, always rooted in our own personal perspective. Social time is what mediates between natural temporality and psychical temporality and the common field where our conscious individual time is formed and integrated within our collective history. No society could exist on a 'no future' assumption and the terror of such a possibility nurtures the most nightmarish dystopias.

Future dystopias are a recent social-historical construction based on a sense of collective hopelessness and a modern feeling of fatalism. But this occurs only because we are individually excluded from the central political decision-making that brings forward future possibilities. In our nation-state societies, the official past, embodied in established authorities and official historical narratives, which function as the justification mechanism for established authorities, casts its shadow over the present both as authority and as tradition. Instituted attitudes, norms and stereotypes that reproduce social inequality and exploitation invest on the repetitive dimension of temporality and try to control the future, thus securing the status quo.

But, change and alterity are immanent in time. Time passes and this passage is manifested in the emergence of alterity, the appearance of the new, the questioning of the traditional and the opening up of unforeseeable futures. Social injustice, inequality and exploitation erode the foundations of social belonging and identification with authority.

The creative dimension of time erupts without warning in rebellions, revolutions and the rise of new significations. These are the moments where the arbitrary foundations of establish authorities are exposed as such and the political question regains its full existential depth, being rephrased as a questioning of society's institution as a whole and a collective impetus toward the reclaiming of the future, which means the re-institution of the present.

So, at this moment, we, as co-existing social individuals face an unprecedented dilemma between a fervent, agonizing presentism without pause, or a different, radical present, based on the anti-systemic and humane values of equality, freedom and respect for nature. It is not a free option that we can freely decide. It is rather a cause of struggle against the system, in order to create the free public space and time where we can actually have an option. Then there are the countless grassroots movements around the world that demand a radical systemic change toward a common future for all. Sometimes consciously and sometimes not, many demand a paradigm shift oriented toward a project of direct democracy, which will allow to all people participate in the shaping of institutions and all spheres of public life. These movements provoke a break from the déjà vu effect of capitalism and nation-states and lay the foundations of a democratic and ecological future. This means that we have to radically alter our present, thus reclaiming the future.

Political Ecology and Democratic Theory

The first two chapters of the book are dedicated to exploring the theoretical outlines of political ecology and direct democracy as the foundational basis of a plethora of common futures. Both are viewed as intrinsically interconnected and timely as never before.

The first chapter is dedicated to political ecology. As a rich body of theory and practice, it is crucial for understanding the root causes of the ongoing climate crisis and environmental degradation. Through the lens of political ecology, the ecological catastrophe we are facing is not due to some naturally occurring events, or something which humanity did recently. Its roots span long before the emergence of capitalism, back to the first traces of patriarchy and gerontocracy. In other words, it is the early forms of domination and oppression that have gradually shaped humanity's imaginary to obtain a sense of pseudo-mastery over nature and exploit it.

Political ecology also goes beyond contemporary fallacies like economic growth and overpopulation scaremongering as they both aim to maintain the contemporary regime. Furthermore, it is not a scientific discipline, but instead it has to do with the ability of human societies to self-limit their activities in relation to nature. In this sense, ecology is essentially political and is interlinked to democracy, as they both involve active social self-limitation.

The second chapter thus introduces us to certain theoretical outlines of direct democracy. The term direct is being used as to indicate the active and participatory nature of democracy. In this sense there is a clear distinction that must be made between the current oligarchic regime and democratic theory and practice. To equate the contemporary parliamentary system with democracy means to strip the term from any real meaning as then everything can be described as democratic—from constitutional monarchies like the UK until the Zapatista caracoles and Rojava's cantons. The absurdity of describing as democratic every liberal oligarchic system is evident from one such comparison.

As it is defined by Rousseau, direct democracy, first and foremost, is a regime of self-limitation. This implies that the whole citizenry will take an active part in the law-making, self- instituting and all the limitations that will be set before their actions. The essential difference with the current regime is that it will be through a process that allows to all members of society to participate and voice their concerns, proposals etc., unlike the current setting, in which it is governmental elites, consisted of professionalized politicians and technocratic elites, that do that behind closed doors or as part of media spectacle.

The project of direct democracy is incompatible with the current parliamentary regime and its tools. In this line of thought political parties are viewed as obstacles to democratic self-management, as they tend to become entities interested mainly with their hold on power. The concept of the need for roots is also presented as an integral part of direct democracy. Unlike capitalism and nationalism, who both uproot people from their organic communities, democracy strives at rooting people through the detaching of politics and history from the sterilization of the Nation-State and linking them instead to the organic experience of life in our cities, towns and villages.

Finally, there is the question of ideology. In the last piece of chapter two, we attempt to differentiate politics from ideologies. Exploring the works of diverse thinkers, ranging from the Situationist International, Friedrich Nietzsche, Cornelius Castoriadis and Claude Lefort, a clear distinction is being drawn. While ideology is being presented as an imaginary that saturates space and time, hindering the flow and clash of ideas, direct democracy comes as the exact opposite—the creation of public space and time, in which history is being viewed as creation and dissensus is being maintained.

The target of chapter two is to find the common linkages between democracy and ecology and to suggest that tackling environmental catastrophe requires collective efforts from below. In this way, it paves the way for the following chapter that focuses on the specificities of concrete social practices and movements.

Social Movements

The agents of radical change in our time are neither political parties nor traditional forms of organized struggle, like the syndicate, but rather horizontal and leaderless social movements, that move beyond representative politics. During the 21st century, grassroots social movements have manifested their power in rebellions and insurrections that seem to erupt successively throughout the globe. From the anti-globalization or alter-globalization movements of the early 2000s to the insurrections in Chile and Hong Kong that began in 2019 and continued well into 2020, societies rebel against State and corporate politics. The common features of these rebellions are their use of ICTs to globally diffuse their message, the absence of formal leaderships and their horizontal, direct democratic manner of organisation. Another, emergent common property is that refute and refusal of traditional representation mechanisms, thus formulating informal channels of communication that bridge the local and the global, the particular and the universal, transgressing the national level of state politics. However, they face an array of problems, ranging from traditional ones, like how to defend themselves against state oppression and violence, to new ones, like how to address issues of representation, decision-making and decision-enactment. Direct democracy and community seem to provide a fertile ground for solving those issues, albeit the historical forms that both direct democracy and community have taken in the past, namely the commune-form seem inadequate. Modern communities cannot be closed in themselves but need to remain open to the world, whereas direct democracy cannot be locally restricted, since there are social and environmental problems that transcend locality. A possible answer can be found in the form of social transnational networks, supplemented by the new digital network technologies. But there is neither place not time to freely experiment with these, without a direct confrontation with established authorities.

We devoted the second part of the book to a research on the temporal, contextual, and conceptual challenges raised by the recent social movements of our century, focusing on our experience in Greece and Europe. In the third part, we present a brief timeline and description of Greek and French social movements, starting from their historical rooting in the 1960s and before and proceeding to examine their qualitative elements as they struggle against the establishment toward a common future, as we engage in a theoretical dialogue with thinkers such as Jacques Ranciére, Kristin Ross, Cornelius Castoriadis, Murray Bookchin, and others.

In the fourth part, we delineate some of the conceptual challenges that these movements have faced or brought about, like the questioning of nationality, representation and temporality in terms of freedom, equality, ecology, social, and individual autonomy. The convergence of direct democracy and social ecology in a free public space and time seems to be the necessary ground from which we can collectively, equally and deliberatively project the radical horizon of a common future.

Yavor Tarinski & Alexandros Schismenos,
Athens, July 2020

NOTES
1 Karl Marx, *The Eighteenth Brumaire of Louis Bonaparte.*
2 The Castoriadis Reader, ed. David Ames Curtis, London: Blackwell, 1997, pp. 218-238.
3 Paolo Virno, *Deja vu and the end of history.* London: Verso Books, 2015, p. 18.
4 https://publicseminar.org/2015/02/virno-and-history/
5 Luciano Floridi, *The 4th Revolution*, 2014, Oxford: Oxford University Press, p. 20.
6 Ibid. p. 23.
7 https://www.theguardian.com/environment/2020/jan/27/terror-police-list-extinction-rebellion-shared-across-government

I. Political Ecology and Social Change

Yavor Tarinski

INTRODUCTION

> [I]t is one thing to establish international treatises, national laws, and environmental ministries and agencies; it is quite another to effect the concrete changes in attitudes, practices and institutions necessary to resolve the ecological crisis.
> DIMITRIOS ROUSSOPOULOS[1]

NOWADAYS, the need to act against the ongoing environmental degradation seems more than evident, as well as its relatedness to other social, political, and economic problems that we are facing today. From marginal activist groups to governments of the strongest countries on the planet, all appear to be concerned with how the future of our shared world will look like. However, what does not seem so obvious is how we are going to deal with the deepening ecological crisis.

The mainstream environmentalist strategy, strongly propagated by governments and big business, strives at situating the current ecological challenges on the level of nation-states and global markets. According to it, it is the national governments and the multinational corporate players, the very ones responsible for the current mess in the first place, that should agree on how to protect nature. For many years, a significant part of the environmental movement had its imaginary entangled with the bureaucratic dynamics of political parties or green consumerism. But renowned author Dimitrios Roussopoulos masterfully points at the inability of nation-states and intergovernmental technocratic institutions to successfully tackle the crisis, despite thousands of international agreements and protocols:

"In 1886, the first international environmental agreement was signed; today there are over 250 agreements, most of them concluded since the 1960s. Since the 1972 United Nations conference on the environment in Stockholm, almost all-important international bodies, from the Organization for Economic Cooperation and Development to the World Bank, have adopted environmental protection programs. Since the Stockholm conference, some 10,000 new environmental groups have come into being adding to some 15,000 such groups that had been formed prior to the conference.[2] [...] [T]he state management of the environment, along with the rigmarole of intergovernmental institutions and agreements, have overwhelmingly failed."[3]

It is clear that it is up to the people themselves, in their role as active citizens, to organize on grassroots levels and bring a holistic change that will create a more democratic and ecological future. This is the very essence of political ecology. But, for such a horizontal strategy to be initiated, one must first understand the social and political roots of the environmental crisis, the relationship between ecology and direct democracy, and then to move on to analyzing and researching ongoing struggles and social movements that already have made practical steps in this direction.

Roots of the Contemporary Crisis

Domination and Oppression

"The notion that man must dominate nature emerges directly from the domination of man by man."
MURRAY BOOKCHIN[4]

The mainstream environmentalist opinion, strongly propagated by governments and big business, strives at identifying the primary ecological challenge as being the preservation of wildlife or wilderness, while blaming overpopulation, technological development or individual behaviour. This view, however, seems highly unsatisfactory. If we begin examining the roots of various sources of environmental degradation, we will see the systemic nature of the problem. Behind massive oil spills in oceans, extensive deforestation of rainforests, pollution of air etc., is the capital-nation-state complex and its crusade for more power and domination. For this reason, Murray Bookchin has concluded that the real battleground on which the ecological future of the planet will be decided is clearly a social one.[5]

On Hierarchy and Domination

The ongoing environmental crisis is rooted in the social relations of hierarchy and domination. It can be argued that the human feeling of superiority over nature has been developing hand-in-hand with the idea of superiority of one man over another. Thus, the domination over nature precedes capitalism, unlike some trends of eco-socialists would like to believe.

Thinkers like social ecologist Dimitrios Roussopoulos and the Kurdish revolutionary Abdullah Öcalan have been arguing that the phenomenon of elites attempting to dominate over nature and other people can be traced back to the rise of patriarchy and gerontocracy. The gradual enslavement of the young by the old and of the woman by the man led to major shift in social imaginary: There was a replacement of feminine conceptions of symbiosis within society and with nature by masculine conceptions of strong authority and exploitation.

With the emergence of statecraft, domination and hierarchy were further internalized by society through the bureaucratization of everyday life, imposed by the State. Bureaucratic management dehumanized people by turning them into taxpayers and vote casters, while destroying the traditional organic relation communities had with the land and the commons.

Environmental degradation was much worsened when older forms of domination and hierarchy were compounded with capitalism. The capitalist trend toward unlimited economic growth and utilitarisation of everything increased exponentially the destruction of ecosystems. This was so because the synthesis of the State with capitalism established a system of domination with global dimensions which views life as insignificant and in narrow utilitarian manner. Business elites and ruling politicians formed global stratum, whose power expands over the entire planet and those on it, creating preconditions for unseen exploitation, both of nature and human beings.

Social Structures and Nature

The way our societies view and treat nature is reflecting the way they are being socially structured. Thus, in the current reality of social stratification, where a narrow stratum manages and exploits the vast majority of the population, dominates the idea of humanity's pseudo-mastery over the vast world of complex ecosystems that covers the planet. But it also means that our social relations can be radically restructured so as to reflect the complexity of the natural world.

The primitive people of ancient times lived in what Bookchin called "organic societies," i.e. communities whose members had non-hierarchical and highly egalitarian relations with each other and with the surrounding environment. They were not patriarchal, but "metricentric," which does not mean that they were run by women, but that they had internalized "feminine" values like care and mutual aid.

Later on, societies became more centralized and authorities emerged that regarded those they ruled, and the land they ruled over, as inferior. Ancient Athens was an important exception to this trend, because of a political project that emerged among its people—direct democracy. Athenian democratic politics created space of equality between men and respect for nature.

Athenians created a system through which citizens directly managed the public affairs of their city and chose their magistrates by lot. And while they did not allowed women to participate in political deliberation, and neither abolished slavery, something that definitely shouldn't be overlooked, it is important to note that in most places of the ancient world exclusion of women and slaves from public life was very common. What was exceptional for its time was the notion of democracy: The idea that ordinary people, without titles or professional skills, can participate consciously and equally in the management of their society. On this last point, Bookchin noted that the Athenian experience represented an advance over the primitive organic societies.[6]

Athenians were conscious of the consequences their acts could have on nature, thus adopting an attitude of stewardship. They viewed themselves as stewards, i.e. not masters or exploiters, but beings who depend on the natural environment, hence responsible for its protection and sustenance. This was an attitude that highly resembled direct democracy. People like Theophrasus, who came to Athens at an early age, regarded the interaction of society with nature as relationship between two autonomous equal entities.[7]

There is such exception also today, one of whom is located at the heart of the war-torn Middle East—these are the communities of Northern Syria or Rojava, who are under the constant threat of the current authoritarian regime of Turkey. The emancipatory project that these societies are building is called Democratic Confederalism and it is based on three pillars: Autonomous society, ecological sustainability, and gender equality.[8] Out of the rubbles of war-torn cities, the people of Rojava launched an ecological campaign to "Make Rojava Green Again."[9] Through it they aim at addressing and dealing with issues related to cultivation of food beyond monocultures and chemical fertilizers, reforesting large swaths of land, providing alternative forms of sustainable electricity, limiting fossil fuel usage, preserving water supplies, and even developing waste management solutions.

Fighting Environmental Degradation

To successfully tackle the ongoing environmental crisis, we need to go beyond green reforms, whose aim is to only maintain the status quo. The current dominant imperatives of grow-or-die economism and exploitation, even in greener forms, will always be degradive to our common world. We need to focus on the root-cause of the problem.

All forms of domination, not just capitalism or statecraft, must be confronted by collective action and by major social movements that challenge the social (and thus political) sources of the ecological crisis, not simply by individualistic forms of greener consumption or New Age spiritualism, but by the creation of spaces of popular participation and sustainability. An important strategy in this direction can be the concept of Libertarian Municipalism, introduced by Bookchin in the 1980s, according to which people should liberate their neighborhoods and cities by managing them collectively through popular decision-making bodies, simultaneously connecting them in democratic confederations.

Such an approach does not require a Grand Revolution for it to take place but can begin taking shape here and now. Every workplace, educational institution, neighborhood square or condominium can become a political arena in which domination and hierarchy to be challenged. The seeds of one democratic and ecological future are already being planted by social movements and communities around the world and it is up to each one of us to help them flourish.

Janet Biehl has posed the dilemma of our time to be "Ecology or Catastrophe." If it is to avoid the latter and embrace the former, we need to democratize our societies to such a degree, so there will be not even the slightest trace of domination and hierarchy. Nothing more, nothing less.

The Fallacy of Economic Growth

"The insistence on work and production is a malign one."
Giorgio Agamben[10]

The contemporary engine of domination is being called economic growth. We are being told by all dominant institutions that we always need more of it in order to overcome the present multi-layer crises. Actually, we have been hearing this for quite some time now. Both right and left, capitalist and socialist governments, offer their theories about how we need more production and consumption, in order for our societies to progress and overcome the present difficulties.

The Narrative of Constant Economic Growth

But a question arises—isn't our economy already more than big enough? Our production and consumption levels are already outgrowing our planet's biocapacity by nearly 60% each year.[11] Constantly expanding, material extraction and consumption on a global scale have peaked to almost 70 billion tonnes annually.[12] And the current projections show that this rapid growth will continue—it is expected that, by the year of 2100, we will be producing three times more waste than we do today.[13]

This constant process of large-scale resource extraction and consumption has triggered a severe degradation of nature. Scientists are warning us that we are witnessing the greatest mass extinction of species in more than 65 million years.[14] Due to human economic activity, a climate change has been set in motion (with each year passed being hotter than the previous) that threatens to trigger large-scale displacement of people (climate refugees). In many parts of the world, soil fertility is being degraded by GMO crops, while water and air are being polluted to levels dangerous for human health. Whole islands consisting of garbage are being formed above the deepest points of our oceans.[15] The list goes on and on. Having said this, we can go as far as to talk of a war on nature.

It is not clear how we will be able to reverse the ecological crisis provoked by the Anthropocene if we continue down the same path. The global leaders admit the problem and call for keeping CO_2 emissions down, in order to keep up with the "below 2 degrees Celsius" requirement,[16] while paradoxically insisting on more resource extraction, industrial production, long-distance shipment, consumption etc.

According to the dominant narrative, we need economic growth, even at the price of irreversible ecological catastrophe, in order to cope with inequality and poverty. And here, another question arises—with the growth acquired until now we should have made some significant progress in this direction, shouldn't we?

Instead, in most contemporary societies, despite their growing economies, there is an increase in inequality. According to Jason Hickel, from the London School of Economics, the world's richest 1% have increased their profits by 60% for a period of more than a decade before the 2008 financial crisis,[17] during which global economic inequality was rapidly rising—a period of constant economic growth on a global scale.

This is so, because economic growth does not indicate general social wellbeing. If a few bankers get much richer, the indicator of average income can go up, even as most individuals' incomes are declining. The growing indebtedness also potentially can contribute to economic growth, as was the case of Ireland, before it descended into crisis. For example, if the incomes of the slum dwellers rise, it will be an insignificant gain for the economic sector, while the same does not apply for the richest strata of society, whose expanding piece of the economic 'pie' consists of most of the global economy.

These negative effects of the doctrine of constant economic growth were already noticed in 1897 by Errico Malatesta, who in his book *At the Café* wrote[18] "These evils [social inequality, poverty, unemployment] generally are more intense in countries where the industry is more developed, except if the workers themselves didn't manage, through organizing at the working place, resistance or revolt, to achieve better living conditions."

The Paradigm of "Fair Growth"

The Left's interpretation of the growth doctrine[19] comes with the promise of more just sharing of the economic "pie." But still, as if it is not already big enough, it must grow further. It is unclear why this should happen and why we cannot just share the plenty we already have. Is the ruling Left just trying to buy itself more time in power?

The poster child of "left-winged" growth is the so called *progressivismo* of Latin America. It is based on the paradigm of supposedly progressive governments conducting large-scale extractivist policies, in order to improve the general wellbeing of society. Despite the obvious ecological costs such projects usually have, it is also worth noticing the negative effects that they have on rural and Indigenous communities.[20] By the enclosure and commodification of common-pool resources which accompany the extractivist policies, traditionally sustainable ways of life are made practically impossible, thus forcing the members of these communities to search for livelihoods in megalopolises, often ending up in the urban slums.

For the enrichment of the metropolitan middle and upper classes, sustainable ways of life are being sacrificed. And what are they being sacrificed for—for a life of increasing dependence in an unhealthy environment. That's why much of the critique and resistance against the pink-tide in Latin America is coming from those located at the bottom of the pyramid—the Indigenous communities, the first that are being sacrificed in the name of "progress."

We can assume therefore that economic growth is incompatible with ecological and self-sustainable ways of life. In order to continue growing, the modern economy needs to absorb as much commons as possible, making impossible human interactions outside of it. Some, such as Google and Facebook, the two fastest growing corporations in the history of capitalism, are going as far as to commodify our very existence in the datascape, squeezing our digital life for surplus value.[21] And by doing this, economic growth actually strengthens the capitalist system, which is, alongside the state apparatus, responsible for the deepening social inequalities.

Thus, the Left's promise that constant economic growth could lower the current levels of inequality and poverty is at least unrealistic. We can assume that in reality it is nothing more than a move that strives at getting them to position of power by giving hope. On the one hand, it is a promise toward the many that are in need, stricken by the crisis. On the other—toward the richest strata, promising them that the current social imbalances will not be disturbed.

But even if somehow reduction of poverty and inequality is being achieved in the distant future through constant economic growth, it will be at the price of irreversible environmental changes that will affect human health, like the unbreathable air of the Chinese megapolises, or the inflammable water in American towns where shale-gas fracking is taking place. But there will be a cost also on the socio-political level. In this process self-sufficient and democratic ways of life will be sacrificed and absorbed by unstable capitalist entities and the state that strive to commodify and bureaucratize everything. Thus, alternative approaches will be pushed even further away from the social imaginary.

Overcoming Economism

Instead, we should abandon the growth doctrine altogether and direct our attention at the already existing enormous economic "pie." There is no point at enlarging it even further; on the contrary, if we want to have any future on this planet, we will have to de-grow it. But this can have meaning only if we decide to share it equally. And this cannot be done by the state or other hierarchical extra-social structures, for equality require equal participation in the decision-making by all citizens. Thus, here we speak for major paradigm change: an altogether abandonment of the capitalist economism of *homo economicus* and embracement of the social ecology of active citizens, impassioned about public affairs and conscious of their symbiotic relationship with nature.

This implies that, instead of elected representatives, economic oligarchs or artificial economic indicators to determine where the pieces of the economic "pie" should go, this should be done by interconnected direct-democratic institutions like popular assemblies and councils of revocable delegates that give the opportunity for direct participation to every member of society.

In such a way, actual social, individual, and environmental needs, reflected by the above-mentioned deliberative bodies, will direct the size and purpose of economic activity. Therefore, already existing and functioning technologies could be put to serve people and nature, reducing the workday and creating more time for creativity, philosophy, politics, art, enjoyment etc. Energy could be acquired through decentralized and renewable means, fostering local self-sufficiency and sustainability. Tools and devices could be made long-lasting, by designing them to be upgradable, rather than replaceable. All these and many more are already possible with the current state of our development.

The rejection of economic growth does not mean a retreat to primitivism, but rather a different use and understanding of what we already have and will acquire in the future. Scientific research and experiments need not cease taking place, but they shouldn't be navigated by the economism of short-term profits for the few, but by the general commonwealth of people and nature. And this includes conscious self-limitation, i.e. the possibility of society itself to decide, in a deliberative manner, which directions to progress in and what technology (or knowledge) should be dealt with cautions, or even restrained.

Here, it is worth noticing that the technological progress that is being praised by the advocates of capitalism and economic growth is, quite possibly, not their strongest side. In his book *Utopia of Rules*, David Graeber points at the unfulfilled popular hopes of technological miracles we should have acquired by now. Instead, the imperative of constant economic growth, bureaucratic hierarchy and short-term market competitiveness have made companies and scientists indulge mainly into developing information technologies,[22] i.e. technologies of simulation, or what Jean Baudrillard and Umberto Eco call "hyper-real"—the ability to make imitations more realistic than the original. Thus, real advance in this field was replaced by a spectacle.

Grassroots Resistances to Economic Growth

We can already see that in many parts of the world projects aimed at enforcing economic growth, are being met with hostility from local communities. From India's farmers burning GMO crops, which are degrading their land, to Indigenous and environmental groups in the US that have managed during the last couple of years to stop some mega-projects—like the Keystone XL and the North Dakota pipeline, that were supposed to transfer large quantities of oil over drinkable water sources, putting in danger the lives of the locals.

But, even in the countries that can be considered as pioneers of the "Fair Growth" concept we see such reactions. In Bolivia *comunarios* (communal peasants)[23] are protesting against the government's extremely extractivist policies that are contributing to the warming of the climate and the drought that impoverishes local farmers. In Ecuador, Indigenous and ecological movements have gained such a momentum, that Correa's administration went as far as to criminalize environmental activism, classifying it as "terrorism."[24]

We can conclude that economic growth, either Right or Left, cannot solve the present social problems. Instead it strengthens capitalism and statist hierarchies, which only deepen the roots of the present crisis. For their successful tackling a completely different paradigm is needed, one that will not aim at cursory "fix-ups", but will deal with the real causes of our problems in a holistic manner. We all need to support and participate in such struggles and movements by connecting them with each other, introducing them to alternatives like decentralizing power, giving it back in the hands of interconnected local communities, and making all of us conscious of our dependence on nature.

THE OVERPOPULATION MYTH

The idea of overpopulation has been with us for a long time, and has often been used by apologists for the wealthy classes to decry the excess of poor people in the world.
BRIAN TOKAR[25]

Another fallacy, which is being spread today and works to preserve the status quo is overpopulation as a driver of climate extinction. This logic is based on the relics of eugenics and racism, and it basically suggests that 'more mouths to feed' automatically means a ravishing of the planet's resources to the full. This analysis wrongly presumes that all people on the planet have an equal access to its resources and are therefore all equally guilty for the environmental devastation we see today. After just a quick fact check, one can easily see that this is obviously not the case.

The "Overpopulation Myth" highlights low-income countries in the Global South as a driver of environmental degradation, indirectly implying that their cultures are somewhat inferior to the Western civilization. In reality, however, it is exactly these rich "first-world" countries that do most of the pollution.

In fact, the poorest half of the global population, some 3.5 billion people, are responsible for only around 10% of global emissions (while living overwhelmingly in the countries most vulnerable to climate change).[26] According to the Hampton Institute, "The richest 10% of people in the world are responsible for around 50% of global emissions. There are 7.7 billion people. 95% of us occupy only 10% of the land. We produce enough food to satisfy 10 billion people and can double that, in a more sustainable way. We have a profit & distribution problem (capitalism), not a people problem."[27]

The advocates of the threat of overpopulation draw their arguments from Malthusian works like Paul Ehrlich's "The Population Bomb", spreading racist ideology in the environmental movements. This logic cultivates within Northern climate activists a certain feeling of superiority—they perceive themselves as planetary guardians who have to enlighten the people least likely to contribute to climate extinction on family planning for a sustainable future while forgetting the devastating impact Northern lifestyles have had historically and presently on the climate.

This helps shift the blame from the impact domination and oppression have on society and nature to those most disempowered and least responsible for the current situation. It is the same scapegoat logic that allows to the current capitalist oligarchic system to continue existing.

Political ecology, on the other hand, urges us to centre our environmental struggles on transnational and intergenerational climate justice. That means righting the historical wrongs that have created the situation we see today and that will continue to fuel the devastation of the world's most vulnerable populations, which necessarily include radical social change.

Ecology Beyond Narrow Technoscience

> *[T]he passivity of contemporary man rests*
> *on the following imaginary signification:*
> *technoscience as capable of resolving problems in his stead.*
> Cornelius Castoriadis[28]

One of the contemporary arguments that keep our society from adopting a more ecological attitude is technoscience—the idea that we can place our faith in the hands of technology without implying any form of social limitations.

Contemporary technoscience has become the practical equivalent of religion. It has managed to reinforce the dominant ideological mystification in a time in which authority has become ostensibly desacralized. If, in the past, the power of the ruling elites was explained through its divine God-given origin, today it rests on the scientific knowledge that they claim to posses and allows them to continue their destructive activities. This is an evident form of domination, which derives from ancient times and the emergence of gerontocracy (the power of the all-knowing elders over the unknowing youth).

The emerging new totalitarian forms are being described as technocracies—rule by experts and scientists. And the very structure of contemporary techno-science resembles the dominant organizational structure of society—that of heteronomy.

The depth that this logic has reached is even more evident from the space that it occupies among youth countercultures. If in the 1960s, they were deeply submerged into radical politics from below, modern-day hacker culture, for example, has given birth to supposedly-alternative tendencies like the Zeitgeist movement, in which technological and scientific expertise has replaced popular self-instituting, thus essentially reproducing the heteronomous nature of the present system.

Like religious sacralized regimes of the past, contemporary technocracies claim to know what the people actually "need." They can calculate it through the means of science and deliver it through economic growth and extraction. But what they actually do is to express the needs, embedded in one specific imaginary. In reality we can say that there are no predetermined natural human needs. Every society creates its needs and the means for their satisfaction. For one truly religious person, the ultimate need is to make a pilgrimage to a holy (to his faith) place, spending all his savings if required. For the anthropological type of capitalism, the need to constantly replace his belongings and gadgets with newer ones that are slightly different and supposedly improved, seems as unquestionable and as natural as their very existence. Thus, "need" is a social construct that can be altered.

If this paradigm today manages to function it is because it can still successfully manage to provide the means for satisfaction of the needs that it fabricates. And the debate between the two opposing fractions for the seats of power—the Right and the Left—is centred on this matter. The right-wingers advocate market deregulation as engine of growth, while the leftist forces often tend to blame the current close ties between multinationals and governments for the lessened buying power of local populations and promise, if elected to power, to fix that. And both sides insist on the scientific nature of their claims. In this sense the current paradigm is less threatened by traditional ideological criticism, rather than from the danger of running out of oil, for example.

Castoriadis took issue with the absence of prudence and the inability of our societies to take precautions when transforming the world. If scientific research cannot determine with certainty whether something harms the environment irreversibly, then precautionary limitations should be established with a political, direct-democratic process, he argued. Ecology therefore is incompatible with the current technocratic approach. As Castoriadis suggested,

> "…profound changes must take place in the psychosocial organization of Western man, in his attitude toward life, in short, in his imaginary. The idea that the sole goal of life is to produce and to consume more—an idea that is both absurd and degrading—must be abandoned; the capitalist imaginary of pseudorational pseudomastery, of unlimited expansion, must be abandoned. That is something only men and women can do. A single individual, or one organization, can, at best, only prepare, criticize, incite, sketch out possible orientations."[29]

Just as contemporary techno-science has become sacralized, however, ecological thinking can evolve into a new religious cult or neo-fascist ideological project, too. The Nazis turned human health into a dogma that led to the extermination of thousands of people with disabilities. Faced with environmental catastrophe, one can imagine the birth of an authoritarian regime that will impose draconian restrictions in the name of preserving nature. Hence Castoriadis proposes to integrate ecology into a political project that goes beyond narrow concerns for nature. Such politics will not be based on romantic, mystic notions of the love for Mother Gaia or the superiority of pristine nature over technology and science. Instead, it will take into account the balance between humanity and the planet, without glorifying the one and diminishing the other. Ecological politics should recognize that for the continuation of our species, we do not have to abandon technology and science, but find out a position within the fragile planetary conditions.

The future seems uncertain. The environmental crisis develops into an existential crisis. It is difficult for one to remain optimistic with all the negative predictions coming from scientists. Some claim that what we need is new technological innovations. But as Castoriadis has demonstrated, this will not prevent ecological catastrophe. An existential crisis requires creative human power to draw a new direction—a drastic paradigm change—to navigate humanity toward completely new direction, based on collective stewardship and not domination.

INTERCONNECTEDNESS OF ECOLOGY AND DEMOCRACY
Theoretical Outlines

> An ecological conscience, aware that we inhabit, with all mortal beings, the same living sphere (biosphere). Recognizing our consubstantial bond with the biosphere we can give up the Promethean dream of dominating the universe and nurture our aspiration for conviviality on this earth.
> EDGAR MORIN[30]

Philosopher Murray Bookchin saw the interconnectedness of humanity and the natural environment around us. He wrote that "human nature is derived from nonhuman nature and social evolution from natural evolution."[31] We can agree with him, by suggesting that nature is the body of all living beings, including humans. Humans are part of it and are not necessarily destined to dominate it. Instead, they can assume a more symbiotic and ecological role—that of the steward.

Nature has a multidimensional effect on human life and is essential for the development of culture and identity. It is the source of food, housing, and all other material needs of life but its significance spreads beyond that. As

French philosopher Simone Weil suggests, despite the purely physical human needs, there are also ones that are related to the soul.[32] And nature played an important role in this second category, providing inspiration, motivation and creativity for human imaginaries.

One can argue that ecology echoes democracy in the relationship it implies between humans and space. In the former, there is direct relation between human beings and their surrounding natural environment, while the former, that there is direct relation between individuals and their social setting.

Unfortunately, our societies today are organized in heavily non-ecological and non-democratic basis. This is due to the fact that the main incentives today are domination and the paradigm of constant economic growth, which are always unsustainable and environmentally degrading. The current growth-based model's main aim is the continuous commodification of resources, natural elements, even human relations. There is constantly decreasing space for communal, sustainable and democratic ways of life, which are detached from capitalist markets and state control. Furthermore, the very idea of such alternatives is being made more and more distant from the social imaginary.

The way of life imposed on us by the capital-nation-state complex implies the disconnection of people from their natural, social and cultural heritage, promoting instead detached and individualistic lifestyles. This produces an existential crisis which, as Simone Weil explains,[33] uproots individuals from their organic communities and solidarity-based relations. In this way, a fertile ground is being provided for xenophobic and nationalist sentiments. Such uprootednes creates anthropological type that is much more amenable to exploitation, consumption and mob mentality—all ingredients for an authoritarian and oppressive political system. Statecraft and the current capitalist order detach people from each other by introducing mundane bureaucratic procedures and financial speculations in the social relations, thus degrading them into nothing more than transactions between consumers.

While the system today tries to separate society from nature, many oppressed communities find expression of their resistance in the latter. For them the natural world stands for the creative and vibrant organic social bonds that are threatened by the bureaucratization and privatization of life. Nature is at the heart of the struggles of Indigenous people from Latin

America, Middle East, and elsewhere, whose history of colonization by foreign invader coincides with the exploitation of the environment.

The degradation of nature has serious impacts on humans; thus, it can be viewed as social degradation as well. The effects of extractivist industries, immense dams, oil pipelines etc. cause much harm to the environment, but they also affect local communities, either by degrading ecosystems that are vital for local economies or by endangering the health of locals. Such threats often mobilize communities to stand against the profit-driven appetites of the Capital-Nation-State complex.

In this line of thought, ecology can offer a perspective that can provide common ground for various antagonistic to the status quo movements and political trends, combining anti-capitalism with struggles for self-determination, sustainability with urban self-management etc. As explained above, it is tightly related to gender liberation and democratic practices, and thus it can be considered as one of the pillars of a holistic project of direct democracy.

Ecology presupposes the creation of an anthropological type that will be different from the careless consumer of capitalist modernity. What it implies instead is the emergence of politically active stewards that are conscious of their dependence on the complex and dense network of ecosystems that are covering the planet. Or as Castoriadis puts it: "the creation of human beings living with beauty, living with wisdom, and loving the common good."[34] Such anthropological type will be the basis of a society capable of self-limiting its activity so as to not exploit neither nature, neither other people. Such self-limitation, as demonstrated by Castoriadis,[35] can only be based on direct democracy. In this sense, ecology and democracy are intrinsically interconnected. Such an imaginary will imply that all living beings have the right to exist due to their natural occurrence, and humanity must find a way to coexist with it, without endangering it.

Struggles against environmental destruction and extinction of species are essential, but it is important, as social ecologists suggest, to be placed in a political context. The protection of nature requires a systemic critique on the current organizational model of our society and the advancement of alternative model: one that will offer radical break with capitalism and statecraft, proposing instead ecology and direct democracy. For this reason, Castoriadis said that "[e]cology is essentially political; it is not "scientific." Science is incapable, as science, of setting its own limits or its goals [finalités]. If science were asked the most efficient or the most economic means of exterminating the Earth's population, it can (it should, even!) provide you with a scientific answer. Science qua science, it has strictly nothing to say about whether this project is "good" or "bad." One can, one should, certainly, mobilize the resources of scientific research to explore the impact that such and such an action within the sphere of production might have upon the environment, or, sometimes, the means of preventing some undesirable side effect. In the last analysis, however, the response can only be political."[36]

Andrew Flood has suggested back in 1995, that "in a society where we democratically control production we will decide not to pollute or to limit pollution to a level that can be absorbed."[37] This is not a mere speculation, but an expression of the connection between ecology and democracy: both imply direct relationship between individuals and their immediate space—be it the community or the natural environment. As Kurdish researcher and activist Ercan Ayboga puts it: "In order to defend nature and ecological relations, destructive and exploitative projects need to be stopped and the models of housing, production, consumption, mobility etc have to be altered radically. All this can be done only if democratic decision-making structures are dominant in the society, i.e. radical democracy is developed, and no more small circles in the society can influence via lobbying the political decision."[38]

Toward a Democratic and Ecological Strategy "From Below"
In order to give a positive response to the dilemma ecology or catastrophe, as formulated by Janet Biehl, we are in need of developing a strategy "from below," which to correspond to the interrelatedness between ecological sustainability and direct democracy. One such approach will go beyond parliamentarism and narrow environmentalism, seeking instead connection with other movements on the basis of participation in public affairs and the strive toward holistic system change.

Inhabitation and Durability of the Struggle

The temporality of a struggle is of crucial importance, and as such it cannot be overlooked by social movements aiming at radical social change. If it expands within a long period of time, or it is a momentous eruption, creates different conditions for the forms it will take. Often environmental struggles have protracted time span, due to their non-negotiable character. Either certain area will remain as it is –wild or in symbiosis with local communities – or it will be integrated into the capitalist paradigm of unlimited economic growth through some kind of development project. As author Kristin Ross writes, "An airport is either built or it is not; farmland is either farmland or it has become something else - housing developments, say, or an army training ground."[39]

Another important aspect of environmental struggles is the element of inhabitation, which implies that often communities are living within the areas they protect. This places locals in opposition to the frames of the contemporary statist-capitalist order, and thus in need of thinking beyond it.

When durability and inhabiting are combined, the struggles for protection can transform into struggles for defense. And what is being defended changes over time. As Kristin Ross suggests, "Where once what was being defended might have been an unpolluted environment or farmland or even a way of life, what is defended as the struggle deepens comes to include all the new social links, solidarities, affective ties, and new physical relations to the territory and other lived entanglements that the struggle produced.[40] It is important to note that there is no determinist relation here, just preconditions that can allow, if accompanied by other circumstances, a deeper sense and practice of democratic politics to appear.

The zad (zone à défendre) at Notre-Dame-des-Landes, France, is one such case where durability and inhabiting helped for new and creative ways of coexistence and collaboration to be found. It became clear to the zadists that the state and capitalism do not have to completely collapse in order to begin living in relatively free and egalitarian manner. During the defense of the zad, participatory and collective practical ways of satisfying basic needs, both material and social—housing, food, education, health care—were created in a relative independence from the statist, capitalist and other forms of domination.

The autonomous communities of the Zapatistas in Chiapas and the Kurds in Northern Syria have also experienced enormous development in their political projects and practices during the decades of inhabiting their struggles. Their very communal and sustainable ways of life, by being threatened by neoliberal globalism and statist bureaucratism, became a site of struggle. During prolonged temporalities of opposition to domination and oppression from foreign power-structures, the political nature of the Zapatistas and the Kurdish liberation movement became increasingly anti-authoritarian, embedding deeply democratic and ecological elements in all spheres of their social life. Highly indicative of this is the way women liberation gradually proliferated amidst their struggle.

Localism and Translocal Confederalism
The question of space as a site of genuine political deliberation is crucial for the implementation of a democratic and ecological project. The way our societies are being politically structured today places the main decision-making power on an extra-social level, beyond the reach of most people. It is the modernist realm of bureaucratic technocrats and economic elites. This level expands over vast areas, within national borders and/or transnational agreements. This organizational form is among the main vehicles of domination today, as it creates a culture of social alienation, political immaturity and environmental commodification.

Direct democracy, on the other hand, as a deeply egalitarian and ecological project, strives at creating genuinely public space, i.e. a political arena on which all citizens can deliberate and decide on all issues that affect their common life: political, economic, social and ecological. This implies the radical rethinking of the levels of decision-making.

The departure from the extra-social space will take us to the local in the face of cities, municipalities and neighborhoods. In them citizens themselves will have to institute democratic and ecological institutions like popular assemblies and councils. This would mean the creation of public space where genuine political deliberation can take place and allow for equal redistribution of power among all members of the community.

But since such localities cannot exist in a state of isolation, they will have to establish another level of coordination with each other, which to go beyond the extra-sociality of the nation state. Such is the proposal of direct-democratic confederalist approaches, in which local communities maintain their sovereignty by electing revocable delegates and not voting for representatives. There is an essential difference between the two: In the latter case, people give their power away to professional politicians, while in the former they delegate to revocable individuals certain decision(s) of the local community which to be coordinated with other social collectivities. This is a break with the logic of expertise in political decision-making, since as Castoriadis suggests "There are not and cannot be 'experts' on political affairs. Political expertise—or political 'wisdom'—belongs to the political community."[41]

Ocalan writes that in democratic confederalism "higher levels [of decision-making] only serve the coordination and implementation of the will of the communities that send their delegates to the general assemblies. For limited space of time they are both mouthpiece and executive institution. However, the basic power of decision rests with the local grassroots institutions."[42]

In this way, the local and the community remains the main locus of power, while remaining part of wider and regional social ecosystems. In a sense such self-emancipated municipalities could overcome the limits of isolationism, allowing cities, towns and neighborhoods to sustain a democratic counter-power to the centralized political institutions of the state, while overcoming parochialism, promoting interdependence, advancing a broad liberatory agenda and bringing people closer to their natural environment. As Bookchin wrote, "It is through the municipality, that people can reconstitute themselves from isolated monads into a creative body politic and create an existentially vital…civic life that has institutional form as well as civic content."[43]

DEMOCRATIC TRAITS OF THE EARLY CITIES

The greatest achievement of these human beings was the creation of cities.
DIMITRIOS ROUSSOPOULOS[44]

Cities are an integral part of human history. Furthermore, they are vibrant part of political ecology and as such, carry the seeds of a more democratic and sustainable future.

With the creation of the first cities a public space emerged, which allowed their inhabitants to experience true political freedom. The city gave birth to direct democracy and the concept of the *polis*—both based on the idea that citizens can and should collectively and equally self-manage their common urban life, in all its spheres. Such free cities networked with each other into democratic confederations. Their relation with the countryside was one of symbiosis and mutual aid.

Ancient Mesopotamia

In early Mesopotamian cities, it was not uncommon for public affairs to be managed by a general assembly composed of a community's free men as early as 2800 B.C.[45] Such democratic decision-making bodies dealt with communal conflicts, decided on major issues as war and peace, and could—if the people deemed it necessary—grant certain member of the city with supreme authority (namely kingship) for a limited period of time. A council of elders presided over the general assembly, but they did not hold more authority than the assembly itself. Sovereignty rested in the assembly of free men. Distinguished assyriologist A. Leo Oppenheim writes that "the community of persons of equal status bound together by a consciousness of belonging, realized by directing their communal affairs by means of an assembly, in which, under a presiding officer, some measure of consensus was reached as it was the case in the rich and quasi-independent old cities of Babylonia."[46]

Gilgamesh, the historic king of the Sumerian city Uruk, consulted the assembly in important matters of peace and war. Sources suggest that he first consulted the council of elders and then the assembly, consisted of the free men of the town before he decided to engage in a military campaign. His consultation was not only for advice but for consent as the assembly was recognized as the ultimate political authority.[47]

The democratic traits of these Mesopotamian cities were reflected in the religion beliefs of society. According to the Adad myth, gods and goddesses deliberated at an assembly, held in a large court called Ubshuukkinna. Anu, the god of heaven and father of all gods, along with Enlil, god of the storms, presided over the sessions, with their task being mainly to bring issues for discussion. Then all gods and goddesses deliberated, proposed, and ultimately reached collective decisions. Wise thinking was much admired by the gods, as was the ability to make others listen to one's words. No single god possessed ultimate authority. It was their assembly that had such power.[48]

As time passed, the political structure of Mesopotamian cities became increasingly authoritarian. The position of the king became permanent, and inheritable, without the approval of the general assembly. But even after royal power became entrenched during later periods, community assemblies did not die out completely, although they were methodically stripped out of their powers.

India

Another example of proto-democratic assembly institutions comes from the independent towns of India, often referred as sanghas and ganas, which existed as early as the 6th century B.C. and persisted in some areas until the 4th century. The evidence for this is scattered, however, and no pure historical source exists for that period. Greek historian Diodorus mentions in his works in 1st century BC, without any detail, about the existence of independent and democratic cities in India.[49] While he might have used the term democracy in a distorted manner due to the epoch in which he lived (a time of political centralization as a result of the legacy of Alexander the Great), it is worth noting that his time was nonetheless close to the epoch of stateless, self-managed Greek cities, and thus he might have referred to the authentic meaning of the word.

While there was no complete political equality, as existed to certain degree in Ancient Athens, the structure of these independent cities contained the institution of the popular assembly. In some cases, these assemblies were open to all free men. According to Eric W. Robinson, in the communities of Sakyas (the Buddah's people) participation in the assembly was open to all, regardless of their wealth or status[50]. In other cases, only the members of certain classes or casts were allowed to attend. Decisions were usually taken by consensus, although there are proofs for the usage of voting as well.[51]

But, in any case, the assembly had significant financial, administrative, and judicial authority. It had the power to elect monarch (wherever this position existed). The latter, and all other official administrators had to coordinate their decisions and activities with the assembly and seek its agreement. In certain cases, there was also a council of elders or nobles.

Ancient Athens

Ancient Athens can be described as the birthplace of genuine direct democracy since, at a certain point, it developed a participatory system in which the general assembly was the supreme authority and there were no monarchs or other oligarchic structures/positions existing in parallel to it.

The Athenians called this grassroots decision-making body *ecclesia*. It was the popular assembly, open to all male citizens as soon as they qualified for citizenship. In 594 BC, after Solon's reforms, all citizens were allowed to participate, regardless of class or status. The assembly was responsible for declaring war, military strategy and electing the strategoi (military generals) and other officials. It was responsible for nominating and electing magistrates, thus indirectly electing the members of the Areopagus (supreme court). It had the final say on legislation and the right to call magistrates to account after their year of office. A typical meeting of the Assembly probably contained around 6,000 people, out of a total citizen population of 30,000–60,000.[52]

In the 390s, new measures were passed, which introduced payments for attendance at the assembly so as to allow in practice even the poorest of citizens to participate in the political deliberation. It originally met once every month, but later met three or four times per month.[53] The agenda for the ekklesia was established by the Boule—the popular council whose members were chosen by lot among all Athenian citizens. Votes were taken by a show of hands, counting of stones and voting using broken pottery.

The regular meetings of the general assembly were held on an open-air space at the Pnyx—a hill at the heart of Athens. One the one hand, this location allowed for large meetings with thousands of participants to take place. On the other, it symbolized the openness of the political system: Politics were no longer conducted behind closed doors, but outside, on the open where nothing could be hidden.

Scandinavia's Thing

In Nordic towns, during the Viking age, a public institution called *Thing* emerged. In its essence, it was an assembly where all free men of a community would gather to deliberate on laws, decide on policies, elect chieftain, judge etc.[54] While the *Thing* had both judiciary and legislative powers, it had no power to carry out sentences. Instead, this was responsibility of the injured party's family.

Each town had its own independent *Thing*, with sessions held on regular basis. Larger settlements were structured as confederations of local communal Things, who would send representatives to deliberate at the general assembly of the whole city, as was the case of Iceland.[55]

Following the Viking oral tradition, each *Thing* had a law speaker who would recite the law, which he had to memorize by heart. All free men of the community supposedly had a say at the assembly deliberations, although women could also be present but couldn't take part in the decision-making.[56] The *Thing*'s sessions were presided over by the law speaker and the chieftain. The existence of certain roles with more power created the preconditions for *Things* to be dominated by a local, powerful family or families.

The *Thing*'s sessions would generally last for several days, often accompanied by a festive atmosphere. Traders would bring their goods for sale and merchants would set up stands with products. *Things* were held where water was easily obtained, there was grazing for animals and fishing or hunting would provide food for all. Brew masters would provide the attendees with ale and mead. During the *Thing*, marriages were arranged, alliances were crafted, news and gossip exchanged, and friendships established and renewed.[57]

Toward the end of the Viking age, the political system became more centralized as chieftains began consolidating their power and control over the assemblies, becoming kings. The *Thing* lost most of its political power and, as a result, it began functioning largely as King's court in the later Middle Ages.

Medieval Slavic Veche

The early medieval Byzantine historian Procopius of Caesarea wrote in the 6 AD the following words, regarding the political structure of early Slavic societies (VII. 14. 22-30): "the Sclaveni and the Antae, are not ruled by one man, but they have lived from of old under a democracy…"[58]

In medieval Slavic towns all important decisions regarding public life were made at the so-called *veche* (popular assembly). The term originates from the ancient Slavic word *vet* (assembly or council). Attendance was allowed to the free members of the community.[59] Decisions taken there were obligatory for all the community. Although a certain Veche might differed from the rest, it was still based on popular participation and existed throughout the Slavic world—from the Baltic Slavs to Novgorod.

There is scarce historic information about the structure of the Veche. It is known that in Novgorod, the popular assembly could annul a decision made by the *knyaz* (chieftan) or even expel him from the town.[60] This comes in no surprise since the *knyaz* or *voevoda* was not a bearer of high religious or noble status, but simply a head of the warriors, and the community could even hire one as a means of protection. Despite that, with the passing of time the warriors would gain significant power and would eventually either dismantle popular assemblies or will dominate them. Novgorod was one of the places where the institution of the Veche lasted for the longest time—until the 15th century, although there too its power was strongly deminished.

Most decisions at the Veche were taken through simple majority vote. When strong disagreements were present one session could last for up to five days. There were however cases of popular assemblies where decisions were taken through consensus. Such were the veches of the Lutichi, one of the Baltic Slavs tribal unions. According to German chronicler Thietmar von Merseburg, in the Lutichi tribal union a person who dared to question a common decision could be beaten by sticks and his house could be burned.[61] This was a means to keep people from going "against the stream." This comes as a reminder that consensus can lead to conformism.

New England Town Meetings

The New England town meetings are much more recent example of democratic traits in emerging cities. As puritan colonists began settling at the Massachusetts Bay in the 1630s, they formed autonomous towns with democratic characteristics.[62] Although the public life of these settlements was centred around their churches, the people of each city self-governed themselves through covenants that all members of the community wrote together at town meetings.

The supreme political institution, which governed these towns, was the town meeting (general assembly). Its sessions were held on regular basis. In the beginning these meetings were attended only by church members, but with the passing of time, they became open to all male citizens who had any property or regular income (even minor sums).[63] At the town meeting citizens would gather to decide on all aspects of public life.

The ownership of the land was distributed among all male citizens in a relatively egalitarian manner, reflecting the democratic governance of these communities, with all of them receiving plots enough to sustain a family.[64] This helped for inequalities to be avoided for a significant period of time. All able-bodied males were also part of the town militia and received a training.

As town meetings evolved and empowered colonists, they were increasingly viewed as a threat to the British Empire. It was the town meeting that fueled the spark that ultimately led to the American Revolution, and was at the heart of the latter.[65] However, as with the previous cases, town meetings were gradually stripped from their authority by other, much more centralized institutions, such as the presidency. Nowadays they still exist in cities like Burlington, but the scope of their decision-making power has been significantly narrowed.

Toward Democratic and Ecological Cities

[I]f sustainability requires a sustainable democracy, then cities may be the places where democracy is most sustainable.[66]
Benjamin Barber

With the expansion of empires, nation-states and capitalism, cities were submitted to the paradigms of political oligarchy and unlimited economic expansion. But the paradigm of democratic and ecological cities is not yet forgotten. Increasing popular dissatisfaction with the current state of urban life contains the seeds of a different city for the future. Growing amount of people desire cities that will be viewed and managed as commons by their residents. Democratized urban space that will allow for genuine right to the city to be experienced by the entire citizenry. Cities based not on fortification and stratification, but on inclusion and interaction. Urban spaces, focused on the quality of everyday life of all their inhabitants and surroundings, and not on financial profit and unlimited economic growth. In short, cities that don't pollute but heal; where the citizen has direct interaction with his social and natural environment.

The foundations upon which such democratic and ecological spaces can once again be built are still present—like municipalities and neighborhoods. It is from within this grassroots level that we can steer our societies toward politically free and environmentally sustainable future.

Democratic Institutions

> *The famous hymn to the glory of man, the builder of cities and creator of institutions, ends with praise for the one who is able to weave together the laws of the land and the justice of gods to which he has sworn.*[67]
> CORNELIUS CASTORIADIS

The basis on which such democratic and ecological cities should be built is a process of constant popular self-institution. In other words, this implies that the collective creation of participatory decision-making bodies, through which the citizens to be able directly to shape the laws and rules of their common urban habitat. Such democratic institutions will be nothing like the current bureaucratic ones that keep power away from the grassroots, but they also go beyond the anarchist slogan "make war on institutions, not on people,"[68] which implies that institutions as such are the obstacle to emancipation and self-determination. An institutional structure, based on direct citizen participation, will allow people to self-limit their activities so as for genuine freedom to emerge. This comes in line with Rousseau's idea that "the impulse of mere appetite is slavery, while obedience to a self-prescribed law is liberty."[69]

People from the independent cities of the Antiquity and the Middle Ages sought, through such self-institution of laws and constitutions, protection from kings, tyrants, nobles and oppressors. The oligarchic structure of the modern city, on the other hand, allows for growing inequality and precarity to reign. This is so due to the fact that the power is being centralized in the hands of the bureaucratic and business elites, while the citizens' participation is being limited to vote-casting in elections.

The role of such democratic institutions is to make the exercise of nonstatist, non-opresive and non-capitalist power possible. Suitable decision-making bodies for this framework are the neighborhood assemblies and municipal councils, as demonstrated by the Ancient Athens. The ancient

Athenians based their city management on the *ekklesia*—popular assembly in which all citizens had the right to directly participate in the management of public affairs—while choosing their magistrates by the means of sortition (choosing by lot), in order to avoid demagoguery or professionalization of the political realm. While the Athenian society had many shortcomings—like slavery and patriarchy—it still offered us the concept of the *polis*: A free city managed directly by its citizens.

The political foundations of our cities then, could be based not on centralized bureaucratic mechanism, but on network of popular assemblies, each one operating in neighborhoods or areas with population between 30,000–50,000 (the number of citizens in Ancient Athens that had the right to participate in the general assembly). These bodies will be the main locus of power, through which the citizens will shape the common framework of policies and laws to which all urban dwellers should abide to.

Besides the assemblies, there is the need of municipal councils as a supplement for the exercise of grassroots power. Their members could be chosen by lot, following the democratic tradition, and remain revocable at any time if deemed that they exploit their position. Such institution will deal with routine tasks and will be responsible for monitoring the implementation of the decisions, taken by the general assembly. The councils should hold their meetings (which must be public) as often as necessary (for example twice a week). The regular rotation of delegates (once every two, three months or more) will prevent the emergence of a hierarchy and will allow broader participation in the council.

One such democratic and ecological project is genuinely stateless, and thus strives to connect cities by means that radically differ from those of the Nation-State. Instead, it unites them in confederations, in which every city maintains its sovereignty. Murray Bookchin describes that one such democratic confederation "should be regarded as a binding agreement, not one that can be canceled for frivolous "voluntaristic" reasons.[70] A municipality should be able to withdraw from a confederation only after every citizen of the confederation has had the opportunity to thoroughly explore the municipality's grievances and to decide by a majority vote of the entire confederation that it can withdraw without undermining the entire confederation itself."

Post-capitalist Municipalized Economies

> *An alternative [economic] system would be one that has both the desire and the ability to curtail or eliminate profit seeking in favour of humanistic values, practices, and institutions.*[71]
> JANET BIEHL

The paradigm of democratic and ecological cities implies that the economy will be municipalized, i.e. directly owned and managed by the citizens. In one such city, economic activities will be placed in the hands of the urban communities, under the direct control of the popular assemblies, councils and confederations. As author and activist Janet Biehl suggests, in this way "the citizens would become the collective "owners" of their community's economic resources."[72]

In one such paradigm, the inhabitants of the city don't vote as workers and/or consumers. Instead, they participate directly, as citizens, in the formulation and approval of economic policies regarding their neighbourhoods and city. The citizen body will collectively determine its needs, as well as distribute the material means of life, decide how to use available recourses etc. The democratic institutions will allow for everyone in the community to have access to the means of life, regardless of the work he or she was capable of performing. Furthermore, with citizens forming collectively the economic policies of their city, there will be no space left for capitalist antagonism, as all economic entities will have to adhere to ethical percepts of cooperation and solidarity.

Regarding the economies of wider regions, which include more than one city, it will be up to the democratic confederations, as described above, to exercise power "from below." As Biehl writes, the wealth expropriated from the property-owning classes would be redistributed not only within a municipality but among all the municipalities in a region.[73] If one municipality tried to engross itself at the expense of others, its confederates would have the right to prevent it from doing so. A thorough politicization of the economy would thereby extend the moral economy to a broad regional scale.

The municipalized economy of the post-capitalist city ceases to be, as Bookchin suggests,[74] an economy in the strict sense of the word. Instead, it becomes incorporated within the direct democratic political processes of the community, as it is democratically guided by humane and ecological standards. In one such economy, where people participate primarily as citizens, an ethos of public responsibility emerges. Since it is not only economic prosperity, in the narrow sense of the term, which is being sought, a more general quality of urban life, which includes things like healthy environment and strong communal bonds, becomes the prime target. As Andrew Flood wrote in 1995, "in a society where we democratically control production, we will decide not to pollute, or to limit pollution to a level that can be absorbed."[75] His suggestion stems from a post-growth logic, according to which the increase in production and consumption is not an end in itself. In such democratic and ecological paradigm, stewardship and self-limitation, aiming at the general increase of quality of life, replace the capitalist imperatives of unlimited expansion and competition for short-term profit.

Agriculture

> *I hope that [...] many people will learn what is lost*
> *in a big city - so many people have become detached from agriculture.*[76]
> RITA, URBAN GARDENER FROM GREECE

The relationship between agriculture and the city will be radically transformed in the transition toward post-capitalist democratic and ecological future. Nowadays, food production is zoned away from urban areas. The food which reaches our cities arrives from distant areas in huge containers, produced by multinational industries, which only care for their narrow profits. There is much insistence on the way food is being packaged and promoted rather than its quality. Even products that are labeled biologically or organically produced are intended to make money rather than increase the health of as many people as possible.

Nowadays those who run these agricultural industries have little contact or knowledge with/about the land on which their employees are cultivating. In fact, the way this domain is being managed does not differ considerably than any other wasteful, short-term oriented capitalist industry. This comes in stark contrast with earlier form of agriculture. Ancient cities formed around farmlands. Their people viewed food cultivation as a spiritual activity, and its consumption, as social ritual. There was this attitude of stewardship, rather than exploitation. The people of Ancient Athens, like Theophrasus, regarded the interaction of society with nature as relationship between two autonomous equal entities.[77] For indigenous people like the Cayuses in North America, the ground beneath them was alive, and they listened to it, in order to hear the "Great Spirit."[78]

The high esteem the earth had in many of these societies had to do with their dominant paradigm. Many of them were rather feminine, in the sense that feminist conceptions of symbiosis within society and with nature were the basis of their worldview (except of the Greeks for example, but their departure toward patriarchy and gerontocracy was not as temporally expanded as it is for our modern societies). As it was the ground from which they cultivated their food, they considered it the mother of all life. Even today Indigenous communities like the Zapatistas, who live close to their land, have built their mythology around the earth (and corn especially, as one of their main crops).

In one democratic and ecological future, where city life does not equal environmental degradation, agriculture is being integrated to a certain degree within the urban matter, while non-urban agricultural areas, which will still be vital for the feeding of the citizenry, will have to be integrated into democratic confederations, alongside self-managed cities, which means radical decentralization of the agricultural production into cooperatives and rural assemblies. This implies new democratized approach to agriculture, which as Bookchin suggests:

> "Transcends the prevailing instrumentalist approach that views food cultivation merely as a "human technique" opposed to "natural resources." This radical approach is literally ecological, in the strict sense that the land is viewed as an oikos—a home. Land is neither a "resource" nor a "tool," but the oikos of myriad kinds of bacteria, fungi, insects, earthworms, and small mammals. If hunting leaves this oikos essentially undisturbed, agriculture by contrast affects it profoundly and makes humanity an integral part of it. Human beings no longer indirectly affect the soil; they intervene into its food webs and biogeochemical cycles directly and immediately."[79]

Jane Jacobs explains one such relationship between the urban and the rural in the following symbiotic way: "Big cities and countrysides can get along well together. Big cines need real countryside close by. And countryside-from man's point of view-needs big cities, with all their diverse opportunities and productivity, so human beings can be in a position to appreciate the rest of the natural world instead of to curse it."[80]

In the paradigm of democratic and ecological cities, nature is interwoven within the urban matter. This means that it will be present into the everyday life in an essential manner, unlike today, where large parks are among the few interactions a person can have, and not on a daily basis. While there will be need of certain urban planning toward such natural integration, it will be mostly up to the democratized social, political and economic relations. For example, collectives and individuals could be producing food on unused urban surfaces like terraces, rooftops, parking lots, etc. This would also imply that networks of free, pollution-free, public transport should be expanded to such an extent as to liberate significantly the streets from car traffic (and consequently from the need for parking lots).

The integration of agriculture into the urban life will increase the food sovereignty of cities. But surely it will be not enough. Cities will have to establish a new type of relationship with the countryside (where most agriculture is taking place), based on collaboration and mutual aid, instead of domination and profiteering. Such relations will have to be based on democratic confederations which allow to all involved to maintain their political sovereignty. This means that villages and rural towns will have to adopt the direct democratic approach of the democratic and ecological cities. Through this confederal level urban dwellers could engage in participatory planning, regarding their needs, and send them to their rural allies and vise versa.

Energy

> *The assumption that what currently exists must necessarily exist is the acid that corrodes all visionary thinking.*[81]
> MURRAY BOOKCHIN

The question of energy is of crucial importance when we discuss the future of our cities. Our contemporary heavily urbanized societies consume huge amounts of energy, which is being derived through environmentally degradive means.

The creation of democratic and ecological cities requires departure from our current energetic paradigm. Instead it implies changes in two basic directions: First, by going beyond the logic of technological neutrality, and second, by rethinking how our needs are being formed and toward what ends.

For the modernist Left, the problem is not our current technology but who owns it. For them, technology is violent, wasteful and destructive only when used by the wrong hands (for example those of the capitalists). In their view, every technological innovation is not shaped by the context in which it was created, which in itself is really problematic view.

Driven by this logic, many on the Left imagine the post-capitalist city's energetic needs being supplied by nuclear power. Their answer to the anti-nuclear movement is that our current dependence on fossil fuels is destroying our world and nuclear energy is the quickest way toward salvation. But they seem blind to the characteristics, this energy source has, which were embedded in it by the contextual environment in which it emerged.

First of all, nuclear power is incompatible with decentralized and democratic forms of self-governance. Instead, as suggested by researcher Aaron Vansintjan, it requires large state subsidies and centralized planning.[82] According to him, "nuclear power requires a regime of experts to manage, maintain, and decommission; a centralized power grid; large states to fund and secure them; and, then, a stable political environment to keep the waste safe for at least the next 10,000 years. The technology is only 80 years old, modern states have existed for about 200, humans have only been farming for 5,000, and most nuclear waste storage plans operate at a 100-year timespan. To put it mildly, an energy grid dependent on nuclear means having lot of trust in today's political institutions."

This is deeply political issue. The vision of a nuclearly-powered society implies the creation of a totalitarian-like organizational structure, a powerful state. The scale of such an energy system demands to be situated away from the people, in areas zoned away from the rest of society (even whole cities build around such power plants). In this environment scientists and technocratic elites will naturally play an important role. With all the dangers that come with nuclear power plants, there will be need of high-level security measures, control and supervision. All these requirements make nuclear energy incompatible with direct democratic ecological visions. Instead, it is much more suitable for totalitarian visions such as eco-fascism.

Furthermore, nuclear energy is incompatible with the new climate-impacted planetary conditions, which are highly prone to fires, extreme storms, and rises in sea-levels. With the increase of the probability of environmental catastrophes and extremities, it is questionable to say the least, weather nuclear power can function safely. Professor Heidi Hutner has pointed out that wild weather, fires, rising sea levels, earthquakes and warming water temperatures all increase the risk of nuclear accidents.[83] And on top of that, the lack of safe, long-term storage for radioactive waste remains a persistent danger.

An energy source, compatible with the paradigm of democratic and ecological cities is the one derived from renewables. But simply shifting from fossil fuels to renewable sources will not suffice. We must, first of all, avoid approaching renewables from a modernist perspective. This would mean that we cannot use them mainly in a centralized manned (like industrial-style enormous solar or wind farms), since this would require a bureaucratic managerial apparatus, not much different from the one required by nuclear power. Although it will never be possible to avoid larger scales, one democratic and ecological paradigm would require for us to develop renewables toward the greatest possible decentralization, so as to allow local communities to have direct control over their energy supply.

Then there is another issue that must be seriously considered. As author Stan Cox notes:

> "There's nothing wrong with the '100-percent renewable' part…it's with the '100 percent of demand' assumption that [scientists] go dangerously off the rails. At least in affluent countries, the challenge is not only to shift the source of our energy but to transform society so that it operates on far less end-use energy while assuring sufficiency for all. That would bring a 100-percent-renewable energy system within closer reach and avoid the outrageous technological feats and gambles required by high-energy dogma. It would also have the advantage of being possible."[84]

Thus, from ecological and democratic perspectives, we cannot simply switch to this or that technology. We have to bear in mind the contextuality of every technological innovation and the scale on which it is being implemented. Energy is much more than simply a tool: It has to do with the relationships between people, societies, and ultimately humanity and nature. Furthermore, it is not just a means for the satisfaction of our needs, but a need in itself, and in a democratic paradigm, it will have to be deliberated on grassroots level by all members of society.

Democratic & Ecological Urban Design

> *Hence the citizens of a city are of no less concern to me than the city itself, for the city at its best eventually became an ethical union of people, an ethical as well as social eco-community, not simply a dense collection of structures designed for no other purpose than to provide goods and services for its anonymous residents.*
> MURRAY BOOKCHIN[85]

The creation of democratic and ecological cities is a complex thing. For society's organization to be reorganized on the basis of direct democracy and environmental sustainability, among the many preconditions that seems to be required, is the breaking of alienation and establishment of communalist relationships within the urban realm. A city that would encourage and strengthen community feeling would represent mixture of housing, public, workplace, shopping, green and other spaces, all of which will be within walking distance or reachable by public transportation, in contrast with the modern mainstream way of urban design, based on positioning of fixed zones across vast distances.

A mixed architecture consisted of medium-sized housing cooperations, with adjoined gardens, within a walking distance from schools, public squares, markets, and green spaces will allow for the experience of random interactions between neighbors. The walking element could build feeling of belonging to the city, with citizens developing strong links with their local, social and urban environment. It will also, as author Jay Walljasper suggests,[86] contribute for greater economic equality by allowing everyone the right to freely move across the city, without the need of car.

The shift toward walkable cities would imply the radical rethinking and remaking of roads and streets, today designed mainly as high-speed arteries connecting housing districts with office areas, encouraging driving over walking. As Donald Appleyard's famous 1972 study demonstrates,[87] the denser the car traffic is on a street, the lesser pedestrians andeveryday communal experiences there are. This, except the obvious effects on human health (leading to obesity, heart diseases etc.), contributes to the already high levels of alienation in urban areas.

An approach that could alter this alienating effect, encouraging instead people to walk on the streets and potentially to produce community feeling is the narrowing of streets in urban areas, expansion of pedestrian spaces, introduction of wider bicycle alleys etc. As city planner and author Jeff Speck explains,[88] "people drive faster when they have less fear of veering off track, so wider lanes invite higher speeds." This, in mixture with vast network of free urban public transportation, will allow for daily social interactions on them by pedestrians and passengers. The daily social experiences like nodings, smiles and random chatting with co-citizens potentially could contribute for us to feel more comfortable on our streets.

This would bring with itself other positive features, like drastic reduction of the health problems mentioned earlier, but also with reduction of car speed, responsible for the death of huge number of people around the world, as well as reduction of air pollution of the contemporary private car-dominated metropolises.

Green spaces are another key aspect of the urban environment. According to Bob Lalasz,[89] they tend to make people happier. Furthermore, green spaces bring people closer together. Thus, in one democratic and ecological urban project, nature should be essential part of the urban landscape. The gardens, part of housing cooperations will allow for the experience of shared gardening time by neighbours. It will also potentially encourage the development of communal/solidarity economy, by producing their own food and exchanging it or sharing it with other urban gardeners.

Beyond that, parks and public gardens should be shuffled across the mixed urban architecture. There is a certain trend in the modern metropolitan cities for large scale parks to be zoned away from housing districts and office areas, making human interaction with nature a rare opportunity.

Contrary to this logic, the mixed city, described here, could propose green spaces located in various locations across the city. As Charles Montgomery suggests,[90] this does not exclude the existence of large-scale parks, but that the urban green space will not be limited to them. This will imply that people will have the possibility to get in contact with tiny gardens and parks on their way, let's say, to work etc., as well as experiencing the feeling of being "in the wild" by entering the huge local parks.

The squares play a key role in one city that encourages democratic and ecological culture, since they act as spaces for social interactions as well as forums for expression of civic opinions. Thus, they should be made freely available for popular interventions, unlike today, where bureaucrats decide who, when, and for what reason parks are used for certain events.

But, we also hear critiques about over-crowdedness of modern cities, leading to further alienation and withdrawal into passivity. If this is true, should we abandon city life altogether and return to village life? According to psychologist Andrew Baum's study,[91] the feeling of over-crowdedness is being fed by design that does not allow people to control the intensity of spontaneous social interactions. Baum compared the behaviour of residents of two very different college dormitories. He concluded that students whose environment was allowing them to control their social interactions experienced less stress and built more friendships than students who lived along long and crowded corridors.

Therefore, an answer to the "over-crowdedness" problem could be found in the creation of semi-public/communal spaces, which to represent a middle passage between the private and the public. This would imply the abandonment of the gigantic housing projects in which large numbers of people live together (like the socialist-era gigantic worker "barracks"), never feeling quite alone. Instead, a space could be given to medium-size housing cooperations, with common spaces, in disposal of all the neighbors. Thus, three layers of social spheres will be creating—private, communal and public—allowing citizens to regulate their social interaction, thus giving them sense of comfort and encouraging egalitarianism.

Public Space

You will agree with me if I say that a socialism of traffic jams is an absurd contradiction in terms and that the socialist solution to this problem would not be to eliminate traffic jams by quadrupling the width of the Champs Elysees.[92]
CORNELIUS CASTORIADIS

Of course, many things can be done with urban design to encourage communal feeling across citizens, but it cannot alone do this job without providing space for institutions of public deliberation, which to enable for co-inhabitants collectively to determine the destiny of their cities as well as of themselves. It is difficult to imagine what else could bring people closer as community than the feeling of shared responsibility for their city.

Thus, a democratic and ecological city should always strive at managing itself through direct democracy. This will require the establishment of public spaces, suitable for the accommodation of direct-democratic institutions, like the popular assemblies described above. Such spaces, like public squares, halls or amphitheatres, should most likely, be equipped with sound systems, allowing for single speaker to be heard amongst gatherings of several thousand citizens, as well as live streamed for the rest of the community to be able to observe from distance.

Murray Bookchin points[93] at the cities of the past, before the emergence of the so-called statecraft. In them, the citizens were actively involved in shaping their cities, deeply and morally committed to them. But with the emergence of parliamentarism and capitalism, they were replaced by passive consumers, simply passing through their urban environment, without any commitment to it.

Such step toward reframing the city's role as encourager of community and citizenry is, in a sense, rediscovering the ancient Athenian logic of the *polis*. Of course, the sizes of their times and our own are incomparable, but the logic on which their city was build could be used as "germ," as suggested by Cornelius Castoriadis,[94] by us today. Ancient Athens was encouraging community feeling as well as active citizenry, which gave birth to one of the most influential periods of human creativity to this day. At the heart of the

Athenian urban life were situated the agora and the general assembly. The agora was a market place, positioned in accessible and central part of the city, where the Athenians spent great deal of their time exchanging goods, information and opinions, or in other words—socializing—while in the assembly they were bonding with each other as well as with their city by sharing responsibility for its destiny.

Free Public Transportation

> *Free public transportation implies many changes, a completely new way to look at the city, both in terms of how we move and how we tax, but also how we live, where we live, how we relate to each other as a society, and our broader relationship to the urban, regional and global eco-system.*
> JUDITH DELLHEIM & JASON PRINCE[95]

Free public transport (FPT) as a much more holistic option compared to the atomized, privatized means of transportation that dominates the contemporary streets, can contribute to the creation of democratic and ecological cities by allowing citizens to move freely around the urban space in groups, thus laying the foundations of vibrant communities and agora in the authentic ancient meaning of the term. Some of these benefits include:

1. Environmental friendliness: Reduced air pollution, helpful to mitigate global warming, less oil consumption etc.
2. Health benefits: Reduces illnesses that are linked to automobile generated pollution, as well as helps in the reduction of obesity
3. Safer for the urban space: Reduces car traffic, urban noise, etc.
4. Socially inclusive: It allows people to move around their city, without creating financial barriers for some urban dwellers
5. Creates preconditions for the emergence of agora: Socialization and creation of community feeling

Free public transportation is not some utopian vision for dreamers. On the contrary, it is already functioning in cities around the world. The Estonian capital Tallinn is one of the most famous examples for working FPT. The scheme was such a success that Estonia is expanding it on a nationwide level.[96] In France at least 15 towns and cities are experimenting with different forms of FPT.[97] Similar processes can be observed in Germany[98] and in other parts of the world.

For citizens to be able to feel that their taxes are not going to be spent behind closed doors, a good idea could be the parallel introduction of participatory budgeting on a municipal level. In this way people will be able to determine what portion of the city's budget should be spent in the form of subsidies for FPT, and thus have an idea of what the real costs are and how they can best be covered. As sociologist Erik Olin Wright suggests,[99] public transportation has to be paid for, but it should not be paid for through the purchase of tickets by individual riders—it should be paid for by society as a whole.

> "This should not be thought of as a 'subsidy,' in the sense of a transfer of resources to an inefficient service in order for it to survive," he says, "but rather as the optimal allocation of our resources to create the transportation environment in which people can make sensible individual choices between public and private means of transformation that reflect the true costs of these alternatives."[100]

In one democratic and ecological city the implementation of FPT and its management should be left in the hands of the citizens themselves. What would the specific forms of direct citizen control could be in this case may vary, but we can find some examples from history when people have managed to take their public transportation system in their hands. During the Spanish Revolution in 1936, the rebellious population of Barcelona took the control the entire city. The public transportation system was placed under direct workers control.[101] The various modes—buses, subway, streetcars—were all managed through elected committees, answerable to assemblies of the workers. An engineer was elected to each administrative committee, to facilitate consultation between manual workers and engineers. There was an overall assembly for decisions that affected the transit system as a whole, where all citizens could voice their concerns regarding the transportation system. There was no top manager or executive director. A seven-member elected worker committee was responsible for overall coordination.

One of the first acts of the citizens of Barcelona through this new self-managed public model was the abolition of the fare zone system—a zoning scheme which forced people taking longer commutes to pay more. This in practice affected mainly the poor that lived away from the city centre. They switched instead to a flat fare throughout the metropolitan area, in order to make the transportation system more inclusive. Despite this lowering of the fare, the worker-run transit system operated at a profit. This move was quite radical for its time and can be compared to the contemporary idea for FPT.

Toward a Strategy from Below

> *The freedom to make and remake our cities and ourselves is, I want to argue, one of the most precious yet most neglected of our human rights.*[102]
> DAVID HARVEY

The paradigm of democratic and ecological cities is not just a utopian vision for a future never to come. There are countless grassroots initiatives and struggles that strive toward that goal from today. During these last few years, we are even witnessing a rising interest among social movements in the urban question. More and more people are starting to notice the effects our cities have on us. Different movements, focused on the urban question, are emerging, some focused on municipal elections, others on urban planning. But it seems that most of them do not view this matter in holistic political manner.

On the one hand, the introduction of changes, no matter how great, in the way local elections are being held, won't give cities back to their citizens. This can be done only by introducing new deliberative institutions, which will allow to each and every citizen to directly participate in the determination of his city's destiny. The role of existing local authorities should be reduced to supervision and enforcement of the decisions, already taken by these new institutions, and thus subjected to them through means such as revocability, sortition, rotation etc.

On the other hand, often social movements dealing with city issues tend to limit their activities to narrow urban designing, waiting from local authorities to implement their proposals. Their work remains half-way done, since a city is not consisted only of buildings, roads and squares, but also of people and thus, social relations and forms of organization. As Henri Lefebvre suggests,[103] "The right to the city cannot be conceived of as simple visiting right or as a return to traditional cities. It can only be formulated as a transformed and renewed right to urban life."

Thus, the approach should be focused on linking urban design with politics and decision-making in particular. As we saw above, radical change in the one is difficultly imaginable without such radical change to occur and in the other. But what seems a very good start is the fact that more people are paying attention to the role our urban environment is playing on us, our social relationships and our political projects in general.

Conclusion

> *The city is one of the main fronts on which this battle between equitable happiness and brutal misery will continue to rage. For the sake of all those who wish to enjoy lives worth living, it's a battle we had better win.*
> SAMUEL MILLER MCDONALD[104]

The creation of democratic and ecological cities is a question of radical social transformation. The city has played an important role in human life from antiquity until nowadays. We cannot think of our future without thinking of the future of our urban inhabitant. Oversimplified proposals for the abandoning of city life and retreat to small villages and rural life have either lost touch with reality or are being influenced by primitivism and its anti-political orientation.

If we are to create democratic and ecological society, we will have to rethink and remake our cities along democratic and ecological lines. We must depart from the elements which have negatively shaped the modern city: Modernist thinking (large scales and centralization), unsustainable and short-term profiteering (fossil fuels and monocultures), and exploitation (vertical management and capitalism). New principles must be adopted, such as environmental sustainability (citizens acting as conscious stewards) and democratic participation (all citizens shaping directly and collectively their common city life).

Ultimately, the question of democratic and ecological cities is a deeply political one, as it requires the collective deliberation of the future we want. This includes not only deciding how we would like our common world to look like, but also what characteristics we wouldn't like to see in it. And this is a question of self-limitation—something impossible within the framework of capitalism and statecraft. As Aaron Vansintjan concludes, "talking about limits isn't constraining, it's liberating—perhaps paradoxically, it's the basic requirement for building an ecological future of real abundance."[105]

Political Ecology in Practice

A free, ecological society is possible everywhere.
Debbie Bookchin[106]

Today there is a strong tendency, which may agree that political ecology is desirable in theory, but nonetheless it is impracticable. Among the most prominent arguments used by this tendency is the infamous "Tragedy of the Commons"[107] theory, developed initially by William F. Lloyd, and later on by Garret Hardin. In a neo-Malthusian way, they argue that individuals acting independently and rationally according to their self-interest behave contrary to the best interests of the whole group by depleting some common-pool resource and ultimately making their natural environment uninhabitable. Since then, the thesis that people are incapable of managing collectively and sustainably, without control and supervision by institutions and authorities separated from the society, have successfully infiltrated the social imaginary.

Even for big sections of the Left, the resource management in common is being viewed as utopian and therefore they prefer to leave it for the distant future, lingering instead today between variations of private and statist forms of property.[108] Such views remain entrapped in the pseudo-dilemma private-state management of common-pool resources which leads to the marginalization of other alternative forms.

But great many voices, trying to break with this dipole, were always present and currently growing in numbers. For Michael Hardt and Antonio Negri this is a false dilemma. According to them [6]:

"The seemingly exclusive alternative between the private and the public corresponds to an equally pernicious political alternative between capitalism and socialism. It is often assumed that the only cure for the ills of capitalist society is public regulation and Keynesian and/or socialist economic management; and, conversely, socialist maladies are presumed to be treatable only by private property and capitalist control. Socialism and capitalism, however, even though they have, at times, been mingled together and at others occasioned bitter conflicts, are both regimes of property that excluded the common. The political project of instituting the common…cuts diagonally across these false alternatives."

The democratic and ecological management of commons has its roots deep in the antiquity but through constant renewal is exploding nowadays, adding to the Indigenous communal agricultural practices' new urban practices of solidarity and sustainability. The absence of strict ideological frame enhances this constant evolvement.

Ecological and democratic management of resources, according to the anthropologist Harry Walker,[109] could be found in the communities of Peruvian-Amazonia, for whom the most desirable goods were not viewed as things to be competed for, in contrast with modern economics which assume that if goods are enjoyed by one person can't be enjoyed by another. The Peruvian-Amazonian culture was focused on sharing, on the enjoyment of what can be shared rather than privately consumed. Thus they created an egalitarian lifestyle of sustainability, in which there is no imperatives for exploitation of nature and fellow human beings.

The Swiss villages are a classic example of sustainable commoning. Elinor Ostrom is shedding light on this within her field research.[110] In the Swiss village in question, local farmers tend private plots for crops but share a communal meadow for herd grazing. Ostrom discovered that in this case an eventual tragedy of the commons (hypothetical overgrazing) is being prevented by villagers reaching to a common agreement that one is allowed to graze as much cattle as they can take care for during the winter. And this practice dates back to 1517. Other practical and sustainable examples of effective communal management of commons Ostrom discovered in the US, Guatemala, Kenya, Turkey, Nepal, and elsewhere.

Elinor Ostrom visited Nepal in 1988 to research the many farmer-governed irrigation systems.[111] The management of these systems was done through annual assemblies between local farmers and informally on a regular basis. Thus, agreements for using the system, its monitoring and sanctions for transgression were all done on the grassroots level. Ostrom noticed that farmer-governed irrigation systems were more likely to produce not in favour of markets, but for the needs of local communities: They grow more rice and distribute water more equitably. She concluded that, although the systems in question vary in performance, few of them perform as poorly as the ones provided and managed by the state.

Another similar case can be observed in the Bolivian city of Santa Cruz, where the water management is organized in the form of consumer cooperative.[112] It has been functioning for more than 20 years and continues to enjoy reputation as one of the best-managed utilities in Latin America. It is being governed by a General Delegate Assembly, elected by the users. The assembly appoints senior management, over whom the users have veto rights, thus perpetuating stability. This model has drastically reduced corruption, making the water system working for the consumers.

There are many other contemporary examples for sustainable democratic communities that disprove the grim predictions of the tragedy of the commons and the supposedly inherently anti-ecological human nature. The Zapatistas in Chiapas, Mexico, have managed for decades to protect the Lacandona jungle, through an autonomous system of self-governance, from the environmental destruction of the capital-nation-state complex.

Similar is the case with the democratic confederation, developed by communities in Northeastern Syria (or Rojava), as noted in the beginning of this book. The stateless system they developed in the war-torn Middles East, based on popular assemblies and local councils, led them organically to the path of political ecology. They initiated the campaign "Make Rojava Green Again," whose aim is dethatching the local populations from their dependence on oil and other unsustainable economic and energy revenues. Instead it strived at deepening local autarchy, which will deepen democracy further, through sustainable agricultural practices and renewables.

In other words, the idea that humans are inherently anti-ecological is nothing but another fallacy in service of the current system of domination and hierarchy. Communities have proven their ability to collectively and sustainably interact with their social and natural environment, without recreating patterns of oppression and exploitation. In all these cases, amidst vibrant participatory processes, we witness the emergence of anthropological type of socially active and devoted stewards of nature. This means radical break with the dominant nowadays imaginary of economism, which views all human beings simply as rational materialists, always striving at maximizing their utilitarian self-interest. Instead, it implies radical self-instituting of society on the basis of political ecology and direct democracy.

Humanity has proven its creative capacity. But what this creativity can bring in the future is, above all, a political matter. As Castoriadis reminds us, "[m]an, qua creative power, is man when he builds the Parthenon or the Notre-Dame Cathedral in Paris, as well as when he sets up Auschwitz or the Gulag."[113] It is political participation (or the absence of it) that shapes the values and principles of new emerging social forms. Thus, it is up to all of us individually and collectively to create and cultivate one paradigm shift that will navigate us toward sustainable, democratic future.

NOTES

1. Dimitrios Roussopoulos: *Political Ecology: Beyond Environmentalism* (Porsgrunn: New Compass, 2015) pp47-48
2. Dimitrios Roussopoulos: *Political Ecology: Beyond Environmentalism* (Porsgrunn : New Compass, 2015) p15
3. Dimitrios Roussopoulos: *Political Ecology: Beyond Environmentalism* (Porsgrunn : New Compass, 2015) p9
4. Murray Bookchin: *Post-Scarcity Anarchism* (Montreal: Black Rose Books, 1986), p85
5. http://social-ecology.org/wp/1986/01/what-is-social-ecology/
6. https://philebersole.wordpress.com/2016/05/11/the-legacy-of-domination/
7. https://philpapers.org/rec/HUGEIA
8. http://new-compass.net/articles/glimpse-rojava%E2%80%99s-economic-model
9. https://internationalistcommune.com/make-rojava-green-again-picture-gallery-june-2018/
10. http://www.versobooks.com/blogs/1612-thought-is-the-courage-of-hopelessness-an-interview-with-philosopher-giorgio-agamben
11. http://www.footprintnetwork.org/en/index.php/GFN/page/public_data_package
12. http://www.intress.info/fileadmin/intress-docs/Perspectives_and_assumptions_for_setting_resource_targets_01.pdf
13. http://www.nature.com/news/environment-waste-production-must-peak-this-century-1.14032
14. https://theconversation.com/earths-sixth-mass-extinction-has-begun-new-study-confirms-43432

15 https://en.wikipedia.org/wiki/Great_Pacific_garbage_patch
16 http://ec.europa.eu/clima/policies/international/negotiations/paris/index_en.htm
17 http://www.aljazeera.com/indepth/opinion/2013/04/201349124135226392.html
18 Errico Malatesta: *At the Cafe: Conversations on Anarchism* (London: Freedom Press, 2005), p30
19 http://greece.greekreporter.com/2016/08/23/cabinet-discusses-fair-growth-and-governments-work-ahead-of-tif/
20 Naomi Klein: *This Changes Everything* (Bungay: Penguin Books, 2015), pp180-182
21 https://roarmag.org/magazine/socialize-the-internet/
22 David Graeber: *The Utopia of Rules* (London: Melville House, 2015), p110
23 https://nacla.org/article/new-water-wars-bolivia-climate-change-and-indigenous-struggle
24 http://www.aljazeera.com/indepth/opinion/2011/06/201162995115833636.html
25 Brian Tokar: *Exploring the New Ecologies* in Alternatives Vol. 15 No. 4 1988. p35
26 https://www.oxfam.org/en/press-releases/worlds-richest-10-produce-half-carbon-emissions-while-poorest-35-billion-account
27 There are 7.7 billion people. 95% of us occupy only 10% of the land. We produce enough food to satisfy 10 billion people & can double that, in a more sustainable way. We have a profit & distribution problem (capitalism), not a people problem.
28 Cornelius Castoriadis: *A Society Adrift* (Unauthorized translation, 2010), p186 (Available online on http://www.notbored.org/ASA.pdf)
29 Cornelius Castoriadis: *The Rising Tide of Insignificancy: The Big Sleep* (Unauthorized translation, 2003), p113 (Available online on http://www.notbored.org/RTI.pdf)
30 Edgar Morin: *Seven Complex Lessons in Education for the Future* (Paris: UNESCO Publishing, 1999) p38
31 https://theanarchistlibrary.org/library/murray-bookchin-society-and-ecology
32 Simone Weil: The Need for Roots (London: Routledge, 2002), p8
33 Simone Weil: The Need for Roots (London: Routledge, 2002)
34 Cornelius Castoriadis: *The Castoriadis Reader* (Oxford, Blackwell Publishers, 1997), p288
35 http://www.publicseminar.org/2018/02/self-limitation-and-democracy/
36 http://dkantalis.blogspot.com/2011/11/revolutionary-force-of-ecology.html
37 Andrew Flood in '*Anarchism and the Environmental movement*' (1995) (Available online at: http://struggle.ws/talks/envir_anarchism.html)
38 https://komun-academy.com/2018/06/28/ecology-discussions-and-practices-in-the-kurdish-freedom-struggle-with-a-focus-on-north-kurdistan-bakur/
39 Kristin Ross: *The Long 1960s and "The Wind From the West"* in Crisis & Critique Vol.5 Issue 2, p.327
40 Kristin Ross: *The Long 1960s and "The Wind From the West"* in Crisis & Critique Vol.5 Issue 2, p.328
41 Cornelius Castoriadis: *The Castoriadis Reader* (Oxford: Blackwell Publishers, 1997), p277
42 Abdullah Ocalan: Democratic Confederalism (London: International Initiative Edition, 2011), p33
43 https://theanarchistlibrary.org/library/murray-bookchin-libertarian-municipalism-the-new-municipal-agenda
44 https://m.youtube.com/watch?v=o8ScPcVoMtM
45 Benjamin Isakhan: *Re-thinking Middle Eastern Democracy: Lessons from Ancient Mesopotamia* (Paper presented at the Australasian Political Studies Association(APSA) Conference, University of Newcastle, Australia), p.6 http://citeseerx.ist.psu.edu/viewdoc/download?doi=10.1.1.515.6429&rep=rep1&type=pdf

46   A. Leo Oppenheim: *Ancient Mesopotamia: Portrait of a Dead Civilization* (Chicago: University of Chicago Press, 1964), p95
47   https://www.bxscience.edu/ourpages/auto/2017/9/28/78342001/HW2-1—Democracy-in-Mesopotamia.pdf
48   http://www.pwhce.org/apr/apr66.html
49   J.A.O. Larsen: *Demokratia* in Classical Philology vol.68 no.1, 1973, pp. 45-46
50   Eric W. Robinson: The First Democracies: Early Popular Government Outside Athens (Stuttgart: Franz Steiner Verlag, 1997), p23
51   Eric W. Robinson: The First Democracies: Early Popular Government Outside Athens (Stuttgart: Franz Steiner Verlag, 1997), p22
52   Mogens Herman Hansen (editor): *From Political Architecture to Stephanus Byzantius: Sources for the Ancient Greek Polis* (Stuttgart: Franz Steiner Verlag, 1994), pp 51-53
53   http://www.stoa.org/demos/article_democracy_overview@page=all&greekEncoding=UnicodeC.html
54   https://www.britannica.com/topic/thing-Scandinavian-political-assembly
55   Örnólfur Thorsson(editor): *The Sagas of Icelanders: A Selection* (New York: Penguin Books, 2010), pxlvi
56   Natascha Mehler: *Þingvellir: A Place of Assembly and a Market?* In Journal of the North Atlantic, Special Volume 8, 2015, p69
57   Phillip Pulsiano & Paul Leonard Acker: *Medieval Scandinavia: An Encyclopedia* (Oxford: Taylor & Francis, 1993)
58   http://users.clas.ufl.edu/fcurta/Procopius.htm
59   https://www.slavorum.org/veche-the-ancient-popular-assembly-in-medieval-slavic-countries/
60   https://www.slavorum.org/veche-the-ancient-popular-assembly-in-medieval-slavic-countries/
61   https://www.slavorum.org/veche-the-ancient-popular-assembly-in-medieval-slavic-countries/
62   https://slate.com/news-and-politics/2013/05/new-england-town-halls-these-experiments-in-direct-democracy-do-a-far-better-job-than-congress.html
63   https://anarchyinaction.org/index.php?title=New_England_town_meetings
64   https://anarchyinaction.org/index.php?title=New_England_town_meetings
65   https://laurinberresheim.wordpress.com/2018/07/16/hannah-arendt-on-freedom-and-revolution/comment-page-1/
66   https://www.humansandnature.org/democracy-benjamin-barber
67   Cornelius Castoriadis: *The Castoriadis Reader* (D.A.Curtis, Ed., Oxford: Blackwell, 1997), p285
68   http://www.respublica.gr/2015/03/post/thoughtsmunicipalism/
69   Jean-Jacques Rousseau: *The Social Contract* (Ware: Wordsworth Editions, 1998), p20
70   http://www.respublica.gr/2015/03/post/thoughtsmunicipalism/
71   http://new-compass.net/articles/municipalization-economy
72   http://new-compass.net/articles/municipalization-economy
73   http://new-compass.net/articles/municipalization-economy
74   http://dwardmac.pitzer.edu/Anarchist_Archives/bookchin/gp/perspectives2.html
75   http://struggle.ws/talks/envir_anarchism.html
76   https://www.dw.com/en/environment-urban-agriculture-community-gardens-greece-urban-heat-island-effect-sustainability/a-39277047
77   J. Donald Hughes: "Ecology in Ancient Greece" in *Inquiry: An Interdisciplinary Journal of Philosophy 18 Vol.2* (1975), pp115 - 125

78 Angie Debo: *A History of the Indians of the United States* (Norman: University of Oklahoma Press, 1984)
79 https://libcom.org/library/radical-agriculture-murray-bookchin
80 Jane Jacobs: *The Death and Life of Great American Cities* (New York: Vintage Books, 1992), p447
81 Murray Bookchin: "The Meaning of Confederalism," in *Green Perspectives*, no. 20 (1990)
82 https://www.redpepper.org.uk/wheres-the-eco-in-ecomodernism/
83 https://aeon.co/ideas/nuclear-power-is-not-the-answer-in-a-time-of-climate-change
84 https://www.europe-solidaire.org/spip.php?article44271
85 Bookchin, Murray: *Urbanization without Cities: The Rise and Decline of Citizenship* (Montreal: Black Rose Books 1992), pX
86 http://www.commondreams.org/views/2015/10/23/good-place-everyone-walk
87 Donald Appleyard and Mark Lintell: "The environmental quality of streets: the resident's view point" in *Journal of the American Planning Association* (1972), pp84-101
88 http://www.citylab.com/design/2014/10/why-12-foot-traffic-lanes-are-disastrous-for-safety-and-must-be-replaced-now/381117/
89 http://blog.nature.org/science/2015/05/22/science-nature-emotion-affect-feel-better/
90 Charles Montgomery: *Happy City: Transforming our Lives Through Urban Design* (London: Penguin Books, 2015), p110
91 Stuar Valins and Andrew Baum: "Residential Group Size, Social Interaction, and Crowding" in *Environment and Behavior* (1973)
92 Cornelius Castoriadis: *The Castoriadis Reader* (D.A.Curtis, Ed., Oxford: Blackwell, 1997), p250
93 http://new-compass.net/articles/toward-communalist-approach
94 Cornelius Castoriadis: *The Castoriadis Reader* (D.A.Curtis, Ed., Oxford: Blackwell, 1997), p269
95 Judith Dellheim & Jason Prince: *Free Public Transport: Or Why We Don't Pay to Ride Elevators* (Montreal: Black Rose Books, 2018), p.7
96 https://ftnnews.com/other-news/34496-tallinn-s-free-public-transport-goes-nationwide.html
97 http://www.france24.com/en/20171109-france-french-cities-public-transport-free-dunkirk-compiegne
98 https://www.theguardian.com/world/2018/feb/14/german-cities-to-trial-free-public-transport-to-cut-pollution
99 https://bigthink.com/think-tank/should-all-public-transit-be-free
100 https://bigthink.com/think-tank/should-all-public-transit-be-free
101 http://www.workerscontrol.net/authors/worker-management-barcelona-public-transit-system-1936-1939
102 David Harvey: *Rebel Cities: From the Right to the City to the Urban Revolution* (London: Verso 2012), p4
103 Henri Lefebvre: *Writings on Cities* (Oxford: Blackwell 1996), p158
104 https://www.currentaffairs.org/2019/05/the-city-of-tomorrow-is-the-city-of-yesterday?fbclid=IwAR05pE1TkFaxZQRX-ZmavO8krW_l-nEISec7eNoSRNovHciovZ9ZgoG-Qdo
105 https://www.redpepper.org.uk/wheres-the-eco-in-ecomodernism/
106 Internationalist Commune of Rojava: *Make Rojava Green Again* (London: Dog Section Press 2018), p13
107 The concept was based upon an essay written in 1833 by Lloyd, the Victorian economist, on the effects of unregulated grazing on common land and made widely-known by an article written by Hardin in 1968.

108 As Theodoros Karyotis demonstrates in his article *Chronicles of a Defeat Foretold*, published in ROAR magazine, Issue #0 (2015), pp 32-63
109 http://bollier.org/blog/anthropologist-harry-walker-lessons-amazonian-commons
110 http://www.onthecommons.org/magazine/elinor-ostroms-8-principles-managing-commmons
111 Elinor Ostrom in Nobel Prize lecture *Beyond Markets and States: Polycentric Governance of Complex Economic Systems* (2009)
112 http://siteresources.worldbank.org/INTWSS/Resources/WN5cooperatives.pdf
113 Cornelius Castoriadis: *The Rising Tide of Insignificancy* (Unauthorized translation, 2003), p123

II. Theoretical Outlines of Direct Democracy

Yavor Tarinski

Democracy as a Regime of Self-Limitation

[F]or the impulse of mere appetite is slavery, while obedience to a self-prescribed law is liberty.
Jean-Jacques Rousseau[1]

THE PHILOSOPHER Cornelius Castoriadis has often been credited with saying that "democracy is the regime of self-limitation."[2] But since for him the only true democratic form is direct democracy, this claim might seem a bit odd. Direct democracy has come to be conceived by many, including several critics, as a regime that disconnects society from laws and regulations, resulting in its depoliticization and degradation. This concept has understandably raised concerns about what would be the outcomes of the more excessive actions of the masses.

The essence of direct democracy however, as presented by Castoriadis, differs considerably from such chaotic and nihilistic logics. For him, the primary meaning of the term democracy is political, being before all a regime in which all citizens are capable of governing and being governed—with both terms (democracy and self-limitation) thus being inseparable. Democracy, in other words, is understood as a form of explicit societal self-institution, through reflectiveness and self-limitation.

According to Castoriadis, democracy is not mere process for collective decision-making that can exist in parallel to or within non-democratic oligarchic frameworks, as proposed by thinkers like Jürgen Habermas or Chantal Mouffe.[3] For him, democracy is rather the basis of the project of autonomy—a social condition in which society recognizes no external limits to its instituting power. That is, unlike different forms of what Castoriadis calls "heteronomy," societies where laws and regulations are derived from extra-social sources like capitalist markets, nation-states, gods, historic necessity, etc., a democratic community's sole limits result from its self-limitation through collective positing of the law.

Castoriadis observes that institutions and laws that suggest what cannot be done, but also what should happen, are what make society function. Without such regulations, the thought goes, social ties disintegrate. In his own words "society is there precisely at the moment when there is a self-limitation of all the brothers and sisters."[4] His emphasis on democracy is, in this sense, not a rejection of organization and legislation, but rather certain sources of organization and legislation.

Forms of Social Limitation

Every society does not only offer, but in some way, it enforces certain roles, values, beliefs, ways of life, etc to its individual members. Each societal form provides only a certain set of possibilities to its population, since one cannot be everything nor do whatever he wants. Thus, we can speak here of limitation, but despite the negative connotations of this term, it most certainly also carries a positive trait: By forbidding certain things, society simultaneously draws patterns of what should be done, therefore giving distinguished meaning to its form of life.

Every social order determines different sources for this prohibition. But what cultivating an autonomous, essentially democratic setting means is that the limitations will be self-imposed by society in its entirety. In heteronomy, on the other hand, prohibition is being set extra-socially. This does not mean that such extra-social sources (i.e. sources that are external to the actual and living society, such as gods, nation-states, founding heroes or natural laws when they are presented as immune from human influence[5]), are not in some way connected to or reachable by society, but that they monopolize power, taking it away from the general populace. According to Castoriadis, they are still a product of society's self-creating capacity.[6] It is because of this relatedness that a revolutionary political shift is even conceivable.

Of course, although every society is based on some set of limitations, people do not always abide by these. History is filled with examples of single individuals, communities, and even whole societies that break away from established social norms and prohibitions. The question is, "why"? Contrary to what is argued by many critics of autonomy, people transgressing popular limitations is not a phenomenon limited to the seemingly chaotic direct democracy. In fact, it can be argued that, paradoxically, this trend is more common under heteronomy, due to its non-participatory character, because people in those societies feel alienated from the laws and institutions.

This paradox is due to the disharmonious relation between the individual and the social collectivity. No matter what roles society dictates to its singular members, there will always be some among them who will be breaking with the prohibitions. Indeed, one's individuality is never completely determined by the role that is being attributed to him or her. In fact, these oversteppings of limitations, the breaking of the norm, potentially contain the germs of new possibilities and can become the seeds of social transformation.

Under heteronomy, however, limitations are misleadingly conceived as deriving from a source outside of ourselves, often deriving from narrow managerial elites, who are the only ones able to intervene and alter them. This is so because the heteronomous regimes are based on the scepticism of the ability of large collectivities to consciously determine their destinies. Thus, despite the historic democratic experiences of autonomy, such as the Athenian Polis, or the 1956 Hungarian Revolution, as short as they might have been, there is this false world-view of popular inability for self-instituting being constantly reproduced by genuinely heteronomous entities like the State or the capitalist market to justify their own existence.

Democracy, on the other hand, is based on the rejection of fixed and objective laws, actions, and thought. This seemingly 'nihilistic' concept suggests that everything is possible and certain dangers do give reason for people to be wary. For instance, in regard to the absence of a "norm of norms," Castoriadis refers to the Greek concept of hubris.[7] According to him, hubris does not simply presuppose freedom, but the non-existence of fixed norms, the essential vagueness of the ultimate social bearings of our actions. However, this does not mean that we are destined to run amok, but that there is the space for us to create our meanings, laws and limitations ourselves, since as Castoriadis suggests, hubris exists where the only 'norm' is self-limitation.[8]

Castoriadis suggests that despite the danger of monstrous acts that democracy presents, democracy simultaneously opens the possibility for self-criticism and self-evaluation, which are at the core of self-limitation.[9] Traces of such critical re-evaluation could be found in the Euripedeas's play "The Troades" (The Trojan Women), produced in 415 BC during the Peloponnesian War. It represents the critical commentary of one Athenian on his fellow citizens and the slaughter they conducted on the people of the Aegean island of Milos. With his play Euripides attempts at visualizing the Greek hubris, staging it one year after the massacre, warning the Athenians with the words "such monsters, we are." He suggests that, although the people of Athens can decide and do certain things, they should not always implement it in practice, it is up to them to determine which act is "monstrous" and which is not.

Democracy and Self-Limitation

Self-limitation within democracy decisively shapes the relation between the individual will and collective decision-making. An autonomous society allows all its individual members to directly participate in democratic processes, giving them space to express their views, needs and proposals. Here lies the most positive aspect of the democratic self-limitation: It potentially predisposes society toward lawfulness. By allowing all citizens to participate in the shaping of every law and regulation, direct democracy makes the citizenry the only creator of social limitations, thus making the need of transgression of those limits less likely.

However, there will be times and topics on which unanimity will not be reached and some particular opinions will be contradicted by the collective will. In such cases, those that disagree with the given decision will have to comply with it, regardless of the degree of their disagreement. Democratic decisions are rarely unanimous, and however we may organize processes to give everyone the opportunity to express their views, make their needs known and understood, and present their arguments these will still sometimes be contradicted by the collective will. This means that there will be times when an individual's proposal will not only be rejected by the majority of his fellow citizens; this same individual might even be required to comply with laws with which he does not agree.

Some argue that this means that there is an ineradicable element of heteronomy even within the most democratic society, but it is important to make a distinction between decisions that are made without any input by those who are affected by them, and those in which all affected have the effective opportunity to participate. The term 'heteronomy' is best reserved for the former. And although autonomy is characterized by the latter, it inevitably means that sometimes individuals are forced to obey laws they would not have chosen for themselves, otherwise we cannot talk of decision-making.

One example for such a relation is Socrates' attitude toward the laws and institutions of Ancient Athens. He perceived the regulations of the polis as his own, and felt obliged to submit to them, even when he strongly disagreed. This attitude derived, to a large degree, from his recognition of and gratitude for the city's role in his education, not to mention the possibilities it gave him to lead truly free life. He knew that he had joined the Athenian polis voluntarily and had the right to participate in its self-instituting, which made him recognize himself as a part of the social collective, even when disagreeing with some of the collective decisions.

Submission to laws and regulations, however, can never be completely guaranteed. Heteronomous approaches typically prescribe severe punishment to the transgressors through apparatuses of oppression. In such cases, despite the penal threat, there is strong drive among people to transgress laws, since they don't have even the slightest opportunity to take part in their shaping, and thus feel alienated from them. This, however, does not mean that in the democratic conditions of autonomy, obedience to regulations will be entirely voluntary. But because of the participatory nature of self-limitation citizens will feel, to a larger degree, social prohibitions as their own and will be less tempted to overpass them. This does not dismiss the fact that even under democracy, in its most pure direct form, society will have to be able to impose its collective decisions on those individuals that will still proceed in transgressing them.

On the Contamination of the Revolutionary Project

Although democracy is unthinkable without self-limitation, in certain historic moments, multiple contaminations of revolutionary thinking took place that pulled these concepts apart. The workers' movement in general, and specifically Marxism and Marx himself, were from the beginning steeped in an atmosphere in which the growth of the forces of production, worker-managed economic growth, was made the universal criterion for social emancipation. For these thinkers and activists, production was considered the main locus of all public life, and the idea that progress could and would go on indefinitely was taken for granted.[10] This embrace of the capitalist imaginary contaminated the working class' project of autonomy. An autonomous society is completely incompatible with the idea of mastery, advocated by capitalism's paradigm of unlimited economic growth. Rather, an autonomous, de-alienated society would by nature take up the role of steward of the planet.

Castoriadis suggests that, if the projects of autonomy and economic growth have contaminated each other, then one must know how to distinguish them, which is in no way an easy task. This does not mean that we must make choice between material progress or environmentally-minded primitivism. We are not talking of abandoning scientific research on the pretext that some very dangerous things might come out of them, but that there are nonetheless some very dangerous outcomes that can result from the transition from research to its economic application, which raises questions that muse be democratically negotiated by the collective. This is where democratic self-limitation comes in.

Today, more than ever, the question of setting controls on the evolution of science and technology is posed in radical and urgent manner. The unrestrained development of technoscience, driven solely by competition, proves to be destructive for the planet as well as for us, creating a crisis of an existential character. Castoriadis calls for breaking the currently prevailing illusion of omnipotence that humanity feels.[11] It is true that we are, as he suggests, privileged inhabitants of a planet that is perhaps unique in the universe. But our very existence is dependent on it and on certain fragile conditions, which our civilization is about to disrupt and even destroy. To avoid the upcoming catastrophe humanity needs to reconsider all the values and habits that rule over us.

We should abandon knowledge and science and return to primitive forms of existence, as some modern lifestylish trends suggest. Giving them up means renouncing our ability to be free. But the tricky part is that, as Castoriadis explains, knowledge is like power—it requires caution. We should, therefore, at least attempt to comprehend what our researchers are in the process of discovering and be attentive to the possible repercussions of what we are about to learn. Here the question of democracy arises again, in multiple forms. Under the present oligarchic order, and within current hierarchical structures, the final say over all these matters is in the hands of competing politicians, corrupted bureaucrats or business oligarchs, with narrow technoscientists as their advisors. Society-at-large is thus being excluded from the political determination of how should acquired knowledge be used, and what goals must be set before future scientific research.

Self-Limitation and Education

Among the main excuses for the exclusion of the general public from decision-making on matters of supposedly scientific character is the public's lack of appropriate education in these matters. This argument is essentially paradoxical, however, since most often contemporary political representatives and businessmen themselves lack such knowledge and are driven solely by a desire for power.

In a democratic society, the centrality of education is beyond discussion. In a sense, it can be said that direct democracy is an immense institution of continuing education, a permanent process of self-education for its citizens, and it could not function without that. A democratic society has to appeal constantly to the lucid activity and the opinion of all citizens, since by its essence it is of reflective character. This is exactly the opposite of what takes place today, with the reign of professional politicians and all kinds of "experts."

The issue of education cannot be resolved by mere "educational reform," as is often advocated by parliamentary governments of various sorts, since, as Castoriadis suggests, education begins with the birth of the individual and continues until their death.[12] Education takes place everywhere and always. It is embodied by the everyday life and culture taking place within the city. He invites us to compare the education Athenian citizens received when they participated in the self-management of the polis or attended performances of tragedies with the kind of education a television viewer or electoral voter receives today. Therefore, determining certain limitations requires first and foremost the educative inclusion of all of society into political affairs so as self-limitation to be possible.

Ecology, Degrowth, and Self-Limitation

Ecology is tightly connected to self-limitation. The former implies the necessity of human societies developing the ability to self-limit their relation to the environment, on whose fragile conditions the very existence of humanity depends. Castoriadis traces this logic back to the ancient Greek attitude. He argues that theirs was not based on balance and harmony with nature, but from the recognition of the environmental limits on our actions and the need of self-limitation.

But, for ecology to overcome current environmentalism and move toward a revolutionary direction, according to Castoriadis, it must aim at provoking profound changes in the psychosocial attitude toward life of the modern human, or in other words, in humanity's imaginary.[13] The idea that the sole goal of life is to produce and to consume more—an idea that is both absurd and degrading for human beings—must be challenged and abandoned; the capitalist imaginary of pseudo-rational pseudo-mastery, and of unlimited expansion, must be abandoned. Moreover, it must be recognized that such a profound change can be achieved only by people working collectively on grassroots level. A single individual, or one organization, can, at best, only prepare, criticize, incite, sketch out possible orientations and provoke the social collectivity to change. Thus, one ecological, essentially revolutionary, approach can only be social in character.

An important trend among ecological circles nowadays has become the "degrowth paradigm." It is based on a theory of radical reduction of human impact on nature through deliberate negative economic growth. To some extent it is influenced by Castoriadis' critique of the obsession with economic expansion, found among capitalist, as well as socialist, regimes.[14]

One problem with this trend, however, is that it places of economic shrinkage at the centre of social change, as the very name de-growth suggests. This movement often focuses on the technical part of how such process can take place, rather than on how to radically restructure the organizational basis of society as a whole.[15] Thus, people from this tendency have often found themselves proposing reforms within the parliamentary regime, as have happened, in similar manner, with advocates of the commons. In this we can detect reproduction of the pseudo-scientific folly of techno-fixes beyond politics.

Castoriadis' notion of self-limitation differs significantly in this respect. While recognizing the immense importance of degrowing our economies to environmentally sound levels, it nonetheless suggests that this process should be preceded by the de-scaling of political power, i.e. from oligarchic to direct-democratic.[16]

In a sense, degrowth can be viewed as self-limitation that is restricted to the economic sphere, which by itself is problematic in several, mutually supplementing, ways if it is not included into one holistic political project that encompasses all spheres of human life. First, it participates in the current imaginary of economism, viewing the economy as the highest human activity. It thus tries to navigate social change along the economic lines, already sketched by capitalism. In other words, it narrows the possibility of radical social alteration to alternative forms of consumption, renewable energy sources, environmentally sound production methods etc. without taking into account their scale or who the beneficiaries from such practices might be.

Second, by determining as its main goal the creation of a "society of degrowth," it pretty much leaves open the political approach through which it will be implemented. If the sole target is to de-scale the economic footprint of humanity over the environment, then all political strategies can be used.[17] This by itself is very problematic. Environmental sustainability could be enforced, for example, by a totalitarian regime (like eco-fascism) to the expense of democratic and human rights.[18] This could mean that the current ecological crisis might be avoided to only slam humanity into another political, social and cultural crisis, provoked by the dystopian character of totalitarianism. Thus, degrowing the destructive impact of one human sphere through economic means alone will simply not suffice. There is need of general descaling, with authority as the main target for de-escalation, decentralizing it down to the very grassroots, where people themselves to rethink their relationship with nature and with themselves.

Democracy, as inseparable part of the project of Autonomy, is the dual self-limitation of intrasocial regulations and laws, necessary to maintain the integrity of our societies on the one hand; and the limits we set before our activities regarding nature, on the other.

But to be effective, democracy has to be detached from the imaginary signification of universal rational mastery, which has been contaminating revolutionary thought for many years. We can see clearly contemporary economic growth being forced with the cost of most basic democratic rights. So, democracy too, in its direct, most authentic form cannot be achieved through technological progress or abundance of resources, but by the deliberative self-limitation of society itself.

In a world of unlimited economic growth and hunger for power, those who feel the harshest prohibition are the people and communities that strive at limiting the authority of those that exploit humanity and nature for their narrow profit. This should not surprise us since, as Hannah Arendt suggests, the notion of "everything is possible" is an idea that can be found in totalitarian regimes like Nazism.[19] But unlike the numerous "autonomous" and anarchist trends that seek unlimited individual independence in an institutionless world, the democratic self-institution proposed by the project of Autonomy in Castoriadis can give birth to real political freedom for the creative citizens of a vital society. This requires, however, that social movements and politicized individuals abandon the convenience of heavily ideologized activist groups with sectarian character and immerse instead, into the public affairs of their cities and societies, self-organizing alongside their fellow citizens in an attempt to self-institute the public space of tomorrow. Such might be our only hope to preserve the fragile planetary conditions that allow us to exist, those same conditions the current system is in the process of destroying.

POLITICAL PARTIES: OBSTACLE TO DEMOCRACY

If understood to the letter, a Democracy must be a stateless society. Power belongs to the people insofar as the people exercise it themselves
GIOVANNI SARTORI [20]

The contemporary political model is undergoing deep crisis, which can be attributed to many of its systemic features and the political parties are among the main reasons for it. The Party, once encompassing massive social support and powerful movements, has become today synonymous with dishonesty, greed for power and corruption. Many have embarked on journey to recreate it in different ways that strive at mimicking the grassroots, decentralized character of contemporary social movements and the internet.

Some party formations emerged, as they claim, from the movement of the squares that swept Europe in the beginning of 2010's decade, like the Spanish Podemos. Others were influenced by contemporary hacker culture like the numerous Pirate parties. Some former occupy activists initiated the "Occupy the Democrats" campaign, attempting at using the logic of the Occupy movement for overtaking the Democratic Party of the US. All of these and other similar initiatives however remain with questionable results at best.

Authoritarian Birth

The negative outlook that political parties have is not due to some distortion but logical continuation of the essence on which electoral politics rest. The introduction of political parties into European public life in the late 17th century should be considered not as step toward democratization of society but as continuation of the oligarchic tradition.

In England, as political theorist Hanna Pitkin explains,[21] representation was introduced from above, by the King, as a matter of administrative control and royal convenience over non-royal localities. Situated between the monarchical elite and subordinated communities, representatives, with their role being institutionalized, began viewing themselves as single continuing body pursuing its own interests. Political representation, as foundational basis of the political party, slowly became a matter of privilege, to be fought for, rather than a burden or a mere task.

Their oppressive character is also being demonstrated by the philosopher Simone Weil for whom the Party is to a certain extent heritage of political terror[22]. Its role in the popular uprisings of Europe in the last centuries has been expression of its oligarchical nature, sabotaging democratic efforts "from below" in the name of top-to-bottom solutions offered by the State. Weil's conclusion that totalitarianism is the original sin of all political parties echoes Mikhail Tomsky's famous saying: "One party in power and all the others in jail."[23]

In popular uprisings and revolutions societies express certain tendency toward spontaneous grassroots social organizing based on councils and local assemblies. This is what Hannah Arendt calls "lost treasure of revolution"—

the creation of truly public space in which every citizen can freely and equally participate in the management of society.[24] This "treasure," as a break in the bureaucratic oligarchical tradition, becomes target of centralized state power and political parties, whose existance this new social direction radically challenges.

The current system, at whose core is the party politics, has nothing to do with democracy in its authentic sense. Instead of providing the means for people to directly express their views, concerns and solutions on public affairs, political parties tend to exploit popular passions, polarizing societies into majorities and minorities, using the former as a tool to serve their narrow interests.

A common and essential characteristic of all political parties, both on the Left and the Right, as noted recently by author Raul Zibechi,[25] is their obsession with power. For if they are to successfully fulfill their electoral task that justifies their existence, they must secure for themselves vast amounts of authority. Yet, as electoral politics place political parties in constant competition on national level, while foreign states and private companies are also constantly implying pressure on domestic partisan procedures, power is never enough and soon becoming an end in itself. And since there is never limit for the power that each party strives at possessing, it comes as no surprise why so many thinkers have come to view the institution of the party as essentially totalitarian.

Another way in which representative politics hinders democratic deliberation is the former's tendency toward encouragement of antisocial, disordered-like, behaviours. Clinical psychologist Oliver James claims that psychopathy thrives in hierarchical organizations. According to him "triadic [personality disordered] behaviour flourishes where ruthless, devious selfishness is advantageous and where an individual is very concerned to gain power, resources or status."[26] Jacques Ranciere, in an interview for the Greek National Television ERT3,[27] also suggests that political representation and electoralism attracts the worst of people, i.e. those that seek power for power's sake. Thus, the competitive and hierarchical nature of political parties attracts ambitious, narcissistic individuals, turning them into psychopaths (or encourages them to act as such).

Political Betrayal

By recognizing the logical connection between representative institutions (like political parties) and unlimited hunger for power we can easely debunk the widely propagated myth of "politicians's betrayal" of pre-election promises. It's worth noting that this mythical narrative most often comes from electoral candidates or thinkers that support the status quo and through it they strive at scapegoating individual "traitors" so as to maintain the integrity of the party system.

Cornelius Castoriadis compares would-be-representatives with merchants of junk that try to push their stuff on us, even if that means telling lies.[28] As he says, what electoral competitors are doing is trying to deceive, not betray us. Professional politicians are not traitors but servants of other interests. The electoral race requires competing parties to outbid each other on promises they don't intend to keep and images they will maintain as long as they bring them votes.

The notion of public interest, most often depicted as national, is a good example for the kind of deception that is being used by political parties. It is constantly being invoked by governments and electoral candidates to serve them as cover for their quest for authority and generate them popular support. In short, politicians attempt at gaining or strengthening their own power by deceiving the essentially powerless electorate that the immense political inequality, which is constantly being reproduced by representative democracy, is of mutual benefit. Thus, it is no wonder why the language of patriotism and nationalism is among the most preferred by governments of any kind.

It is understandable, however, that people might feel betrayed by political parties. In a representative system that strips society from any meaningful means for effective self-instituting people are left with no other options in the public space but to either place their hopes (and thus their votes) on certain electoral competitor, or resort to abstention from voting. But, in reality, parties were not and can never truly be on the side of grassroots communities, first and foremost because they are immensely more politically privileged than them.

Nowadays, this matter is being further complicated by the dual processes of globalization and financialization. In the contemporary neoliberal era, elected politicians, as Jerome Roos explains,[29] are being reduced to managers whose function is increasingly that of making the state apparatus work for the profits of bankers and businessmen. It is not to say that the representative institutions are stripped from their powers, but they are being separated even further from society by additional layers of multinational corporate interests.

Party membership and individuality

Contemporary representative oligarchies are making it impossible for individuals and communities to intervene in public affairs without joining or intervening with political parties. Official tools for citizen participation like petitioning and referendums most often have non-obligatory character and are doomed to fail if not backed by any party. Citizenship today is nothing but illusory, since people are forced with the dilemma between withdrawing altogether from the public sphere or submit to party interest. Instead of citizens we have electorate whose concerns for social matters are being crushed by the party's quest for influence and power.

Unlike the pluralism nurtured by deliberative bodies for participatory decision-making like councils and popular assemblies, political parties demand the maintenance of a party line, even though nowadays they seem to appear more flexible in this aspect. By joining a party, one is expected to agree to its entire program or at least submit to it, since in crucial moments he/she will be expected to support it or leave. Even if he has not previously been familiar with it, he is supposed to endorse it in its entirity, or to not expect much from his newly acquired membership. Often different aspects of such programs appear to be contradictory with each other, since in their race for power parties sometimes take mutually exclusive positions. As Simone Weil concludes,[30] whoever joins a political party is expected to submit his thinking to the authority of the party.

Although parties claim that they offer space for political participation and education to their members and supporters, the reality appears to be much different. What they do instead is spreading rigorous ideological propaganda through which the party elite to exercise control over the new reqruits and the electorate. Parties that attempt at not doing so find it difficult to achieve significant electoral victories.

As a result of this propaganda party members and supporters tend to adopt certain ideological and political "brands." This "branding" replaces political thinking. One begins approaching public affairs as member of this party and supporter of that ideology, instead of critically evaluating social problems and individually or collectively developing solutions to them.

Parties tend to create positions in favour of or against certain option and call on the electorate to stand behind their position. Taking sides replaces public deliberation with reality being twisted by each party accordingly to its stance, instead of being analyzed in contextual manner. Many have suggested that this logic has spread into all spheres of human life.

Handling Popular Dissatisfaction

As mentioned above, political parties are bureaucratic organizations that breed oligarchy, not democracy. Their electoral hierarchical nature enforces statecraft, rather than direct public participation, while giving the illusion of being the link between the public and the institutions of authority.

The attitude political parties adopt is twofold. On the one hand, they do everything they can so as to reassert their hold on state power through making powerful allies, briberies, backstage schemes and mass propaganda. On the other hand, they have to respond to demands and matters rised "from below," by social movements and popular resistance, either by crushing them or by introducing decorative reforms meant at reducing the pressure.

This second level of handling social dissatisfaction can be separated into two subcategories. The first one includes smear campaigns, briberies and threatenings that are being directed toward activists and community organizers so as their movements's social credibility and integrity to be hurt. This approach is often used by governments on the Right, as recently demonstrated clearly by Donald Trump's administration.[31] The second one is compounded by the cooptation of social movements through offering positions of power to influential activists and inactment of reforms that create the illusion of specific issues being resolved, as was the case with some Pink Tide governments of South America.[32] This is preferred strategy by the Left when in power.

Institutions Beyond Parties

It is important to note here, that the problem with political parties is not that they are institutions, as some of their most vigorous critics would insist, but that they are bureaucratic organizations. Real, direct democracy, where emancipated citizens directly decide on all issues of public life and are actively involved in the implementation of the taken decisions, requires institutions with participatory character, that are however embedded in and nurturing one radical imaginary, that makes the values and goals of democratic life thinkable and possible.

Unlike the above mentioned grassroots institutions, political parties participate completely in the imaginary of heteronomy. Their form, structure, organization and ideology are essentially bureaucratic and strengthens oligarchy, whether in more or less liberal outlook. Their very existence is a potential obstacle to democracy, constantly suggesting that people are not mature enough to participate in the public sphere as citizens and instead guardians must be nominated to govern them.

A society without institutions, as Castoriadis suggests,[33] cannot exist. Thus, the efforts at dismantling the state apparatus and other contemporary bureaucratic institutions that enforce inequality and oppression cannot be proceeded without the establishment of parallel grassroots institutions that nurture equality and emancipation. Their creation and maintenance certainly will have its difficulties as no social activity, including that of autonomous organizations and movements, can go unaffected by the dominant order. No one can completely separate himself or his group from the overall of society, but only this necessary step of exercising democracy can allow transformation toward forms of social organization and civic culture. And this necessarily includes popular grassroots organizing beyond institutional forms of oligarchy, such as the political party.

Political parties are part of the problem, not the solution. The high levels of alienation and passivity in our contemporary societies are essentially product of capitalism and representation. The electoral spectacle offered by competing political parties seems to resemble to a big degree the one, created by the neoliberal market. The hopes of many on the Left that the former could potentially restrain the latter are naive, to say the least. What they essentially are is different forms of heteronomy, i.e. determination of people's life by outside sources, beyond their reach or control.

Democracy, because of its popularity and potential, is being used by the ruling elites and their intellectual supporters, to mask the oligarchic nature of the contemporary party system. This trend has misled many into blaming popular passions for the oppression, theft and exploitation being done by one government after another. Thus, the far-right, with its call for diminishing freedoms in the name of security has grown in popularity.

It is not democracy to be blamed, but the complete lack of it. The absence of broad public participation allows to competing ruling elites to get hold on power and do as they please. For them, popular deliberation is undesirable as it will end their reign over society and thats why they replace it with party electoralism. The dominant institutions, on which their authority is being based are constructed so as to embody this "hatred of democracy," to borrow the phrase developed by Jacques Ranciere.[34]

For significant social change to take place, a mere imitation of politics, a simulation of public action, like the one exercised by political parties, will simply not do. What is desperately needed is what Hanna Pitkin calls real experience of active citizenship. And this necesserily goes through the reinvention of democracy beyond political parties.

Nation-State, Nationalism and the Need for Roots

> *The State is a cold concern which cannot inspire love,*
> *but itself kills, suppresses everything that might be loved;*
> *so one is forced to love it, because there is nothing else.*
> *That is the moral torment to which all of us today are exposed.*
> Simone Weil[35]

The concept "Need for Roots," coined famously by Simone Weil has an important relation to direct democracy, and is of key importance if we are to reinitiate a coherent revolutionary project in the 21st century.

The influence nationalism (an essentially anti-democratic concept) has today can be attributed to the sense of uprootedness people experience in the contemporary neoliberal globalization. The human need for feeling part of a community within familiar territorial and temporal environment remains heavily neglected by the dominant heteronomous paradigm of individualism and exploitation.

Rootedness appears as one of the most important yet overlooked human needs. People are rooted when they not only feel protected, but actively and organically participate in the life of their community, preserving in this way alive certain traits of the past and expectations for the future. When brought to life, every human being is connected to a certain place of birth, cultural traditions and social environment. As Simone Weil writes, "Every human being needs to have multiple roots. It is necessary for him to draw well-nigh the whole of his moral, intellectual and spiritual life by way of the environment of which he forms a natural part."[36]

In the current state of uprootedness, however, The Nation-State, and eventually nationalism, appears as the last remnant of human collectivity related to actual geographical territory and historicity amidst digitalized global flows of authority and capital.

The contemporary pseudo-rational paradigm that places consumption and individual success as the main target of life has come to degrade all social links and bonding imaginary significations. As Castoriadis explains in his article "The Crisis of Modern Society," these processes have come to produce a crisis of insignificance in the so-called developed liberal societies that is slowly spreading to all their satellites in the developing world.[37] In this crisis social bonds are being diminished even on family level and the only entity that remains to provide any sort of identity, both on social and individual level, which links the future, the present and the past, appears to be the Nation-State.

The reality, however, is much different. There has been, and to some extent there still are, many other levels of human collectivities related to common ground on much smaller, decentralized and humane scale like the municipality, the city, the town, the village, the province etc. The nation or in other words—the State—has come to replace all of these, homogenizing the various cultures and traditions within its borders in its effort at establishing its authority as the only legitimate one. Thus, the national identity has come to replace or dominate every other bond of attachment. As philosopher Simone Weil suggests: "[m]an has placed his most valuable possession in the world of temporal affairs, namely, his continuity in time, beyond the limits set by human existence in either direction, entirely in the hands of the State."[38]

The Emergence of Nation-State

Nations are a recent invention, if we take into account the time span it occupies within the whole human history. It is tightly related to the logic of etatism and the emergence of the Nation-State. But before its domination over social imaginary, people's continuity in space and time was expressed, for example, through their shared experiences in medieval cities and towns. There was still a sense of belonging, but it was of a more fluid nature; without being exclusively set within strict territorial borders, specific language or narrow cultural traits.

What did not exist prior to the emergence of the Nation-State was that permanent, strictly defined patriotic devotion, on a mass scale, to a single object. Feelings of belonging and loyalty were much more diffusive and dispersed, constantly varying according to shared similarities and changing threats. Their character used to be far more complicated as they varied between interconnected groups and territories: Belonging to certain professional guild, town, region, community, leader, religion, or philosophical tendency. There was not one single extra-social national identity above all other intra-social interactions.

All this has changed with the emergence of Nation-States. By shifting the role of sovereign from the vibrant public life to the lifeless bureaucratic body of the state, nationalism (as the absolute internationalization of national identity by society) attempts at summing the total of people who recognize the authority of one and the same statist formation. Thus, as Weil suggests, when one talks about national sovereignty, he really means the sovereignty of certain Nation-State.[39] In statecraft, i.e. the art of making statist politics, the authority does not lay in the collective disposal of the people but it is being absorbed completely by the inhumane, merciless and bureaucratic etatist mechanism. The latter's complete hold on power, exercised through constant policing of everyday life, provokes on the one hand, popular feelings of mistrust, hatred and fear, while on the other, the national element demands absolute devotion and sacrifice to the very same structure, strengthening its total domination on material and cognitive level. These seemingly paradoxical characteristics complement logically each other. Total concentration of power in the hands of one extra-social bureaucratic entity requires for it to appear before its subjects as an absolute value, as a loveless idolatry, to which Weil adds the rhetoric question: What could be more monstrous, more heartrending?[40]

Unlike absolute monarchies of the past, in which the kings were being presented as direct descendants of God, modern nation-states present themselves as desacralized. But they are still embedded in a metaphysical imaginary: One that is not related to religion or God, but on hobbesian fears of the people and weberian bureaucratic rationalism. State is not a sacral idol, but a material object which serves "self-evident," nationally determined purpose, that must be forced above everything else. It allocates, as Kurdish revolutionary Abdullah Ocalan suggests, a number of attributes whose task is to replace older religiously rooted attributes like: Nation, fatherland, national flag, national anthem and many others.[41] The notion of national unity comes to reminiscent and goes even further than religious concepts such as the "Unity with God." It becomes divine in an absolute manner.

In order to achieve this total absorption of all social life, it strives at systematically destroying all organized and spontaneous forms of public interaction, so as to remain the only link between the past and the present, as well as the only social and individual signification. This antagonism between State and society, that takes the form of the former's efforts to constantly degrade public space and time, has low but ceaseless intensity. This process is invisible for the social conscience, because of the cautiousness that is required for the statecraft to not lose its supremacy that nationalism provides. The outcome of this national bureaucratization of everyday life is the infliction of traits of servility, passivity and conformity into people's imaginary, so as to make social interaction beyond Nation-State hardly imaginable.

Nation-State and Borders

The dynamics of State and nationalism enclose those that are situated within their frontiers, both on territorial and temporal level. On the one hand, it encloses through its territorial borders, and on the other, through the subordination of people's imaginaries to patriotic identities. Thus, the social flow of ideas through space and time is being obstructed. These national compartments restrain human creativity, and although not dulling it completely, they still seriously limit its potentials by placing border check ups, bureaucratic formalities, patriotic dogmas, and national antagonisms along the way. Simone Weil suggests that a closer examination of history will reveal the striking difference between flow of ideas and cultures in pre-national periods and the modern age of statecraft and capitalism.[42] Without romanticizing the Antiquity and the Middle Ages, one can see in those periods the fluid, creative, curious relationship inhabitants of cities and regions from different cultural and territorial backgrounds had with each other, as well as with their history, present and future.

Today on the contrary, while we are supposedly connected globally with each other, and the planet has become, as the popular saying goes, one "giant village," we see more suspicion to the foreign, more fear from the unknown, than our access to knowledge, science and technology should suggest. One of the main reasons for this is the deepening enclosure of public space and time by statecraft and nationalism. Similar processes have been observed by other thinkers like David Graeber, who in his book *The Utopia of Rules: On Technology, Stupidity and the Secret Joy of Bureaucracy*[43] observed the unfulfilled promises of the highly scientific, technological age we have already entered. These failed expectations he attributes to the civilizational shift from the real to the simulational, which is a direct result of the capitalist and bureaucratic dynamics that have uprooted our societies from organic experience of and intervention with public space and time.

The National Sense of Injustice and Loyalty

In the national context of statecraft, every notion of justice is being expropriated by and submitted to the expansionist nature of the State. As being an entity aimed at concentrating authority, it is always in antagonistic relationship with other similar formations, as well as with social uprisings for power redistribution. States always present themselves to be in position of injustice regarding their national mission for complete domination. According to Hannah Arendt, "tribal nationalism [patriotism] always insists that its own people are surrounded by 'a world of enemies'—'one against all'— and that a fundamental difference exists between this people and all others."[44] Justice loses its meaning and from a matter of public deliberation it is being absorbed by the patriotic discourse. It is being turned into a tool through which the Nation-State processes and condemns its opponents on geopolitical and on inner/structural level (as national threat and as national traitors, respectively). This inflicted sense of national injustice is used to fill the gap left by the uprooted imaginary significations that relate people and their communities to actual territorial environments and vibrant cultures. It attempts at turning acts, done in the name of homeland, into struggle against universal injustice.

But since this feeling of national injustice is of simulative rather than of organic character, it often leads to extreme attitudes like xenophobia, racism, discrimination, etc. Thus, it comes as no surprise when Weil concludes that "fascism is always intimately connected with a certain variety of patriotic feeling."[45]

By breaking all organic bonds of public life and replacing them with patriotic justice, the state becomes the only entity to which one can pledge loyalty. In such way monstrosities that are being conducted by national bureaucracies are being often adopted by the common folk as just. As radical geographer David Harvey explains, "national identity is the primary means by which the state acquires legitimacy and consent for its actions."[46] This is the reason why people willingly engage in wars that will cost them much, if not even their lives, while empowering, without to place in danger, their rulers, which have provoked the conflict in the first place. It is because of this imaginary signification of national loyalty against the ultimate injustice that has led societies to massacre each other. It is also most certainly the engine of the current rise of xenophobia and racism among people in the developed countries. Nationalism leads them to view themselves as victims of those that seek refuge from the rubbles of the Third World, neglecting the fact that it was the pillage and exploited conducted by their own nations that have provoked these current migratory waves.

Reproduction of Hierarchies

The sense of uprootedness slowly penetrates the social imaginary. The long tentacles of the dominant bureaucratic mechanisms embed themselves within the everyday lives of people, making it almost impossible to not view everything in terms of nations, states, and capitalist relations. Thus, the current heteronomous worldview is often being recreated by those who rebel against it. Social mobilizations that rise against authoritarian regimes or exploitative/parasitic capitalist systems tend to slowly replace the initial democratic traits with erection of hierarchies and leadership cults that mimic the patriotic loyalty to the Nation-State. This is especially true for, but unfortunately not limited to, movements that strive to achieve social change on representational level since, as Max Weber correctly concludes, "no party, whatever its program, can assume the effective direction of the state without becoming national."[47]

By being uprooted from their physical and temporal environment, with only the lifeless bureaucratic machinery of the State as a linkage between the human being and the world, people are compelled to embrace leaders whose role resembles that of the statist Leviathan. We can see this logic in pop culture, and particularly in cinema, where manufactured stars play characters that resemble contemporary popular perceptions of the state: either the flawless superheroes and top agents from the Cold War era, or the cynical and vulgar, but effective, antiheroes that have sprang during the ongoing crisis of political representation.

Thus, uprootedness breeds further uprootedness, or better yet, it expands itself, constantly securing the continuation of dominating bureaucratic organisms and power relations. The dangers of these processes have been examined by thinkers like Hannah Arendt, for whom the loyalty to religious or national groups and identities always leads to the abdication of individual thought.[48] But, we are not doomed to remain uprooted and thus easily controlled and manipulated. Possibilities for rooting can be found all around us that lay beyond the ideological mystifications of the contemporary heteronomous system.

Putting Down Roots
Putting down roots means restoring the sense of belonging that one feels toward their social and cultural environment, through shared responsibility. There is the need to make, as Andre Gorz suggests, "one's territory" livable again.[49] People should be linked to their cities, towns, and villages, through grassroots direct participation in their management and shape them according to actual social needs in the constantly changing world, instead of following predetermined and sterile bureaucratic planning. As Gorz puts it, "[t]he neighborhood or community must once again become a microcosm

shaped by and for all human activities, where people can work, live, relax, learn, communicate, and knock about, and which they manage together as the place of their life in common."[50] Democratic confederations, instead of Nation-States, can ultimately coordinate the activities of such emancipated and rooted communities, allowing them to reclaim their public space and time from the nationalist supremacy.

This requires for the constant creative activity of the public to once again be irritated. The Ancient Greek notion of Astynomos Orgè,[51] i.e. the passion for institution-making, must become vital social and individual signification that gives meaning to life, so as to allow for the responsible participation to replace the irresponsible consumption propagated by capitalism.

Such rooting cannot be "ordered" from above by "artificial" (i.e. extra-social) structures like electoral parties or powerful leaders, for reasons that we already explored above. Instead they should be guided by democratic organizations that emerge in ecological manner in the midst of everyday life by day-to-day necessities. Germs of such organizational type already exist on embryonic level in our contemporary surroundings in the form of neighbourhood assemblies during urban insurrections, markets without intermediates during economic crises, and even the regular meetings between neighbours that live in the same condominium. Political activists and organized groups should encourage and nurture the political element in such occurrences and spontaneous social movements, since politics is what allows societies to reclaim their space and determine their temporality.

An example of such rooting can be observed in the Paris Commune and how this was indicated by certain changes in the language. By taking direct control of their city, Parisians' reclamation of public space and time could be observed through the replacement of the terms *mesdames* and *messieurs* (ladies and gentlemen) by *citoyen* and *citoyenne* (female and male for citizen). As Kristin Ross observes, the former formula, used mainly by the French bourgeoisie, indicated the saturated time of Nation.[52] It confirmed and inscribed the existing then social divisions (i.e. the superiority of the bourgeoisie over the working class) and the continuation of a certain politico-historical tradition of statecraft and hierarchical stratification.

The introduction of *citoyen* and *citoyenne* by the communards, according to Ross, indicated a break with the national belonging. Instead, we can suggest that it addressed revolutionary withdrawal from the artificial/extra-social national collectivity and heading toward popular rooting in another politico-historical tradition, dating back to the emergence of the Athenian *polis*. It indicated new politicized relationship that people obtained with their surrounding and temporality and the way they linked themselves to their city and history: On the one hand, they began viewing themselves as stewards of their city, managing it collectively; on the other, they began conceiving of history as creation, in which they take an active part. *Citoyen* and *citoyenne* was not a reference to a certain social stratum, part of national entity, but an expression of equality and shared passion for political participation in public affairs. We could only imagine how this new democratic culture could have developed in the long run if the Commune was not brutally suppressed by the French army after only three months of existence.

Today, we see how our society of uprooted people willingly embraces narratives like that of nationalism that provoke hatred and fear, which ultimately leads to social degradation and cannibalism. The pseudo-dilemma before the modern individual is either to stick up with the Big Brother, i.e. the Nation-State, which to offer him a sense of belonging, or to become a kind of neoliberal "space cowboy" that wonders the world on his own in search of things and experiences to consume without any sense of self-limitation or ethical boundaries. But both these options strengthen each other and create a vicious cycle.

What seems to be hidden from the "naked" eye is the third option of rooting people through the recreation of public space and political time on the basis of direct democratic self-emancipation. This means detaching history from the sterilization of the Nation-State and linking it instead to the organic experience of life in our cities, towns, and villages. Historic facts should not be distilled by the means of statecraft but by the imaginary context of each epoch and society, allowing communities to determine their temporality. This would also mean that the spaces we inhabit become truly public, i.e. controlled and managed directly by those that inhabit and depend on them, and not by bureaucrats or capitalist markets.

This approach will not solve all our problems, neither will put an end to history, but it will get us closer to the paradigm of social and individual autonomy, which in its essence can provide people with the freedom to determine their past, present and future. The historic popular efforts at self-emancipation have shown the potential of such paradigm shift, offering us germs for us to use in our efforts today. It is in our hands to determine how our societies will move on.

Time and Ideology

Beyond Ideology: Rethinking contextuality

> *We are indeed conditioned by the contexts in which we live, but we are also the creators of our political and social constructions and we can change them if we are so determined.*
> Mary Dietz[53]

In the debate[54] between Simon Springer and David Harvey on what ideological frame the radical geography should adopt, Harvey's proposal for letting radical geography free of any particular "ism" seems to make a lot of sense. And although their polemical texts discuss, at first sight, the matter of radical geography, in my opinion, they have also a wider importance for the whole question of the role of ideology in the project for social liberation and emancipation. With small exceptions, the proposal of freeing ourselves from ideology seems highly neglected from the movements for social emancipation, and I think this is a big mistake if we want to actually involve more people in them and act constructively.

We see activists and thinkers busy trying to keep their ideological/identical "purity," often engaging in endless discussions on what is "anarchist," "marxist," or whatever. Don't get me wrong, I do not mean to abandon theory as such in the name of direct action. On the contrary, I think that theoretical research and critical thinking are essential for effective action. But Ideology must not be mistaken with theory.

Ideology and Non-contextuality

The Situationist International defined Ideology as a doctrine of interpretation of existing facts,[55] which can be understood as thinking in a non-contextual way. What this means is that the *ideologue* creates a certain type of analysis, influenced by his local context (social environment, economic development, culture etc.) and constantly tries to fit in its realities, born in different contexts, which often leads to non-understanding. We can see this clearly, for example, in the reactions of certain anarchists and marxists (having purist class analysis based solely on realities of 19th-century industrial Europe), which are judging the events in Rojava, searching there for "proletariat," that does not exist in the classical Western sense.[56]

In this line of thought, Ideology castrates the ideas one has, turning them into sterile/mummified dogmas that cannot exist beyond their initial form. The "ideologized" ideas become incompatible with realities/contexts that differ from the ones that have given them birth, and in a way, they become useless. The ideological non-contextuality obstructs both the theoretical research and the subsequent from its activity. Ideology creates the dogmatic notion of utopia and excludes everything that does not fit in it, even if there are some common principles (as we saw above in the case of Rojava), creating a sort of self-alienating elitist subculture.

Thus, ideology becomes more self-expressive than instrumental. It morphs into specific identity, often serving as an excuse for abdicating from broad social affairs. Instead, it creates its own circle of self-interest, open mainly to like-minded (sharing same Ideology) individuals who remove themselves voluntarily from the institutions and social networks of the society which they potentially could influence,[57] As Jonathan Matthew Smucker points out, "when we do not contest the cultures, beliefs, symbols, narratives, etc. of the existing institutions and social networks that we are part of, we also walk away from the resources and power embedded within them. In exchange for a shabby little activist clubhouse, we give away the whole farm. We let our opponents have everything."

Because of its non-contextual character, Ideology can be viewed as part of the dominant nowadays imaginary, based on bureaucratic logic, which needs to frame everything into "comfortable" fixed boxes, i.e. strict social and political roles, thus creating and strengthening identity, rather than ideas. In her book *The Emergence of Social Space*, Kristin Ross describes how during the Paris Commune, Catulle Mendès (representing the pre-commune order) is not really mourning the drop-in production but rather his anxiety stems from the attack on identity, since the shoemakers stopped making shoes, but barricades.[58] She traces this bureaucratic logic of narrow identity back to Plato, for whom in a well-constituted state a unique task is being attributed to each person; a shoemaker is first of all someone who cannot also be a warrior.[59]

One characteristic of the bureaucratic logic is its inherent predisposition toward hierarchy, since some tasks and roles are more important than others. David Graeber, in an interview for the Greek political magazine Babylonia, defines ideology as the idea that one needs to establish a global analysis before taking action, which presupposes that the role of intellectual vanguard (narrow ideologues-experts), have to play a leadership role in any popular political movement.[60]

Beyond Ideology: Context is All

In order for modern social movements to really challenge the existing order, they will have to overpass the limits of the contemporary imaginary, based on bureaucratic logic and fixed political roles. In practice, this means moving beyond ideology, i.e. locating desirable principles and results, and simultaneously making efforts at adjusting them to the local context. This does not mean to leave aside our ideals and to "go with the flow," but, on the contrary, to try to share them with as more people as possible, who most probably don't share the same (or any at all) Ideology/dogma/political lifestyle. In so doing questions such as "is EZLN anarchist or not?"[61] will become obsolete and replaced by "what do they propose, on what basis and principles, how and do we agree with what they do?" and so on.

In the end, it depends on the goals we target with our struggles. As author and activitst Modibo Kadalie suggests, "If politics is about action, then our political character and values—be it an individual, organization or group—appear while in motion. You cannot determine whether someone is an ally based upon their appearance or even their words."[62] If we strive to build a democratic and ecological society, then only if most of its citizens want to decide policies themselves can such a process be realized, and thus we must strive toward broad and intersectional alliances.

Steps toward this direction were made by Larry Giddings, who replaced the ideological label "anarchist" with the broader "anti-authoritarian."[63] He did so after acknowledging that whether he recognizes non-anarchist struggles or not, they still exist, and by ignoring them because they don't reflect his own notion of a "non-nation-state future," he ignores his own desire for such. He reached the conclusion that de-centralized social and economic systems, organized in democratic, non-statist manner, will only come through common struggles by various movements and broad social involvement.

So, instead of constantly trying to define what "true" anarchism is, he decided to try another approach: To locate the anti-authoritarian characteristics of various already existing social movements and to identify their common enemies (oppressors) and thus to connect them. And in order for such connections to be made, narrow ideological narratives had to be abandoned and replaced by general anti-authoritarian culture, which can simultaneously be determined and itself to determine the context in which it was created.

Moving beyond Ideology does not mean abdicating from our ideas and principles but their constant reevaluation and development. To the fears that without ideological identities we will be absorbed by the dominant culture of political apathy and mindless consumerism we can answer with the creation of a broad citizen culture of autonomous individuals who are, before all, speakers of words and doers of deeds.[64] Such a broad concept, based, as proposed by Mary Dietz, on the virtue of mutual respect and the principle of "positive liberty" of self-governance (and not simply the "negative liberty" of non-interference), will keep the anti-authoritarian spirit while allowing for interaction with large sections of the society and the implementation in practice of our ideas in different contexts. Only one such approach will help us escape the "sectarianism" (with all the separatism and lifestylishness that stems from it) of the political movements haunting them from the beginning of 20th century until nowadays.

Ideology and the Saturation of Time and Space

> "Time and space are modes by which we think and not conditions in which we live"
> ALBERT EINSTEIN[65]

According to the Situationist International, ideology[66] is essentially a type of analysis, developed in specific politico-historic context, that have internalized the latter's temporal and spatial characteristics completely. In this way ideologies are meant to present every other contextual reality (no matter how different) in the light of their initial environment.

Thus, cultural and racial superiority (based on pseudo-scientific theories from the past) remains as relevant as ever for heavily ideologized fascist trends, despite the immense scientific body of proofs that disband their theories. The industrial proletarian worker (of the 18th and 19th century industrial Western Europe) remains the main actor for genuine social change for a large section of the modernist Left, despite the fact that its social environment has long entered into a post-industrialist era of service-oriented economies. Space and time are thus being saturated by ideology, which prevents the recognition of alterations in temporality and spatiality.

Friedrich Nietzsche, in his work *Dawn of Day*, notes the similarities between Christianity and the radical ideologies of his period, regarding their attitude toward time.[67] According to him many on the Left, just like priests, preach among the oppressed for a future without oppressors. But like the mythical for Christians "day of judgment," socialist and other "revolutionary" utopias are eternally delayed. Nietzsche concludes that these ideologies ask you to be prepared and nothing more, waiting for something external, but otherwise you continue to live in the same way as you had lived before.

In similar manner, the situationists proclaimed ideologies to have long been dead,[68] since their effect saturates time and space, lacking essentially any vibrancy. The Situationist International maintained a philosophical opposition to every ideology, because it serves to sterilize everyday life. For them, ideologies are the despotism of a social fragment imposing itself as pseudo-knowledge of a frozen totality, as a totalitarian worldview.

Every ideology, regardless of its philosophical base, tends, like everything else in capitalist society, to rigidify, become fetishised and turn into one more thing to be passively consumed.

In order for real life activity to continually experiment and correct itself, i.e. to remain vibrant, it must not be ideologized, otherwise it will only have an illusory character that pushes the past and present into a cycle of *déjà vu*, making the notion of future meaningless. In other words, ideology tends to sterilize the present, subordinating it to the past, while excluding the future. This illusory character is evident from Guy Debord's magnum opus *The Society of the Spectacle*, where he argues that ideology is being "legitimated in modern society by universal abstraction and by the effective dictatorship of illusion."[69]

Levels of Ideology

There are several levels on which ideology affects social and collective perceptions of space and time. According to the analysis of Cornelius Castoriadis, developed in his critique of Marxism, we can detect two such levels: Of the established power and of the political sect. In both of them he detects problems that arise when one tries to gauge real activities after the mythical standards of a certain ideology:

1. When ideology serves as the official dogma of an established power in a country, it is a tool for this authority to conceal reality and to justify its policies, no matter what its actions are. Socialist states from the past, for example, claimed that they strive toward social equality and classless society, while simultaneously creating an all-powerful class of party functionaries and strengthening the authority of the already existing state bureaucracy. Signs and symbols were placed around public spaces, as a reference to supposedly ongoing Revolution, at a time when authoritarian counterrevolution was actually raging, with temporality and spatiality having been saturated artificially by the socialist ideology of the state.

   The same is happening today with the capitalist system. Its ideological veil presents it as the kingdom of diversity, individuality and freedom, while in practice we witness uniformity on a global scale and the merger of state and private sector. Ideological phrases such as "global village"[70] (neoliberal globalization) and "end of history" (Fukuyama) indicate, in the former case, that all space has become known to us and there is nothing new to be discovered since all has come under the same order, while the latter refers to the inalterable temporal character of the current situation.

2. Ideology, as the doctrine of a multitude of political sects, is the self-evident, self-justifying reason for small groups to act in a certain way. By abiding to a certain ideological purity, such sectarian collectivities voluntarily abdicate from public affairs, as a result of the conception of space and time they have adopted. Their temporality and spatiality have been saturated by their ideology, and new developments in society are being faced with hostility as they appear foreign to their non-contextual analysis. Because of this, groups that claim to be fighting for social emancipation disconnect their political activity from the ongoing social processes, entrapping themselves instead in a past-without-a-future, thus ceasing to be essentially revolutionary. The attempts to gauge real activities after the mythical standards of a certain ideology most often leads to political inaction.

Direct Democracy versus Ideology

French philosopher Claude Lefort argues that "[w]hile ideology emerges from within the social order, ideology dissimulates and conceals the conflicts that ensue from the internal divisions of the social. The discourse on the social can maintain its position of being external to its object only by presenting itself as the guarantor of the rule which attests, by its very existence, to the embodiment of the idea in the social relation."[71]

Direct democracy, on the other hand, as a non-hierarchical project that is antithetic to the oligarchic order of political representation, breaks with the symbolic closure that is typical of modern ideologies (which seek to incarnate rationality and appear to be immanent in the social order) and pre-modern religions (that present the social order as deriving from some extra-social source, or as german-american historian Ernst Kantorowicz puts it—monarchies were the embodiment of two orders of reality: The transcendent (or divine) and the immanent, that is, the king 'gave society a social body'[72]).

Direct democracy is a political form that creates public space and time, since it allows for constant interrogation and self-instituting to take place. Instead of concealing internal clashes within society, as ideologies do, direct democracy is based on what Jacques Ranciere calls *dissensus*—an activity that cuts across forms of cultural and identity belonging and hierarchies between discourses and genres, working to introduce new subjects and heterogeneous objects into the field of perception.[73] This does not mean that such democratic project is nihilistic or institutionless; on the contrary, it is essentially the constant self-institution of society itself which allows to wide deliberation and exchange of ideas and opinions to be constantly taking place.

In other words, direct democracy is the creation of a different relation of society with its past, present and future, a new relation with its traditions based on critical reflection and re-creation, and, as Castoriadis suggests, "the emergence of a dimension where the collectivity can inspect its own past as the result of its own actions, and where an indeterminate future opens up as domain for its activities."[74] It creates a new public space of social deliberation and political decision-making, where power belongs to all, while also establishes a temporality that is grounded in the present, but also directed at the collective creation of the future, without metaphysical reassurances of a religious or ideological eternity.

Direct democracy is incompatible with ideology, since the social order and the conflicts that may emerge from the grassroots of society are interlinked. There is not a separated source of power that can conceal itself. This is due to the democratic contradiction observed by Lefort, according to which democracy is the power of the people and the 'power of nobody,' because power cannot be identical or 'consubstantial' with a particular individual or group.[75]

Renewing the Revolutionary Project beyond Ideology
Danish philosopher Søren Kierkegaard has said that:

> "A revolutionary age is an age of action; ours is the age of advertisement and publicity. Nothing ever happens but there is immediate publicity everywhere. In the present age a rebellion is, of all things, the most unthinkable. Such an expression of strength would seem ridiculous to

the calculating intelligence of our times. On the other hand, a political virtuoso might bring off a feat almost as remarkable. He might write a manifesto suggesting a general assembly at which people should decide upon a rebellion, and it would be so carefully worded that even the censor would let it pass. At the meeting itself he would be able to create the impression that his audience had rebelled, after which they would all go quietly home–having spent a very pleasant evening."[76]

His words are, more than ever, abreast with our times. Populist ideologies have created the illusion for whole nations that they are rebelling through their vote for far-right or far-left parties and leaders: From Trump in the USA, through Victor Orban in Hungary, until the Coalition of the Radical Left (SYRIZA) in Greece. Such new governments dress the old normality in certain ideological mantle, leading in turn to increased popular cynicism. Unfortunately, among the enemies of the current capitalist nation-states there is still the tendency of embracing ideologies. The groups they form tend to prefer to relive historical events instead of daring to attempt to alter the future and rethink the past.

For the renewal of a truly revolutionary project, there is the need to rethink our perception of time and space: To not be afraid to live in the present and participate in the formation of the future, but also drawing on the lessons from (and rethinking) the past. For this reason, the project of direct democracy appears to be truly revolutionary, unlike the pseudo post-ideological discourse of neoliberalism, which still draws heavily on ideological concealment of boiling social conflicts. Only by incorporating the project of direct democracy into our struggles and visions we can go beyond the current saturation of time and space.

NOTES
1   Jean-Jacques Rousseau: *The Social Contract* (Ware: Wordsworth Editions, 1998), 20.
2   Marco Deriu: *Democracies with a future: Degrowth and the democratic tradition* (in Futures vol.44 issue 6, 2012), 556
3   Cornelius Castoriadis: *The Problem of Democracy Today* (in Democracy & Nature, The International Journal of Politics and Ecology vol.3 issue 2, 1997), 18-35
4   Cornelius Castoriadis: *The Rising Tide of Insignificancy: The Big Sleep* (unauthorized translation, 2003), 27
5   Chiara Bottici: *Imaginal Politics* (New York: Columbia University Press, 2014), 147

6   Jeff Klooger: *Psyche, Society, Autonomy* (Leiden: Brill, 2009), 7
7   Cornelius Castoriadis: *A Society Adrift* (unauthorized translation, 2010), 193
8   Fisher & Katsourakis: *Performing Antagonism* (London: Macmillan Publishers 2017), 295
9   Nana Biluš Abaffy: *The Radical Tragic Imaginary: Castoriadis on Aeschylus & Sophocles* (in Cosmos and History: The Journal of Natural and Social Philosophy, vol. 8, issue 2, 2012), 48
10 Cornelius Castoriadis: *The Rising Tide of Insignificancy: The Big Sleep* (unauthorized translation, 2003), 226
11 Ibid, 94
12 Cornelius Castoriadis: *Democracy and Relativism: Discussion with the "MAUSS" Group* (unauthorized translation 2013), 56
13 Cornelius Castoriadis: *The Rising Tide of Insignificancy*, 113
14 Cornelius Castoriadis: *The Imaginary Institution of Society* (Cambridge: The MIT Press, 1998), 101
15 http://www.onthecommons.org/stirrings-degrowth-movement#sthash.rNGHboto.dpbs
16 David AmesCurtis (Editor): *The Castoriadis Reader* (Oxford: Blackwell Publishers, 1997), 417
17 Serge Latouche: *Farewell to Growth* (Oxford: Polity, 2009)
18 Cornelius Castoriadis: *The Rising Tide of Insignificancy*, 116
19 Hannah Arendt: *The Origins of Totalitarianism* (San Diego: A Harvest Book, 1979)
20 Amadeo Bertolo: *Democracy and Beyond* in "Democracy and Nature" Vol.5, No.1, 1993
21 http://www.athene.antenna.nl/ARCHIEF/NR08-Parlement/Pitkin-REPRESENTATION.html
22 Simone Weil: *On the Abolition of All Political Parties*, New York Review of Books 2013, p.15
23 Op. Cit. 3
24 Hannah Arendt: *On Revolution*, Penguin Books 1990, pp215-282
25 https://freedomnews.org.uk/venezuela-state-power-when-the-left-is-the-problem/
26 http://new-compass.net/articles/will-disordered-always-rule-us
27 Interviewed for the series **Τόποι Ζωής (Topoi Zois) of the Greek National Television ERT3** (available online here: https://www.youtube.com/watch?v=6zmzJxlw2GM)
28 Cornelius Castoriadis: *The Castoriadis Reader* (ed. David Ames Curtis), Blackwell Publishers Ltd 1997, p.41
29 https://roarmag.org/essays/autonomy-revolution-movements-democracy-capitalism/
30 Simone Weil: *On the Abolition of All Political Parties*, New York Review of Books 2013, p.43
31 https://newrepublic.com/article/144592/trump-creating-propaganda-state
32 http://isj.org.uk/latin-america-new-left-governments/
33 Cornelius Castoriadis: *Figures of the Thinkable*, Stanford University Press 2007, p.124
34 Jacques Ranciere: *Hatred of Democracy*, Verso 2014
35 Simone Weil: *The Need for Roots* (London and New York: Routledge Classics, 2005), p111
36 Simone Weil: *The Need for Roots* (London and New York: Routledge Classics, 2005), p40
37 Cornelius Castoriadis: *Political and Social Writings: Volume 3* (London: University of Minnesota Press, 1993), pp106-117
38 Simone Weil: *The Need for Roots* (London and New York: Routledge Classics, 2005), p97
39 Simone Weil: *The Need for Roots* (London and New York: Routledge Classics, 2005), p124
40 Op. Cit. 4
41 http://libcom.org/library/nation-state-not-solution-rather-problem
42 Simone Weil: *The Need for Roots* (London and New York: Routledge Classics, 2005), p119
43 David Graeber: *The Utopia of Rules: On Technology, Stupidity and the Secret Joy of Bureaucracy* (London: Melville House 2015)

44 Hannah Arendt: *Origins of Totalitarianism* (London: Harvest Book, 1973), p227
45 Simone Weil: *The Need for Roots* (London and New York: Routledge Classics, 2005), p143
46 Network for an Alternative Quest: *Challenging Capitalist Modernity II* (Neuss: Mezopotamya Publishing House 2015), p51
47 Max Weber: *Political Writings* (Cambridge: Cambridge University Press, 1994), p106
48 http://www.tabletmag.com/jewish-arts-and-culture/books/254461/hannah-arendt-and-gershom-scholem
49 Andre Gorz: "The Social Ideology of the Motorcar" in *Le Sauvage*, September-October (1973)
50 Op. Cit. 15
51 http://www.athene.antenna.nl/ARCHIEF/NR01-Athene/02-Probl.-e.html
52 Kristin Ross: "Citoyennes et citoyens!" in *Communal Luxury: The Political Imaginary of the Paris Commune* (New York: Verso, 2015)
53 Mary Dietz, Context is All: Feminism and Theories of Citizenship. in Dimensions of Radical Democracy. edited by Chantall Mouffe.1992. Verso Books. p79
54 http://davidharvey.org/2015/06/listen-anarchist-by-david-harvey/
55 "There is no such thing as situationis, which would mean a doctrine of interpretation of existing facts." (Situationist International) from Internationale Situationniste #1, Knabb, p45
56 https://roarmag.org/essays/zapatistas-rojava-anarchist-revolution/
57 http://www.alternet.org/visions/why-we-cant-depend-activists-create-change
58 Ross, Kristin. The Emergence of social space. Verso 2008 p14
59 Ibid. p13
60 http://www.crimethinc.com/texts/recentfeatures/ideology.php
61 Back in 2002, the US journal Green Anarchy published a critical article of the Zapatista movement, named "The EZLN are not anarchist!"
62 https://roarmag.org/essays/the-stories-we-need-pan-african-social-ecology/
63 "Why Anti-Authoritarian?" an essay by Larry Giddings
64 Mary Dietz, Context is All: Feminism and Theories of Citizenship. in Dimensions of Radical Democracy. edited by Chantall Mouffe. Verso Books. 1992. p75
65 Aylesa Foresee: *Albert Einstein: Theoretical Physicist* (New York: Macmillan, 1963) p81
66 Situationist International: *Internationale Situationniste #1*, Knabb, p45
67 Shahin: *Nietzsche and Anarchy: Psychology for Free Spirits, Ontology for Social War* (Croatia: Elephant Editions/Active Distribution, 2016) p67
68 https://libcom.org/library/internationale-situationiste-8-article-6
69 Guy Debord: *Society of the Spectacle* (Canberra: Treason Press, 2002) p55
70 https://pdgc2015a.wordpress.com/2015/11/13/globalisation-is-the-world-becoming-a-global-village-2/
71 Vrasidas Karalis: *Cornelius Castoriadis and Radical Democracy* (Leiden: Brill, 2014) pp208-209
72 Ernst Kantorowicz: *The King's Two Bodies: A Study of Medieval Political Theology* (Princeton: Princeton University Press, 1957)
73 Jacques Rancière: *The Thinking of Dissensus: On Politics and Aesthetics,* (London: Continuum, 2011) p.2
74 Cornelius Castoriadis: *The Castoriadis Reader* (D.A.Curtis, Ed., Oxford: Blackwell, 1997) p.281
75 Claude Lefort: The Political Form of Modernity (Oxford: Mit Press Ltd, 1986) p.279
76 Søren Kierkegaard: *The Present Age* (New York: Harper Torchbooks, 1962) p.2

III. The temporality of social movements

Alexandros Schismenos

WHAT IS TO BE DONE? LENIN'S QUESTION

WHAT IS TO BE DONE? (Что делать ?) This was the title of a brief political leaflet written by V.I. Lenin in 1901 and distributed in 1902 among Russian revolutionaries. What is to be done?

Despite the question mark on the title, Lenin's response was imperative and would transform the revolutionary movement from inside in the coming decades. In a way, Lenin's answer determined the character of domestic and international politics of the 20th century. In a way, it determined the scope, the means and the horizon of 20th century radical politics. In a way, Lenin's response modernized the territory of the political and social conflict between the labour movement and capital, devising a mechanism that could utilize the revolutionary workers' force as a means for the seizure of State power: The Leninist party.

The title of the leaflet was borrower from a novel by Nikolai Chernyshevsky, written in 1863, which was Lenin's favourite book. In this novel, Chernyshevsky promoted the idea of industrial cooperatives, led by intellectuals that would guide the working masses toward liberation. Lenin adopted that idea and expressed in strategic and theoretical terms his mistrust toward the working masses and his own belief that they should be guided by an enlightened vanguard. This vanguard, the intelligentsia, the Leninist party, had the mission to impose revolutionary consciousness on the workers from without:

> "We have said that there could not have been Social-Democratic consciousness among the workers. It would have to be brought to them from without. The history of all countries shows that the working class, exclusively by its own effort, is able to develop only trade union consciousness."[1]

Lenin opposes the "spontaneity" of workers' struggles and the idea of the spontaneous development of revolutionary consciousness. He leaves no room for the creation of an independent working-class "ideology" that would emerge from the experience of the working-class movement itself and he argues that any deviation from the socialist ideology is nothing more than an adoption of the bourgeois ideology. In this manner he prepares his followers for the persecution of revolutionary dissidents that would follow the establishment of the Bolshevik regime:

> "Since there can be no talk of an independent ideology formulated by the working masses themselves in the process of their movement, the only choice is – either bourgeois or socialist ideology. [...] Hence, to belittle the socialist ideology in any way, to turn aside from it in the slightest degree means to strengthen bourgeois ideology."[2]

The separation introduced by Lenin between two mutually exclusive options, bourgeois or socialist ideology and, consequently, consciousness, destroys from the outset every pluralistic, democratic political ground. The workers' movement and the revolutionary "socialist" consciousness are separated, since, according to Lenin's view, revolutionary consciousness cannot be created by the dynamics and competitions within the social sphere, by the experience of social struggle itself, neither by confrontation and reflection within the political realm, but from the outside, from a fixed theory that, paradoxically, in the Platonic way, is supposed to precede the movement, since: "Without revolutionary theory there can be no revolutionary movement."[3]

The primacy of theory along with the separation of consciousness from actual working experience stripped the revolutionary movement from any autonomy in favour of the party, thereby creating a new kind of orthodoxy, any deviation from which amounted to apostasy or heresy. "We are the party of a class, and therefore almost the entire class (and in times of war, in the period of civil war, the entire class) should act under the leadership of our Party, should adhere to our Party as closely as possible," Lenin explicitly stated in 1905,[4] thus resolving in an autocratic way the essential political question of modernity: The collective representation of an autonomous subjectivity.

The Leninist party was presented as the answer to two key issues of the socialist movement; organization and representation. As he wrote in 1913, the party answered the central question of "the organization of state power." The State was regarded as an instrument that could serve the party, whose task was to strengthen the authority of the State after the seizure of power, in order to facilitate the "expropriation of capitalists."

"This expropriation will make it possible for the productive forces to develop to a tremendous extent [...] The development of capitalism, in turn, creates the preconditions that enable really "all" to take part in the administration of the state,"⁵ Lenin insists after the February Revolution of 1917, while the Bolsheviks get ready for the seizure of State power and the dissolution of the Soviets.

Would that really be his party's objective, the creation of a participatory democracy, where all could partake in State authority? He was as sincere as he was in his support of the Soviets before October. In April 1918, Lenin will abandon this inclusive attitude toward popular participation in the administration. In the following years, the new Leninist orthodoxy would be safeguarded by the Bolshevik secret police organization, Cheka (Чекá), which was granted the authority to suppress any resistance with any means necessary, no matter where it came from.

As Murray Bookchin pointed out, in *The Immediate Tasks of the Soviet Government* Lenin completely adopts the authoritarian perspective, leaving aside any libertarian inclination:

> "The main themes of the article are the needs for 'discipline,' for authoritarian control over the factories, and for the institution of the Taylor system (a system Lenin had renounced before the revolution as enslaving men to the machine)."⁶

In this way, Lenin cemented the dominance of the capitalist imaginary signification of "development" or "growth" and the autocratic imaginary signification of "State authority" over the traditional revolutionary movement. The only option left to other revolutionary factions was to either submit or be banned. The Socialist Revolutionary Party (SR) was banned in 1918 by official decree, something which led revolutionary Fanny Kaplan, who condemned Lenin as a "traitor of the revolution", to carry out an assassination attempt against him on August 30, 1918. She managed to fire three shots at him, which injured but did not kill the Bolshevik leader. However her bold and desperate attempt proved that the Bolshevik establishment was threatened mostly from revolutionary, not reactionary, resistance. This lesson was not lost to Lenin, who, while recovering from his wounds, proclaimed the necessity and urgency for the preparation of "the terror."

After 1921 and the suppression of both the Makhnovtchina anarchist farmers' movement in Ukraine and the sailors' uprising at Kronstadt by Trotsky's Red Army, any alternative voices within the socialist movement, from Rosa Luxemburg to the Emma Goldman, were silenced either by brutal force or by oblivion. We should remember that Rosa Luxemburg warned against Lenin's attitude as early as of 1904:

> "The social democratic movement is the first movement in the history of class societies to be premised in its every aspect and in its whole development on the organization and the independent direct action of the masses."[7]

Luxemburg remained a strong advocate of the creativity of the working masses, in contrast to Lenin, whom she considered "imbued, not with a positive creative spirit, but with the sterile spirit of the night-watchman state. His line of thought is concerned principally with the control of party activity and not with its fertilization, with narrowing and not with broadening, with tying the movement up and not with drawing it together."[8]

After the events of October 1917, in her manuscript entitled *The Russian Revolution*, written in September 1918, she condemned the newly founded Bolshevik regime in Russia, where she saw "the use of terror in so wide an extent by the Soviet government, especially since the Bolshevik politicians developed it as a theoretical system recommending it to the international proletariat as a socialist model."[9]

Similarly, the well-known anarchist and feminist Emma Goldman described her horror after the massacre of the sailors' uprising at Kronstadt:

> "I saw before me the Bolshevik State, formidable, crushing every constructive revolutionary effort, suppressing, debasing, and disintegrating everything. [...] Rarely has a revolution been fought with as little violence as the Russian Revolution. [...] This was demonstrated by the spirit of fellowship and solidarity which prevailed throughout Russia during the first months after the October revolution. But an insignificant minority bent on creating an absolute State is necessarily driven to oppression and terrorism."[10]

However, as we now know, these warnings and renouncements did not manage to weaken the tight grip of the Leninist and later Stalinist regime on the international workers' organization and imagination. The traditional workers' movement would make a last revolutionary stand in Spain during the civil war of 1936–39, and that defeat would be a prelude of the Second World War.

In 1965, philosopher Cornelius Castoriadis renounced Marxism all together, concluding that, both in theory and in practice, it had become, an ideology, according to the definition that Marx had given to that word: "a set of ideas that relate to a reality not in order to shed light on it and to change it, but in order to veil it and to justify it in the imaginary, which permits people to say one thing and do another, to appear as other than they are."[11]

However, Marxist parties refused to acknowledge this reality up until the fall of the Soviet Union, which, for a moment, seemed to signify the end of, not only Marxism, but of the revolutionary project altogether. Of course, this was a brief moment that now seems past us.

The Question Before Us

The Leninist model that revolved around the seizure, strengthening and totalisation of State power did not solve the social issue of inequality and representation. Instead, it made even more acute, by manipulating the workers' movement and subjugating society under the firm boot of totalitarianism. The Leninist model was quickly adopted by conservative, counter-revolutionary regimes of the extreme Right, when traditional elites entrusted fascist and Nazi 'storm-parties' with absolute State power, thus creating another creed of totalitarianism that did not derail the development of the capitalist system.

Today's neoliberal domination and its worldwide expansion have led the socialist project to moral and political bankruptcy after the collapse of the Soviet Union. Even European Social Democracy, Bernstein's most successful Marxist alternative to Leninism, has simply become another, albeit more or less reluctant, advocate of neoliberal politics.

The ideology of the "End of History," expressed by Francis Fukuyama, a prominent neo-Hegelian, in the 1990s, signified a brief era of consumer frenzy and social insignificance, when the spread of globalization seemed to offer limitless possibilities to capitalist "development" or "growth."

But the full implementation of the neoliberal project of capitalist control over society and nature seems to be hindered by three main factors:

1. The depletion of natural resources and the accompanying extreme ecological disturbances caused by the overheating of the planet.

2. The collective resistance of societies and the psychical resistance of individuals who create new horizontal social networks at a time when traditional institutions of socialization and identification are being destroyed.

3. The fundamental antinomy within capitalism itself, which tends to objectify human beings, while depending on human ingenuity, free peer communication and innovation in order to operate and expand.

As long as the financial motive of unlimited profitable growth remains the dominant social imaginary signification, the tension between the capitalist policies and the swift self-destruction brought about by their implementation is a breeding ground for societal crisis.

The political question we are facing now is deeper and more urgent. It cannot be answered by resorting to some fixed theory of history. It brings us before difficult tasks; to clarify the current crisis, to identify the possibilities inherent in social movements, to outline the horizon of a common, free and equalitarian future.

As Cornelius Castoriadis wrote, clarifying our social reality means to recognize the creativity of social movements, and acknowledge the primacy of action over theory:

> "Doing constitutes the human universe to which theory belongs as a part. Humanity is involved in a multiform conscious activity; it defines itself as doing (which contains the elucidation in the context of and in relation to doing as a necessary but not sovereign moment). Theory as such is a specific doing, it emerges once the moment of elucidation becomes a project for itself. In this sense one can say that there is actually a 'primacy of practical reason'. One can conceive of, and indeed there existed for millennia, a humanity without theory; but there cannot exist a humanity without doing."[12]

Our research is theoretical, but its horizon is practical. The concept of social transformation cannot be isolated in any one side of the action-theory polarity; it must transcend the polarity itself. This circular feedback of action and theory can be seen in the historical development of political praxis. Any action that transforms reality also transforms the knowledge provided by that reality, while also transforming the actors' conceptions, which are informed by this knowledge. Consequently, the active subjects, the social environment and the historical horizon of a political movement cannot be predetermined, since their relation is constantly modified, depending on the content of collective activity within the context of the broader social-historical field of human existence.

Those of us who have actively participated in modern social movements have experienced such transformations during major political events that have created temporal ripples in recent history, changing our perspective of the past and our aspiration of the future by creating a conscious collective present. In this sense, we cannot pretend as if there was any isolated point of observation available that would provide the ground for an "objective" historical analysis of our contemporary social reality. Instead, our view should be considered as more of a testimony and an attempt to partially clarify an ongoing collective experience. As Enzo Traverso pointed out, the distinction between subjective memory (Erlebnis) or lived experience and collective memory or inherited experience (Erfahrung) should also take into consideration their inner correlation and interdependence, since our collective representation of the past in public space depends on a continuous regression between social history and personal memory.

If we critically examine the representations of our own recent collective experience, we may clarify the conditions for recreating a different free public time toward a common future. As Jacques Ranciére explained during a meeting in Athens in 2017, what is important about contemporary social movements is their form, which combines the particular and the universal, the local and the global, in a common horizon of emancipation, "the idea that the question of the universal is really at play in the very form of the movement."[13]

Of course, the Zapatista communities and the revolution in Rojava are the best examples of societal democratic institution-building and future-creation in the world today.

However, the Zapatista communities remain a communal structure of Indigenous minorities situated in a rural region outside the main urban centres of the Mexican State, whereas the democratic confederation of Rojava was established after the collapse of local State structures during the Syrian Civil War. They create an autonomous social temporality in the periphery of the capitalist world, in places where dominant social time is either insignificant or has collapsed. Although they use modern networks of global communication to diffuse and spread their message and advance global solidarity among societies, their internal temporal existence is autonomous, except for the points of collision with external State authorities, which expand and contract as their struggle continues.

So, in the following chapters I will try to examine the temporality of social movements primarily in Greece and secondarily in France, two countries in Europe, with a stable and reinforced State apparatus that provide us with a relevant but different view of social temporal change in the centre of the capitalist normality. Greece is a small country, with little financial or military power but with a particular historical significance for Europe that amounts to an inexhaustible symbolic capital. I have personal experience of the social movements in the country. France has the largest military force and second largest economy in the EU and its own particular historical significance; social movements there are of great importance, drawing from a vast revolutionary history and within a multinational society. I do not have a personal experience of them, so my presentation will depend on texts and analyses offered by their actors.

Of course, social movements outside Europe are equally significant. In Latin America and Asia, uprisings continue, that share the ideas of direct democracy, horizontal organization, equal participation and direct confrontation with State authorities that characterize this contemporary current toward autonomy. The fact that they are not mentioned in the following chapters is due to the need to narrow the scope of my research in favour of depth rather than extent.

LESSONS FROM THE PAST: THE LEGACY OF MAY '68

In the late 19th century, Wilhelm Dilthey asserted that social sciences, the sciences of *Kulturwissenschaften* (culture) or *Geisteswissenschaften* (spirit) are grounded on the correlation between experience, cultural expression and *Verstehen* (historical understanding),[14] in contrast to natural sciences which use observation and experimentation. Social sciences understand their subject from within, whereas natural sciences examine their subject from without.

Since humans are historical beings, personal lived experience is the necessary condition for any understanding of the past. The imaginary revival of past experiences, the ability to put oneself in the position of the people of the past, presupposes a common substratum of human experience, a common ground for understanding. Dilthey thought that this common ground is offered by the unity and continuity of our historical-cultural social reality, which he called *Leben* (life). The unity and continuity is sustained by persistent elements, historical categories that frame distinct cultural, temporal and spatial phenomena within a common field of understanding. Historical categories arise from human historical existence itself, which means that their content is set only *a posteriori* and not *a priori*, like the epistemological categories of natural existence. Historical categories are abstractions of inherited past experience and among them Dilthey identifies as "meaning, value, purpose."

Meaning is the central category of historical existence, manifested in the interaction of the individual with his or her social environment, which "signifies the relations of parts of Life to the whole"; it signifies the unity of historical and cultural reality ex post. Since meaning is not an a priori category, "our conception of meaning is always changing [...] the purpose which we set for the future conditions our account of the meaning of the past."[15]

Obviously, it is easier to understand a past meaning if it intertwines with our own present aspirations in accordance to our own social imaginary significations, if it belongs to our own tradition. In this case, instead of being distant 'researchers' of that past, we are actually 'descendants,' because we can find remnants of that past co-existing with our present, albeit transformed by it. Their associations and transformations, their invisible connective threads and the history of their transformations create the common human history that unifies what it also differentiates, encompassing, within the historical continuum, social becoming and the discontinuous ruptures that generate it.

But also, in order to understand the past, we must look at the testimony of past actors and their texts. Again, these are open to re-interpretation, since what is revived through understanding is not an object, a separate entity, but a relationship, a correlation, a transformative connection of heterogeneous experiences on the common ground of human universality, the universality that made the ancient Roman poet Terence say "homo sum, humani nihil a me alienum puto" ("I am human, and I think nothing human is alien to me").

As Castoriadis pointed out, human universality is not based on rationality; it is not like the univocal Kantian universality of reason. Instead, it is rather a potential universality based on creative imagination, which produces significations that may be alienating or familiar but are always representations of a meaning that we can re-imagine, since "[w]hatever has been imagined strongly enough to shape behaviour, speech, or objects can, in principle, be re-imagined (re-represented, wiedervorgestellt) by somebody else."[16]

So, it is a common re-imagined meaning and a common re-represented history that connects the past and us. But understanding also implies choosing a point of view; a point of view close to the imaginary point of view of past actors. We understand history differently, we create a different representation of our common past if we adopt the point of view of the ruling elites and another one completely if we adopt the point of view of society. This is also the difference between formal, dynastical history and informal, social historicity.

How do we choose a starting point? When do the lessons of history begin? Every choice is essentially arbitrary since there is no distinct starting point of history. But there are events that are more relevant to others, not just in terms of temporal distance, but also in terms of inherent meaning. Moreover, according to Reinhart Koselleck, the space of past experience influences directly the horizon of future expectations, experience delimits expectation. Koselleck argues that "events can only be narrated, while 'structures' can only be described."[17] When we want to describe a temporal structure, like the correlation of present social movements to the past, it would be wise to start from the selection of the events that constitute the modules of this structure. Temporal structures can be materialized in institutional entities and can be represented by the symbolic systems of mnemonic institutions which crystallize social temporality.

By temporality we mean the dynamic inner rhythms of individual interaction and social cooperation that leans on an explicit set of rules of social engagement and organizational structures but also expands beyond it, creating a distinct social form of life within the social-historical field which envelops both individual and natural time, investing them with a common meaning. The creative feature of temporality is, in brief, the emergence of alterity or otherness and social temporality is the emergence of alterity or otherness that stems from the collective activity of conscious actors. Creativity is the qualitative dimension of social time. Repetition is the quantitative or identitary feature of social temporality, since collective activity creates temporal structures, social institutions and significations invested with functions of duration and reproduction.

A common spirit of social revolt and temporal rupture permeates the history of modernity, from 1789, to 1871, to 1917, to 1936, to 1968, to our present. These are years that represent abrupt ruptures of historical continuity and peaks of a temporal structure characterized by the emergence of radical temporalities against the dominant social time. Each year represents a historical originality, a new historical starting point, from where new possible futures stemmed, even if their full potential remained only imaginary.

In terms of formal logic this continuity-discontinuity complementarity seems contradictory and paradoxical. But logical terms of explanation are inadequate as regards historical categories. We could say that what links so different events into a meaningful continuity, what characterizes the historical-cultural narrative within which they belong, is precisely discontinuity inspired by a common project, social autonomy. But these events can only be structured *a posteriori*, since while they are still unfolding, the potential horizons of future expectations multiply, converge and diverge. Among them, May 1968 may be the closest to us, since in many ways it designates a revolution whose history has not yet been completed. This gives us a different perspective. When talking about social movements and historical events whose actors may still be living, whose collective memory is still rooted in lived experience, we should rather, instead of temporal structures, talk about temporal modes.

How are we to understand the temporal mode of the continuity/discontinuity complex of the events of May 1968 in Paris? It would be helpful to listen to those who participated in them. Castoriadis was one of them, and his brief brochure entitled "The Anticipated Revolution" is of particular importance to us. It is both a testimony and an intervention, since it was written and distributed by the end of May 1968 with the intention to influence developments, to appeal to the insurgents and to help shape another future. From the beginning of the text, the continuity/discontinuity polarity is evident, as Castoriadis stresses the originality of May 1968 by comparing the 'qualitatively new' features of that revolt to the revolutions of the past:

> "In past revolutions—the Paris Commune, 1917, Catalonia 1936, Budapest 1956—one can find antecedents and seeds. For the first time in a modern bureaucratic-capitalist society, however, no longer is there just the radical demand, now there is the most radical revolutionary affirmation ablaze before everyone's eyes and spreading throughout the world."[18]

This radical revolutionary affirmation consisted of a double rupture, which was abrupt and shook the idle normality of French society, starting from the occupation of the University in Nanterre. On one hand, there was the public denunciation of the fundamental imaginary significations of the system itself, of the authority of experts, of citizens' passivity, of individualism and consumerism. On the other hand, there was a burst of collective creativity emerging spontaneously from the occupied University of Nanterre, where the rebellious student movement assembled in large gatherings, practically put into question the hierarchy of education and the monopoly over knowledge and information while " beginning to bring about the autonomous and democratic self-management of collectivities."[19]

The seeds of another institution of society began to flourish within the direct democratic forms of political decision-making and collective deliberation exercised in general assemblies, in free lessons, in the removal of the divisions between teachers and students, university and society, thought and action, which created a new sense of free public time and space where "the exemplary forms of modern revolution have gained popular currency and become a reality."[20]

This collective experimentation with direct democracy in practice is what we could call the "positivity" of the Parisian May 1968. However, in Paris this positivity remained partial to the students and did not expand to broader social strata, something which also marks a sharp difference between 1968 and the revolutions of the past. The student movement that started, expanded and carried on the revolt soon faced the limits of its identification as a movement of and by the students. Castoriadis had warned against the danger of exclusiveness:

> "The movement of revolutionary students, however, cannot play a general role while remaining merely student oriented. This would amount to trying to act on other social sectors from the 'outside,' an attitude both false and sterile. The student movement has already acted 'from the outside' on other social strata of the population by providing them with an example, by teaching them once more the meaning of struggle, by prompting a general strike."[21]

A general strike was indeed proclaimed, but the workers' unions and parties did not trust the students' movement. The French proletariat of the time was proven less willing to assume the role of the 'revolutionary subject' that was designated to it by traditional revolutionary theorists. In 1968, it was apparent that nothing remained among the proletariat of what made it a revolutionary class. Castoriadis highlights the absence of a common "negative objective" between the students and the workers' unions besides opposition to the government. This absence of a revolutionary consensus divided students and workers on that moment that a unifying project was necessary. The gap of aspirations between the workers and the students reflected a situation where each group drew inspiration from the same space of experience, the traditional revolutionary workers' history, but, nevertheless, projected divergent horizon of expectations:

> "Among the students, at least among their revolutionary and active elements, the negative objective of opposition to the government was understood in a different sense than it was by the workers. For the former, the aim is to eliminate the government, whereas the great majority of workers, even though they do not favour the government, are absolutely unprepared to work toward its overthrow."[22]

The distance and disunity between students and workers was a dead-end for the unfolding of events in a revolutionary way. After the initial social explosion of May had slowed down, there remained little resistance before the re-instatement of the established order.

For their part, the students hesitated before the threat of cooptation, realizing a contradiction between action and theory, spontaneity and organisation, praxis and reflection. We discussed how Lenin resolved this contradiction in favour of theory and organisation, downgrading spontaneity and proclaiming that the workers could not be revolutionized by themselves. Is this actually the fatal dilemma of any uprising? Cooptation or disillusionment?

Castoriadis points out that if we accept this contradiction as irresolvable then we will end up justifying the existing status quo and affirming the dominant bureaucratic-capitalist imaginary:

"It is to accept the existing philosophy and reality. It is to reject a real attempt at transforming the world. It is to integrate the revolution into the established historical order. If the revolution is only an explosion lasting a few days or weeks, the established order (whether it knows it or not, whether it wants it or not) can quite easily accommodate itself to such an outbreak. Moreover, contrary to what it believes, the established order has a deep-seated need for these explosions."[23]

Nevertheless, the students could not become a "revolutionary subject" in and by themselves. Not only was their movement limited in the degree of participation, since it could not, by definition, encompass the whole or larger parts of society, but was also limited as regards public space, since the centres of the movement, colleges and universities, were semi-exclusive institutions and semi-closed places of academic interaction. Of course, the demonstrations and clashes with the police took place on the open public space of the Parisian streets and squares, the barricades were erected once again in the central points of urban life, but the political deliberation and decision-making processes were restricted to the university grounds and the amphitheaters. Even if the latter were open to anyone, not everyone felt familiar within those temples of authorized knowledge and many, especially the workers, refused to participate in an alien to them public space. The ideas that the students brought forward in university meetings, their horizontal organizational novelties, the direct democratic forms of organization that began to take shape remained restricted within the student movement. How could these be transposed into the centre of social life? Castoriadis acknowledged the difficulties of that problem:

"To transpose them in a fruitful way requires reflection. Otherwise, it is just repetition-the bureaucracy of thought to which the refusal to think inevitably leads. Attempts at mechanical transposition were made possible and continue to be nourished today by a false image of social reality, by a lack of understanding of modern capitalism, in which the mythology of 'workerism' plays a preponderant role. The student movement has acted almost all the time as though the working class were just one great revolutionary powder keg and as though the sole problem consisted merely in finding a good spot to place the fuse."[24]

Castoriadis' warning is very important, but emancipatory movements have rarely taken it into consideration. As we know, although the student uprising of 1968 managed to provoke the largest general strike in modern French history and inspire factory occupations and social mobilizations, it failed to permanently disrupt the temporal continuity of the French state which it had deeply challenged, it failed to overcome the tension between continuity and discontinuity, reflection and action, duration and moment.

The assimilative power of the capitalist imaginary is related to the flexibility of its identification and commodification mechanisms, but above all, it depends on the "positivity" of its central social imaginary significations, the technological dominance of nature, the capitalist ownership of labour and the state's authority over society. The workers' movement has transformed, through years of struggle, some particular areas of capitalist production, but the affirmation of these social imaginary significations by Marxists and Leninists made those struggles complementary to capitalist development. Moreover, any radical challenge against state bureaucracy became also a challenge against the bureaucratic organization of labour-unionism, dividing the workers' movement in terms of bureaucratization and sectarianism.

The originality of May 1968, therefore, lies in the encounter of the partial and hopelessly limited positivity of the students' movement with the general (and assimilated by the dominant capitalist positivity) negativity of the workers' movement. This is another point of discontinuity along the continuity of social struggles. This heterogeneous continuity of rebellion consists of a succession of discontinuities in contrast to the homogenous continuity of the tradition of authority.

We could understand this schema better if we look into what this "tradition of authority" means.

It is a concept brought forward in the works of Hannah Arendt and, later, Paul Ricoeur. In his lectures on ideology and utopia, Ricoeur emphasizes the central role of the "tradition of authority," which incorporates new institutions into long-lasting historical narratives.[25] Ricoeur locates the main social antagonisms within the tension between tradition and innovation, since tradition sets the framework for innovation and social transformations are more successful when they are part of the tradition of authority. Somehow, the "evil" of dominance, authority and alienation seems to remain as a residue through social transformations, although each social construct is in itself new in relation to the former. Thus, history can be understood through the historical narrative that refers to a historical structure, which of course remains open to restructuring. Temporality is considered a nexus of chronological and historiographical narratives, as analyzed in Ricoeur's later work *Temps et Récit*.

May 1968 formally ended in June, with De Gaulle's return (after a brief period of self-imposed exile) and his call for general elections. The Parisian rebels failed to overcome the antithesis between reflection and action, between creative rupture and 'revolutionary' tradition. Does this prove that the tradition of authority cannot be transgressed, as Ricoeur implies?

On the contrary, Castoriadis insists on the possibility of overcoming social heteronomy through the institution of social autonomy. For him, the tension exists between the instituted social imaginary and the instituting social imaginary, in other words, between the consolidation of institutions and the creativity of society. Thus, autonomy means direct and reflective self-government, where institutions are placed under public democratic deliberation and individuals, as free subjectivities, are equally involved in political power.

Castoriadis, on his part, was in favour of the destruction, not overcoming, of these 'antinomies' that separate reflection from action, experience from innovation and reality from consciousness, because, as he argued, they stemmed from the conditions of the system, not the human condition per se. As he insisted, if the project of autonomy is to proceed, "it will not be by 'making a synthesis' of these antinomies, or by 'overcoming' them. It will be by destroying the very ground from which they inevitably arise."[26]

However, this destruction cannot be completely negative, and it cannot be restricted to a mere reaction or a nihilistic trend. There should be an autonomous positive side to rebellion, an institution-building process that would materialize the imaginary significations of freedom, equality and autonomy into actual social institutions. What could be the content of those institutions?

Castoriadis, addressing the rebels in 1968 raises the prospect of direct democracy:

> "What is to replace the social division between directors and executants and the bureaucratic hierarchy in which it is embodied is self-management [autogestion], namely, the autonomous and democratic management of various activities by the collective action of those who carry them out. [...] The actual exercise of self-management implies and requires the permanent circulation of information and ideas. It also requires the elimination of partitions between social categories. It is, lastly, impossible without the plurality and diversity of opinions and tendencies."[27]

In this way, the movement could inaugurate a real opening to another future, toward an emancipated and autonomous society. An opening that would not mean lawlessness, but autonomy, that would not be restricted to a moment of rebellion but would expand in the course of social time. The contradictions between the rebellious instance and social duration can only be overcome creatively by the openness of society by itself:

> "Openness is that which constantly displaces and transforms its own terms and even its own field, but can exist only if, at each instant, it leans on a provisional organization of the field."[28]

The only safeguard against bureaucratization, authority and assimilation is the creative collective activity of autonomous individuals within a direct democratic social organization. This way the dominant distinction between means and purposes is overcome and the temporality of discontinuity, the social-historical threads of meaning that constitute the discontinuous pattern of autonomy vis-à-vis the established continuity of hierarchy and exploitation can manifest in a free public time and a free public space. The self-management and, even more, self-institution of social movements is also the only safeguard against their cooptation by the system, since it means instituting forms of collective action, decision-making and deliberation that are incompatible with the dominant hierarchical form of representation, "i to give [them] a form that will convey its content for all time and make it utterly impossible to coopt—that is, capable of being conquered again and again, in its ever-new truth, by living beings."[29]

Was there such an activity that moved beyond the moment of rebellion and produced a different kind of autonomous duration visible in 1968? I believe that there was, and this kept the memory of May enduring against all efforts to mummify it. In order to locate it we should move our gaze away from the Parisian streets and universities, to the countryside, the fields and other peripheral places that equally rose up that year worldwide. There we will find another temporal aspect of 1968, stretching beyond May, in direct reference to a communal way of daily life.

The American professor of comparative literature Kristin Ross visited Athens on 2018 as the keynote speaker of that year's B-fest antiauthoritarian festival. In her speech and during our discussion later, she spoke to us about the temporal mode of duration. She focused on the need to criticize the dominant narrative about May '68, which is promoted officially and reduces the significance of the events to the personal experience of a few celebrated protagonists, by decentralizing our perception of the events:

> "You have to, as you say, decentralize the images that come to peoples' minds which were put into place very powerfully by a whole industry of memory [...] Now, what has disappeared from that picture was the workers, the outskirts, while the entire country was involved, not just Paris. [...] And then you had the trope of the generation that comes in as the narrative. Now, to go further to what you are talking about, then what completely disappears is anything outside of France. The situations in the USA, in Mexico, in Japan, in South America. It is Immanuel Wallerstein who was the first person to argue that, if '68 has any kind of significance at all, it is because it was a worldwide event."[30]

If we proceed to examine this worldwide event, we may find ourselves surprised by the plurality and diversity of the rebellious manifestations and the organizational forms that originated in 1968. Besides the workers and students, Ross helped us understand the importance of the farmers' implication in rural social movements, movements that occupied space and created a temporality of duration which expanded over decades.

One of the most prominent examples is the ZAD movement that began in 1968 and continues today, both as a living experience and as an organizational model for land-occupying movements. It is a grassroots social movement that initially opposed the creation of an airport in Notre Dame des Landes, a fight that was won after 50 years, in 2018, when the government dismissed the airport plan. However, the movement soon evolved toward the permanent creation of a community. The acronym ZAD was originally derived from the designation of the area by the State as *Zone d'Aménagement Différé* (deferred development zone). But then the members of the movement adopted the term, translating it to a *Zone A Défendre* (zone of defense). Over time, ZAD became a communal, direct democratic and collective form of life, creating a different social temporality of duration, offering an alternative to systemic social time. With amazement, we heard Ross describe her experience with ZAD, where she visited and lived for long periods of time over the last decades, as a radical change in the temporal flow of daily life:

> "Obviously we are not talking about a situation that is entirely outside " time moves differently, because salary labour has been pushed to the outskirts of peoples' life. And that means, that, for example, interruptions are different, or what counts as an interruption is different. Because people engage in a task and everybody works on a task and you are constantly interrupted by people who need something [...] so the flow of time, the flow of peoples' pursuits is very different."[31]

With that different flow of time comes also a different sense of personal identity and collective identification. Duration means that the act of rebellion is not temporally restricted and that the participants in that duration see themselves being also transformed over time, as their daily lives converge in a communal lived experience and their activities progress toward proactive institution-building, not just reactive resistance. New forms of social relations are born and change over time and new familiarities develop that transgress the traditional contradictions between theory and action toward new modes of socializing and new forms of shared co-existence. Ross characterized this as a 'Commune-form,' which is a way of expressing both a communal way of life and a continuation of the imaginary significations and the value-content of the Communes of the past, more prominently that of 1871. In that manner, the autonomous temporal duration created by the people in ZAD becomes an original, but not isolated, part of the history of social struggles, connecting the past and the future within daily life:

> "In order to inhabit a struggle over a long duration as they have, you constantly have to transform yourself. You have to transform yourself in order to transform the situation that you share, and you have to transform your own identity, your own personal position. So, it's not really about a political view or a form of organizing, it is really about a lived existence."[32]

However, we may now ask: What kind of community is this? We can think of enclosed communities that are internally hierarchical and exploitative and externally competitive, like the Muslim and Hindu communities in India. So, the important question as regards the character of a community would be: What is the value content of communal living? Does it promote exclusiveness and self-closure or inclusiveness and openness? It is not just the fact of common being but also the political functions of equal and free decision making and public deliberation, that are necessary to be instituted in a direct democratic way, based on the autonomy of the free individual. In order for the individual to retain her uniqueness, freedom and autonomy, the community must evolve into an open, democratic society, creating a free public time and space, where the bonds of solidarity can be sublimated into institutions of equality and political emancipation.

The importance of the concept of the citizen, as an autonomous political agent is that is transgresses the communal identities that are based on other, heteronomous modes of affiliation, like religion. The free and equal citizen that constitutes the political collectivity is linked to autonomy, since her individuality and subjectivity embody individual autonomy in the context of social autonomy.

So, we are talking about open communities based on direct democracy, reciprocity and individual freedom with their definitive features being horizontality and interconnectivity. Being decentralized, they should form centres and hubs for public decision making and self-governance based on the control of second order translocal institutions by the base local units. The form of the network in lines of democratic confederalization is an organizational pattern that emerges from actual social interconnectivity and inter-complementarity.

This kind of communal lived existence combines the temporal mode of rupture that is the rebellious event with the temporal structure of continuity that is duration, creating a living history. We can imagine how the inherited antinomies between the particular and the universal, the discontinuous and the continuum are washed away by this combination of memory and experience that is oriented toward building a common future on the grounds of a common present.

The contradictions of the dominant representation of time, as something externally imposed on us, and of political events, as something that comes from above, crumble before the actual social reality created by the direct democratic institution-building, which transforms both the landscape and the individuals that reside on it. Only if we inhabit the struggle, as Ross said, can we hope to make our collective existence more than a struggle. That is, when we move from the initial stage of resistance, which is the main feature of the temporality of May '68 in Paris, toward the stage of collective institutions, which is the main feature of the temporality of 1968 in the provincial fields, we can find ourselves in a position to defend something positive. As Ross described to us, "there is a change in what Bachelard calls the muscular consciousness of the land which has become part of the value that you are defending. And still, you have eclecticism within the group, nothing of that has solidified as homogenous."[33]

If we don't recognize the temporal mode of duration, we will not be able to comprehend why the events of 1968 still resonate with our contemporary struggles and movements. By this conjunction of different temporal modes and structures, a radical social temporality that unifies a multiplicity of heterogeneities, without leveling them beneath a homogeneity imposed from above, emerges.

And it is this affiliation of significations, this endurance of the values of equality, direct democracy and collective freedom that connects 1789, 1848,

1871, 1917, 1936, 1968, etc. with our present. It is up to us, those that are living today, to guarantee the continuation of the project of individual and social autonomy, not by repetition, but through innovation, not by enacting the authority of past tradition, but by inspiring the values of a common future.

At this point, it is time to move forward, from 1968 to the social movements of the 21st century, in order to re-connect these historical threads.

Lessons from Experience: The Brief Summer of the Anti-globalization Movement

Starting from the Zapatista movement in 1994, social movements have emerged in a direct confrontation with State authorities around the world. One common feature is the resistance against the dominant neoliberal policies. Another is the quest for a different kind of societal organization, in accordance with the direct democratic, horizontal, equalitarian structure of these movements.

Should we want to designate a symbolic starting point for this social-historical phenomenon, we might as well set it on January 1st, 1994, when the Zapatista movement made its first global public appearance by occupying the cultural capital of San Cristóbal in Chiapas, Mexico. The influence of the Zapatista movement spread across the globe, in part due to the novel organizational elements that it brought forward: The absence of a separate, authoritarian leadership, the use of digital communications to promote their project globally, the emphasis on communal assemblies and direct democracy for self-government, the refusal to endorse the traditional Leninist policy of State power seizure, the creation of a different mode of co-existence with the land and nature. For a brief period of time during the last years of the 20th century, it seemed as if Zapatistas were an anomaly within a global system that was establishing a new, unchallenged worldwide normativity.

In 1994, the future looked bleak for radical movements in Greece. The collapse of the USSR had justified the anarchists' rejection of Communist parties that had defined Greek radical politics even before WW2, although this did not prevent anarchists from being overwhelmed by the rise of insignificancy, as Castoriadis called it, meaning the rapid de-politicization of

Western societies. By 1994, trends like the DIY and punk lifestyles had permeated the anarchist movement, which was quite juvenile, since it had only re-emerged in Greece after 1974.[34]

And then, in 1999 the huge demonstrations in Seattle against the World Trade Organisation Ministerial Conference happened. They signified the beginning of a new era for radical social movements because it was a revolt taking place in the centre of the globalized capitalist world, a revolt whose voice and images spread across the globe in real time and which in a way reinvigorated the project of direct democracy.

An article from the Institute for Social Ecology summarizes the significance of those demonstrations that also resonated with many of our aspirations in Greece:

> "In the 1999 anti-WTO demonstrations in Seattle, the spirit of direct democracy was in the air.. [...]This chant, "This is What Democracy Looks Like," repeated passionately, over and over, summoned a new way of thinking about political reconstruction. When taken to its logical conclusion, this chant means not only that we must take to the streets but that we must take to our communities, where we may demand the power to rebuild a vital and passionate political life. This chant inspires us to develop a new understanding of citizenship defined not in relation to a state or nation but in opposition to nations and states. It is time to redefine citizenship in relation to local communities and regional, continental, and even global confederations."[35]

The call for direct democracy projected on a global level, the need for an alternative form of grassroots globalization in direct confrontation with the capitalist globalization of transnational and interstate mechanisms of financial growth and social exploitation, the feeling of a new sense of solidarity beyond borders, were the political issues at the core of the Seattle uprising that resonated across societies, becoming common elements of an alternative future horizon. These were the significations that arose in the centre of radical political discourse along with the anti-globalization movement, as it was called. However, this spirit was not shared by everybody in the movement, since there were also religious or nationalistic groups promoting the general anti-globalist cause in a completely different, isolationist framework, and soon ideological contradictions and oppositions resulted in the fragmentation of the movement.

In Greece, a group of people with an anarchist background assembled and organized our participation in the anti-global demonstrations that followed, in Prague on September 27, 2000, against the IMF and World Bank and in Genoa on July 20–22, 2001, against the G-8 summit. For us it was a definitive experience that changed the scope and depth of our political vision.

In Prague, we felt this new sense of global solidarity among social movements actualized, as we joined comrades from all around Europe in direct clashes with the police forces under the music of drums performed by a group from North America. On the other hand, we also felt the hostility of the local society that had just exited a Communist regime and was extremely suspicious against everything remotely anti-capitalist. We were both delighted to meet with people from countries like Turkey or Macedonia that shared our common vision for social emancipation from State and capitalist authorities and a bit disappointed to find out that we also shared a common confusion and ideological frustration before the new state of things brought up by the unification of capitalist markets on a transnational level.

As capitalist markets were expanding everywhere and the implementation of the Shock Doctrine, later described by Naomi Klein, destroyed traditional societies and corroded the foundations of social identification and bonding, the character of the system itself was changing, with neoliberalism becoming the undisputed dogma and profit accumulation mechanisms moving away from traditional commodity production markets toward stock exchange markets. A definitive element that intensified all social problems and brought about a new temporal sense of urgency was the awareness of impending ecological disaster due to the neoliberal policy of unlimited growth. As Murray Bookchin observed:

> "At the same time capitalism has produced a new, perhaps paramount contradiction: the clash between an economy based on unending growth and the desiccation of the natural environment. […] At present the most promising struggles in the West, where socialism was born, seem to be waged less around income and working conditions than

around nuclear power, pollution, deforestation, urban blight, education, health care, community life, and the oppression of people in underdeveloped countries—as witness the (albeit sporadic) antiglobalization upsurges, in which blue- and white-collar 'workers' march in the same ranks with middle-class humanitarians and are motivated by common social concerns."[36]

Bookchin was right as regards the sporadic and fragmented character of the anti-globalization uprisings of that time, which would lead to the quick decline of that movement, without, however, uprooting the seeds of global solidarity and grassroots connectivity that it helped plant.

In Genoa, the situation was different in many respects. For one, the demonstrations took place in a Western European country, Italy, which had not experienced a Communist regime but had, on the contrary, experienced severe capitalist exploitation and severe State oppression. There, society was expressing its solidarity with the demonstrators in moving ways and the anti-capitalist sentiment was widespread. However, police brutality was also harshest. When, during the first day of demonstrations, we learned of the assassination of Carlo Giuliani, both rage and fear took over us. But on the next day, the huge demonstration of hundreds of thousand people was again brutally attacked by police and para-military forces, whereas at night police raided most demonstrator camps and, violating every human right, ambushed, beat, arrested, tortured, and raped protestors. Fourteen years later, in 2015, the European Court for Human Rights ruled against the Italian state for the use of torture against demonstrators residing at the Diaz-Pertini school.

As the BBC reported, "[t]he Strasbourg-based court also urged Italy to ensure it has proper sanctions against torture, saying current law 'was inadequate for the punishment of such acts and not an effective deterrent against their repetition'. In 2012, several officers were found guilty of falsifying evidence concerning the raid."[37]

We were lucky enough to be located at another place, a stadium at the outskirts of the city constantly monitored by a police helicopter flying above our heads, but without any raids happening there.

"*Libera Genova!*" and "*Assassini!*" were the slogans echoing across and over a city that was chained by police blockades in every street. These slogans expressed society's rage and frustration against the murderous police brutality, which would, nevertheless continue to intensify after each insurrectional event in the future.

Our conclusion after the demonstrations in Genoa was that traditional radical politics and ideologies had reached a dead end. Anarchists had failed to escape the nihilistic lifestyle of a fringe counterculture, whereas Marxist organizations had become strict hierarchical structures and sects, that sought to dominate their respective social sphere of influence.

New ways of grassroots networking had to be invented in order for the project of direct democracy to be diffused to broader social strata. An article by Nikos Ioannou published the following year in the anarchist ContAct magazine summarized our experience:

> "In Genoa, the most massive demonstration of the anti-globalization movement took place, not because the movement is on the rise, but because the divisive conditions and the terrorist attack by the Italian State have united a popular movement whose culture can rarely be found elsewhere. After the massive demonstration on Saturday, which followed the bloody demonstration of Friday, everybody hid something in their reports. They hid the nakedness of the anti-globalization which was made more obvious under the garments of nationalism and left fundamentalism."[38]

Nevertheless, the anti-globalization movement did not have time to mature organizationally and theoretically, since on September 11, 2001, international politics changed dramatically after the attack against USA by Al-Qaeda fundamentalists. State authorities of the West armoured their police forces both in terms of armament and in terms of legislative immunity, whereas social movements contracted within their respective national borders. But the final act of the anti-globalization movement was staged in 2003 in Thessaloniki, Greece, which provided the spark for a new emergence of political collectivities with a new orientation toward direct democracy, social ecology and openness to society.

A decisive moment for the evolution of that prospect was the creation of free social spaces (or centres), starting with Nosotros at Exarcheia, Athens in

2005 and later in other parts of Athens like Vyronas (Lambidona) and Pireaus (Favela) and also in Thessaloniki (Micropolis), Ioannina (Alimoura), and Komotini (Adelante). Free social spaces or centres were self-governed entities on a common ground, mainly a building, managed by direct democratic open assemblies, where cultural activities, lectures, lessons, concerts, and political events could be organized without charge or exclusions.

Free social spaces open up a common ground for collective activities and direct democracy. In that manner, they also create a different form of common daily temporality that is interrelated but also distinct from the temporal modes of a political collectivity or a social movement.

In this way, a horizontal political network became the connective temporal tissue between the more determinate daily temporality of free social spaces, which create forms of co-existence and the more indeterminate long-term temporality of social movements, which create forms of resistance.

As Dimitris Roussopoulos explained during a meeting in Athens, flexibility and openness is vital for social movements:

> "So, what is important is not to pay too much attention to the traditional Left, the authoritarian Left. What you have to do are two things; you have to create broad coalitions with people who you may have disagreements with but whose support you need. And you have to be able to bring in ordinary people. And you have to be very patient with ordinary people, because ordinary people do not have the skills to get up in front of a microphone to speak, they don't read as much, you have to find all sorts of different ways to communicate with them, you have to make it personal."

Free social centres provided a space for daily coexistence and common activities in the centre of the city, open to society and closed to State authorities. However, their aspiration was not to create an independent commune or a detached community, but rather hubs of democratic deliberation and limited self-management. This is different than self-government, which implies a higher degree of autonomy and cannot be confided to the limited space of a social centre. They signify, however, a step toward the ordinary problems of ordinary daily life, where the seeds of emancipation and democracy are rooted.

The 2006-2007 Greek student movement

From May 2006 to April 2007, the neoliberal Greek government of right-wing party New Democracy (ND) attempted to amend Article 16 of the Greek Constitution, which forbids the creation of private universities. A massive student movement rose up against this policy, occupying every University campus in Greece and organizing populous protest marches in major cities, which were confronted by police brutality. Despite the fact that most occupations were controlled by leftist student organizations like EAAK (Union of Independent Left Movements), there was also a visible and active anti-authoritarian faction that ensured that many occupied universities were self-managed by direct democratic open assemblies without party representation. These direct democratic assemblies also led the demonstrations and were on the first line of the clashes with the police forces, creating a kind of "hegemony" on the streets, which was evident by the, never seen before, majority of the black-red flags over the red ones. However, this kind of "hegemony" of the anti-authoritarian manner of activity was not reflected on the demands or the official statements of the movement, which remained defensive and reactive.

The student movement was victorious in the sense that the government bill was withdrawn but never actualized its potentiality, since it did not put into question basic social relations like the professor—student hierarchy, the content of education and the access to education. By definition, any student movement is temporary, since one can only be a student for a brief period of time and abrupt, while student issues rarely touch broader society. But, for the same reason of temporariness, it can also be quickly radicalized. In Greek universities, only the political parties' youth organizations preserve the collective memory of students' struggles alive in university campuses, since theirs are the only enduring structures, while the individual actors of those struggles have finished their studies and moved elsewhere.

So, the temporality of the student movement is a combination of a spontaneous present, constrained by political structures of a fossilized past; this produces a short and narrow collective memory that may become ultimately dispersed into personal histories that can never return to their imaginary place of origin. The student movement is unique among social movements in that it is delimited by age and its lack of direct self-reflection.

As such it is easy for its political creativity to be hindered by the persistence of outdated revolutionary icons and ideological dogmas that affect emotion rather than reflection. The minority of direct democratic student assemblies failed to produce a critical democratic plan as an alternative to the traditional leftist fixations, despite the fact that in practice they had moved beyond leftist representational mechanisms and toward open assemblies. So, while the organizational forms of the student movements became open and horizontal, the agenda under discussion continued to be restricted to the opposition to the educational bill until that bill was withdrawn. But there were no improvements in Greece's educational system, neither did the creativity of the students continue. As the movement withdrew, traditional roles and processes were re-established, and the next generations maintained a distant memory of the events. This was the narrow effect of the movement.

The broad effect, however, was that it diffused anti-authoritarian ideas and direct democratic practices to a wider audience, outside traditional radical collectivities. Many of the college students were politicized during the movement and a culture of solidarity and resistance spread across Greek society, strengthening the social-historical conditions for the popular uprisings that followed.

Rural Movements toward Social Ecology

An alternative temporality and a more radical discourse against traditional political narratives would come up on a different sphere of social collision, that of local communities against State environmental and energy planning, where the elements of direct democracy, social ecology and antiauthority would be combined in a more radical synthesis. This also implies a radical reconfiguration of the relation between locality and universality.

Locality is related to personal and social daily temporality, since it provides the daily social environment of the individual, the space of lived experience and the time of co-existence. It is the now-and-here of the individual, where time and space are formulated in actual social relations.

Locality, being an existential category of self-identity and self-history, is also the essential foundation of every mode of political representation. Even when local authorities are devoid of decision-making power, they remain necessary as the only means of base representation. Locality, thus, is an empirical category that permeates all levels of social being – it constitutes the ground of the existential, the roots of the social, and the territory of the political.

Universality is the a priori logical condition of every locality and the imaginary dimension of our common being as humans. It is not attached directly to daily personal existence but forms the basis of mutual recognition; modes of understanding that constitute the ontological condition of both the existential and the social level. Universality is what gives substance to the sense of a common good, a common future and a common responsibility.

Universality can be interpreted both as immanent and transcendental. As a transcendental category, it goes beyond our experience, like the idea of humanity. As an immanent category, it is constitutive of our experience, as both the condition of historical consciousness and the logical a priori of every other form of social belonging. Universality creates a horizon of solidarity for equalitarian social movements and the basis of humanism.

Locality and universality are inextricably interwoven within human experience. If we start from the empirical point of view of locality, universality forms the imaginary horizon; if we start from the imaginary point of view of universality, locality is its empirical actualization.

Social movements, by definition local but global in aspiration are living examples that transcend and overcome the established borders and fragmented divisions that characterize the dominant bureaucratic and capitalist organization of society.

From 2007–2009, a series of nationwide camping and demonstrations were organized by a grassroots network of direct democratic citizens' assemblies, the Πρωτοβουλία ενάντια στην εκτροπή του Αχελώου (Initiative against the diversion of Acheloos) in co-operation with anti-authoritarian, anarchist, leftist and ecological political collectivities at the upper stream of the Acheloos river, the second longest in Greece, against the operation of the Mesochora dam. The Mesochora dam, rising up to 157 meters in height, was designed to divert the mighty river toward the fields of Thessaly, whose riversystem became polluted and useless due to extensive monoculture and overuse of agricultural chemicals. The local community of the Mesochora village, facing the danger of their homes, heritage and memories being drown under the lake that would be created, had already been involved in a struggle of direct confrontation with the Greek State since 1987.

It would not be an exaggeration to say that antiauthoritarian movements in Greece discovered ecology by reading Bookchin and Castoriadis. When, in 1987, clashes erupted at the mountainous village of Mesochora between police forces and local residents the members of the Ένωση Αναρχικών (Anarchist Union) failed to appreciate the importance of that struggle.

Social ecology provided a different way against the machinations of State policies and representative politics. Murray Bookchin touched on deeper issues, connecting the ecological crisis to capitalist domination, social injustice and the dominant capitalist worldview of mastery over nature. A worldview that promotes the exploitation of nature, originating from a system based on the exploitation of humanity. Bookchin's synthesis evoked a different perspective and a different ethical set of values that combine the democratic ideals of freedom and equality with the ecological understanding of the fundamental interdependence of nature and society and of the ways that domination over nature is rooted in social inequality and the structuring of society along exploitative relations:

> "I believe that there has to be an ideal and I favour an ethical anarchism which can be cohered into an ideal. I believe that it's terribly important to have a movement that is spiritual, not in the supernatural sense, but in the sense of German Geist, spirit, which combines the idea of mind together with feeling, together with intuition. [...] There has to be a body of values. I would prefer to call them ecological because my image of ecology goes beyond nature and extends into society as a whole—not to be confused in any way with socio-biology, which I think is an extremely regressive, reactionary tendency."

In other words, the ideal of social ecology demands a radical transformation of the social imaginary, an understanding of the complementarity between societies and their natural environment and a radical re-imagining of both internal and external social relations in terms of individual and social autonomy and equality that can be institutionalized in political forms of direct democracy. After the global experience of common solidarity in the anti-globalization movement, social movements began interconnecting on a local level as well. Social ecology embedded within the project of direct democracy provided the basic ground for a more inclusive, encompassing both the social and natural worlds, perception of the common good. When the State's project of the diversion of Acheloos was brought up again in 2007, people across Greece joined the struggle of the locals and managed to halt the project. They continue till today the fight for the destruction of the dam. At the village of Mesochora a real direct democratic assembly is held amidst the annual summer demonstrations against the dam or whenever developments deem it necessary, where all the villagers and visitors, of every age and occupation, are gathered to deliberate and decide on their actions in terms of gender equality, free speech and mutual respect.

Similarly, in 2011 in Chalkidiki, local communities came together with ecological and antiauthoritarian collectivities to fight against the gold mining project of the multinational El Dorado Gold Company. The company sought and gained the help of the state, which deployed police forces to protect the mining installations and attack citizens. Legal measures were also deployed, with protesters being accused under the anti-terrorist law for founding a terrorist organization, only to be acquitted in 2019 after a long trial. Having been confronted with fierce State oppression, propaganda, lawsuits and home invasions, the struggle continues, as does the ecological desertification caused by the Company.

More recently, in 2017, in Epirus and Western Greece, a direct democratic ecological grassroots movement has emerged against oil and gas extractions by powerful oil trusts like Exxon-Mobile, Repsol - Energean, Total, etc. Events such as the demonstrations in Ioannina in 2018 and Athens in 2019 where thousands gathered in protest, have been organized in a direct democratic and horizontal manner by open citizens' assemblies that have been created in several places, from Ioannina to Crete. These movements, converging in assemblies and forming networks of solidarity, represent a new social ecological consciousness, a new radical imaginary oriented toward autonomy and democracy.

They share the temporal mode of long discontinuous duration, since they rise against long-term state enterprises and plans. During that duration, in the case of the Mesochora dam, has stretched over 35 years, bonds are formed, people grow, and personal histories are established.

But the movements' temporal modes are neither daily nor weekly but rather abrupt, depending on external factors and long-term social developments. The temporality of those ecological social movements revolves around annual meetings and gatherings that bring together local communities with activists from the urban centres. In the absence of occupied land or space, ecological movements create temporary situations of symbolic reclaiming that cannot however produce a continuous duration of daily co-existence, like it happened in movements like ZAD.

Of special interest are communities like the village of Stagiates at mount Pilion in Thessaly, where people have self-organized their community in a direct democratic and ecological manner, in order to collectively defend and manage the springs of the mountain which are threatened by privatization. It is an experiment that created a continuous duration based on daily co-existence where people can actually realize a different collective life form. The difference between self-organized ecological communities and ecological social movements is also a difference of temporality, the difference between continuous long term duration experienced in daily co-existence, which creates collective and intersubjective relations and bonds on every sphere of life and discontinuous long term duration experienced in annual meetings, planned demonstrations or abrupt events, which creates collective relations and bonds specifically related to situations of political struggle.

The influence of social ecology is also well felt in urban ecological movements, in the city of Athens, the city of Thessaloniki, Ioannina, Volos, where desolation creates urban deserts, movements for the liberation and re-creation of free public space, more recently movements against gentrification and construction. Urban ecological movements in Greece have discussed Murray Bookchin's Democratic Municipalism project in several instances, with diverging opinions. However, while his proposed strategy is of great interest and importance, it remains rather utopian as regards Greece, which is a highly centralized State, with municipal authorities directly dependent on the government and the main political parties.

The Rebellious Event of December 2008

This long-term duration of social ecological movements was intersected by an event that ruptured the temporality of Greek society as a whole.

On December 6, 2008, Alexandros Grigoropoulos, a 15-years-old student was assassinated at Exarcheia by policeman Epameinondas Korkoneas. Almost immediately that night but also on the following days, students and a multitude of people gathered across the country in massive demonstrations that soon started besieging police stations. In the following week, protest marches, public building occupations, and clashes with police forces spread to every Greek city and town, amounting in the biggest riot event in recent Greek history.

Political activist Nikos Ioannou describes vividly the spirit of the demonstrations on Sunday, December 7, the day after the murder:

> "We all understood that this is a rebellion. But shortly before the afternoon rally began, no one could imagine its size. [...] We are tens of thousands, and our numbers grow as the demonstration proceeds. Here the 'average person' disappears and becomes what everyone is.
>
> But the political establishment and the media fail to grasp this reality. They perceive the world only as something over which they want to dominate. They don't see what's going on beyond their perception. They operate on the basis of the 'average person' and from this position they attack what they consider to be a deviation. That is the condition of their power. I did not see gangs in this uprising. I have seen thousands of people break and burn whatever limits their existence. First on the list were the cameras. Police stations, banks and government agencies followed. The flames from the Omonoia police station illuminated the embarrassingly quirky faces of the nearly 1,000 members of the Communist party, illuminating their shame."[39]

December 2008 was a turning point for radical politics. Anti-authoritarian political collectivities acted spontaneously but with maturity during the uprising, opening free public spaces to broader society with the occupations of the Law School in Athens, the Theater School in Thessaloniki, the Cultural Center and the Municipal Radio Station in Ioannina, etc. Those occupations, open to the public, became centres of organizing the struggle, politicizing the people, communicating the spirit of rebellion.

The riots in December 2008 had the temporal mode of a *kairos*, or radical event, a decisive time of rupture with the dominant social temporality, caused by the emergence of instituting society in the central political stage. That radical rupture with established temporality was symbolized by the burning of the Municipal Christmas Tree at the centre of Syntagma square, opposite the Parliament. However, the contingency of the event meant that it was a moment of eruption that had the mode of a double reaction to the initial murderous incident. Both State mechanisms and radical political collectivities were caught unprepared; both were re-acting, without anybody pro-acting. It was an uncontrolled incident that resulted in an outburst of social rage. So, it initially lacked the element of institution building and amounted more to a direct confrontation with the State symbols and forces. What were impressive were the spread of the riot around the country and also the broad participation of society in the demonstrations and occupations.

It was the school students who besieged police stations with oranges and marched along with their schoolmates and parents amidst tear gas bombs and against repression. Certainly, anti-authoritarian, leftist and anarchist collectivities played their part, especially by occupying public buildings and organizing open assemblies, but it was the children's rage that in a way legitimized the riot in the eyes of Greek society as a whole. It was perhaps a riot of anarchistic character, but it was not a riot of anarchists.

In December 2008, the peoples' participation in massive numbers at the demonstrations indicated that, despite the contingency of the murderous incident that ignited social upheaval, the rage, the rejection of State authority, the solidarity among insurgents and the deep mistrust toward police forces and officials were elements that had reached a boiling point within Greek society. The riot came two years before the official announcement of Greek's debt crisis but expressed the peoples' deep resentment and mistrust toward the State.

It is a mistrust rooted in the long-term history of social struggles against the Greek State. We cannot recount that history here, but we can pinpoint one or two historical peculiarities of Greece. The Greek revolution that started in 1821 soon declined into a civil war in 1823 over the distribution of wealth and power (the money of a British loan and the seats of the newly founded government) among the different elites and local aristocracies that effectively ruled over their territories in a semi-feudal manner, owing only allegiance and taxes to the Ottoman Sultan. After independence, the Great Powers of Europe imposed at first a Bavarian and later a Danish king on the newly founded Greek Nation-State in the 1830s. The first Greek police force was established by the monarchy in June 1833, modeled after the French National Gendarmerie of Louis-Philippe, which had been reorganized after 1830 in order to impose colonial order in occupied Algeria. As such it was a military body created to subdue the rebellious local population. The mistrust of the people against the police force was there from the beginning.

Later, during the 20th century, Greece was the only place in the world where WW1 continued until 1922 and also WW2 continued until 1949. After the liberation from German forces in 1945 a bloody civil war erupted in 1946 between the Communists and the Royalists, the first of which constituted the main body of the popular Resistance against Nazi Occupation, whereas the latter were Nazi collaborators. With the help of the United States led by Truman, the Royalists won the war and the Extreme Right reigned for a 30-year period, during which Communist and Socialist organizations where illegal, desolate islands were transformed into exile camps and political executions were held under a special anti-communist martial law. After the restoration of parliament and the abolition of monarchy in 1974, police brutality continued and the autocratic mechanisms of the deep State carried on their background work, under the guise of liberalism.

The Greek nation-state has a peculiar history, since the State apparatus and bureaucracy were just copied from the 19th century Bavarian prototype, only to be violently imposed on local populations that shared a very different, multilingual, multicultural, communal and partially self-administrative tradition of authority, forged during two and a half millennia of successive Empires, the Macedonian, the Roman, the Byzantine, the Ottoman. This meant that from the beginning there was a chasm between the people and the State, which, despite being organized according to Western impersonal rationalism, practically became the biggest patron in a traditionally patron/

client system where personal relations between wealthy families still weigh more that formal laws and institutions.

So, that event of December echoed a long history of tension and frustration between the people and the State in Greece. In that sense, December was a social-historical event the duration of which lasted for more than a month, while the manifestations of public outrage also evolved. It created a mark in history, a "before" and an "after", where the various incidents were interrelated in a distinct temporal sequence characterized by a common meaning, questioning State authority and resisting police brutality. Reinhart Koselleck has argued that an event rises above the "threshold of fragmentation" due to its significant unity of meaning:

> "Thus, for the meaning of historical sequence, there is a *threshold of fragmentation* below which an event dissolves into unrelated incidents. A minimum of 'before' and 'after' constitutes the significant unity that makes an event out of incidents. The content of an event, its before and after, might be extended; its consistency, however, is rooted in temporal sequence. Even the intersubjectivity of an event must, insofar as it is performed by acting subjects, be secured to the frame of temporal sequence."[40]

In that sense, the riots of December constitute a historical sequence whose content extends from the past to the future of social struggles, connecting the Polytechneio uprising of 1973 with the Occupy movement of 2011 that was to follow.

Dimosthenis Papadatos argues that December 2008 had three distinct phases.[41] The first, from the evening of December 6–9 was characterized by large demonstrations in 42 Greek cities, public building occupations and clashes with the police. It was the violent phase, largely depicted on the most violent and popular images of the riot. The second, from December 10–17 was characterized by attempts to organize the people and issue specific political demands, by student unions demonstrations, by the creation of grassroots media and occupations of radio stations, while the political parties were forced to take sides. SYRIZA was the only mainstream party that did not condemn the rebellion, along with the leftist ANTARSYA. From 18–24 the rebellion retreated, while the State unleashed every tactical and legal weapon at its disposal, even charging underage students with anti-terrorism felonies. Whether we accept this chronology or not, there was another decisive element for the retreat of society from the streets, namely the appearance of militant armed groups that shot three policemen on January 5, 2009, an incident which marked the end of the events.

So, as of January 2009, signs of disorientation were apparent, with the State authorities re-organizing and the people finally withdrawing into a post-insurrectional confusion. There was a rift within and between assemblies. In 2009 everyone asked the question: "What comes after the uprising?"

It was a deeply political question that had been raised by reality itself. With all its intensity, the rebellion did not manage to overthrow the government. However, it was a truly widespread uprising, led by students, that involved large parts of Greek society, not just radicals. December's interpretations are many, and for those of us who have experienced it these interpretations have a strong personal element.

At the time, some claimed that "November belongs to everyone, December belongs to no one," meaning that any official political representation of the insurgents would be impossible, contrary to what had happened with the Polytechneio uprising in 1973 against the Junta.

In our interpretation, the main consequences of that December rebellion were:

1. The shaking of the validity of State authority;
2. The shaking of the dominant model of representation;
3. The re-claiming of free public space and time.

But these consequences, which affected new social upheavals following the bankruptcy of the Greek state in 2010, were not acknowledged by the traditional political collectivities. Without a "revolutionary subject," where could the 'revolutionary leadership' stand? The paths that would lead from December to the Occupy movement of 2011 were not visible to all.

The Occupy Movement in Greece

On May 25, 2011 an online call for the occupation of Syntagma square against the Memorandum of Understanding that Greek PM George Papandreou had signed with a Troika (IMF, ECT, and EU) representing the bankrupt State's creditors, was answered by a massive gathering of people at the square facing the Parliament. The Occupation grew, combined with a multiplicity of parallel events, festivals, demonstrations, but mainly, self-organizing the square in terms of direct democracy. The Occupy movement lasted for several months against many odds, while similar direct democratic occupations of public spaces took place in all major Greek cities. State oppression and police brutality was also a daily threat against which the occupants had to defend both themselves and free public space. Oppression reached the heights of severity on June 15 and especially on June 27–30, when police forces attacked with every means at their disposal, finally running out of tear gas and having to order more supplies from Israel. On both cases, the people resisted, did not disperse, re-gathered and not only re-occupied the square but also cleaned it from debris and tear gas cans. The vice-secretary of the ministry of Public Safety called the events of June 28 "the big day of the war," and that wartime attitude was held by the whole cabinet against the people.

The Occupy movement in Greece was a step forward on the paths that had been opened on December 2008. Particularly:

1. The shaking of the validity of State authority escalated into the rejection of State authorities and State jurisdiction over public space. Long discussions and meetings revolved around the idea of a different social organisation without separated authorities, namely direct democracy;
2. The shaking of the dominant model of representation escalated into a rejection of political representation. Appointment by lottery, circular participation to committees and the revocability of delegates by the popular assemblies were proposed as alternatives to the manipulation of the peoples by parliamentary oligarchy;
3. The re-claiming of free public space and time evolved into the re-creation of free public space and time by the people, for the people. The main squares and streets of major cities were transformed from commercial places of commodity circulation to political places of human interaction and deliberation.

Another important element of the Occupy movement was its sense of actualized globality, since it happened in many countries at once, from Spain to USA and was followed by successive rebellions in almost every part of the world, from the Arab Spring of that year to Hong Kong and Latin America in 2019. Having been locally suppressed, the wave of rebellion spread elsewhere, always against neoliberal policies, social inequality and social impoverishment, parallel to the financial crisis that was officially dealt with by bank refunding, depletion of public services and the increase of billionaires at the expense of the middle and lower social strata. This phenomenon of the globalization of rebellion that runs against the globalization of capitalism stresses the temporal mode of urgency that specifies our contemporary world.

Nevertheless, the pragmatic limits of the occupation were also apparent. The popular assembly of Syntagma Square did not occupy an independent place of common living where an actual enduring community could be formed, but the main Square of Athens, a hub in the centre of the city that could provide a space of common meetings and discussion for limited time. Daily interaction did not involve all spheres of daily life. Temporary public services were self-organized, like common lunches, medical facilities, legal teams and even a radio station (Radio Entasi) but there was no challenge against the dominant capitalist model of production, labour and consumption, since there was no self-organization of workplaces. General strikes were called by mainstream unions but not a permanent one, each lasting for a day and without consultation with the occupants.

Moreover, the self-claimed jurisdiction of the popular assembly ended beyond the limits of the Syntagma Square. Whereas the issues under deliberation referred to every aspect of Greek social life, in actuality there was almost nothing practically done to change the real conditions of Greek society except symbolic actions and propositions. The occupants proved that the solutions offered by the State were actually based on false assumptions and deliberate lies but did not have the power to force their own proposals into realization. The occupants shared a lived experience of direct democratic deliberation and direct democratic decision-making, but they lacked the means for decision enactment and project implementation. People stayed in tents at the square for several weeks, but they could not stay there indefinitely, since their homes and the centres of their personal life were elsewhere in the vast city.

This also raised the question of the borders of a direct democratic society. Would those be similar to the borders of the nation-state? Apparently not. But that meant that direct democracy could not be grounded on national representation terms nor could it be limited within national borders. As Castoriadis pointed out:

> "To achieve the widest, the most meaningful direct democracy will require that all the economic, political, and other structures of society be based on local groups that are concrete collectivities, organic social units. Direct democracy [...] requires that [the]citizens form an organic community, that they live if possible in the same milieu, that they be familiar through their daily experience with the subject to be discussed and with the problems to be tackled. It is only in such units that the political participation of individuals can become total, that people can know and feel that their involvement will have an effect, and that the real life of the community is, in large part, determined by its own members and not by unknown or external authorities who decide for them".[42]

This would require not only a multiplicity of autonomous and self-administrated local units, but also a federalization of their network beyond national borders, accompanied by the destruction of centralized State structure. Of course, the Occupy at Syntagma did not amount to so much but was rather a limited local unit of public deliberation.

That is why its temporal mode was that of a short duration of social interaction, rather than that of long duration of co-existence, like ZAD.

The movement carried on into autumn with a multitude of actions, demonstrations and grassroots networks throughout the year, even though the Syntagma occupation ended on October after multiple clashes against police forces. Despite the people's persistence, the State's attitude did not change. On October 31, PM George Papandreou declared a plebiscite about an upcoming new loan accompanied by further austerity measures and that marked the fall of his government. A new government led by banker Papadimos was sworn in on November 11, 2011, with the mission to accept the new loan without questions, as it did.

Popular unrest continued, up until February 12, 2012, which saw a massive demonstration against the second MoU that ended up in further clashes with the police forces and a night of rioting in Athens, Thessaloniki and other major cities of the country. After that, elections were held, which diverted again politics within the walls of Parliament signifying the rise of SYRIZA.

But they also marked the seven-year long participation of the neo-Nazi criminal party of Golden Dawn in the Greek Parliament, which ended in 2019 after the Nazi's had committed hundreds of violent acts against immigrants and antifascists, including the murders of Pavlos Fissas and Shehzad Luqman. For these murders, the leadership of the Nazi party was prosecuted and went to trial, while the antifascist movement managed to contain their presence in public space, with thousands of anti-demonstrations, antifascist events and actions of solidarity to immigrants.

The Rise of the Xenophobic Right

How could a Nazi organization, officially outlawed, be voted into the Greek Parliament in five consecutive elections, the last happening while the party's leadership was imprisoned and awaiting trial for murder? This question appeared as newspaper headlines and TV shows long after the fact, but people in the streets of Athens and in other areas of Greece were asking this question much earlier than 2012. The big chill behind the frozen smiles of journalists when Golden Dawn appeared in the spotlight is characteristic of the atmosphere of the crisis years.

The collaboration between Golden Dawn and the police forces, their financial and legal support by the big right-wing party ND, their funding by Greek tycoons and conservative wealthy families, was well known for more than two decades. What was new was the support given to the national socialist cannibals, not by the nation-state which was built on the same nationalist myths that inspire their own fascist ideology, but by a part of Greek society (around 6% of the voters). Of course, it is support through voting, not through participating, since the actual force of Golden Dawn on Greek streets remains limited, always dependent on the assistance of police forces. But this support didn't diminish, even after Golden Dawn party members, under its leadership's command, murdered anti-fascist rapper Pavlos Fyssas in September 2013. Extraordinarily, the party, while on trial, was yet again voted into Parliament in the elections of January and September 2015.

It is known that conservative nationalist ideas have deep roots in Greece. It is no coincidence that the Kingdom of Greece became the first nation-state to be constituted in Europe after the French Revolution in 1831. It is no coincidence that Greek history textbooks reproduce the most antiquated ideas about "national continuity" and "cultural homogeneity." It is no coincidence that patriotism was adopted by the Left and that Greece, until the elections of 2019, was the only European country to also have a Stalinist political party (the Communist Part of Greece (KKE)), besides the Nazi (Golden Dawn) party, in Parliament. It is no coincidence that Greece remains the only European state that organizes student parades on national holidays. These trends became apparent also in the demonstrations regarding the Macedonian name dispute, when extreme-right groups together with religious zealots organized gatherings against the Prespes treaty between Greece and North Macedonia in 2018.

All these facts are known components of the neo-Greek social imaginary, which combines delusions of ancient grandeur and feelings of present inferiority into a patchwork of images of a mythical past, a deluded present and a bleak future. Some are common elements shared by Balkan nationalism, but these are also strengthened by the reference to a world-famous ancient history. In any case, it is a nationalism of the miserable, morally obsequious and servile toward the powerful, that on occasions voluntarily serves the grand imperialist chauvinism of a Great Power. Such is the official Greek Right and the nationalism expressed by Greek governments.

But Golden Dawn goes much further. The nationalist elements of the neo-Greek social imaginary are necessary but not sufficient conditions of the neo-Nazi phenomenon. Nationalism is the negative identity formation of a heteronomous society by the exclusion of external alterities (which is the other side of the positive identity formation by the perseverance on internal ethnic homogeneity), manifested in archaic attitudes of attraction and repulsion toward the Stranger/Foreigner. However, the racist element that neo-Nazis bring about as a fundamental component and explicit intention is something more radical.

The Stanger/Foreigner in the national-socialist worldview is not the external limit, the difference, the Other, who can be subjected to proselytism, assimilation and incorporation. On the contrary, in the national-socialist worldview, the Other is a dark, inverted reflection of the Ego, an internal division, the Adversary, the antithetical pole that must be eliminated. The very existence of the Other is considered a threat against the existence of the Community, the extended Ego and is rendered to an unacceptable existence, an existential *casus belli*.

Consequently, the differences between the Friend and the Enemy (according to the social anthropology of Nazi political theorist of justice, Carl Schmitt), the characteristics that define the threatening Other cannot be of a cultural or political nature (like classical nationalism supposes, emphasizing on language or religion or custom), namely acquired characteristics. They have to be inherent traits, natural and biological, unchangeable by education or civilization, and here comes the preference to pseudo-physiology, skin colour, bloodlines, and lineage.

If nationalism is manifested as hatred toward the Other as the Stranger, Nazism is expressed as hatred toward the Other as the Enemy. Here, we can locate a further differentiation. Hate toward the Other as the Stranger/Foreigner negatively reflects a positive investment on the Ego, which is presupposed. Imperial chauvinism debases foreigners, founding this hierarchical distinction on grounds of arrogance and pride. It is pseudo-historic, in the sense that it projects a mythical history as a claim to that pride, constructing a past from supposedly glorious historical events. If the Stranger/Foreigner is willing to accept these claims, along with their own inferiority, then they are assimilated into the dominant social hierarchy, as a servant or even an inferior ally. In any case, they are acknowledged as a human being, albeit of the lowest position.

But national-socialist hate for the Other as the Enemy, reflects a deeper hatred. It is a hate directed to the Other but generated by a hatred for the Ego. It is a repulsive reaction of the inner psyche against the socialized Self, who is unconsciously viewed as the realization of personal failure and repressed trauma.

This internal rejection can lead to suicide, but usually changes object by an unconscious metathesis, a transposition of hatred from the actual region of the Self to the fictitious region of a mythical Other/Enemy. Therefore, the Other becomes a constant reminder of egotistic deficiency, a dark reflection and an existential threat. At the same time, this annoying Ego, the conscience of subjectivity, is nullified by the denial of individuality, through the absolute concession of personal judgment to the will of the Fuhrer.

Nazism is anti-historic and proposes a historical racial mythology in order to justify this desire to physically exterminate the Other. It invents pseudo-continuities and legendary entities in spite of any factual reality. It is Myth replacing Reason and nonetheless an absolutely exclusive Myth, in the sense that it cannot be adopted by others. There is no place for the Other except on the altar of ritual sacrifice.

Instead of a mythical past, national-socialism projects a *mythical future*, producing a narrative above and beyond history. While classical nationalism mutilates history to construct its validation myths, Nazism and fascism deny history. Thereof national-socialism develops the ability to organize mystical political rituals and blood ceremonies, to invoke emotions of an imaginary archaic purity among its followers while pertaining in the most advanced technological methods of industrial production. The mythical past of Nazi ideology is not logically prior, like that of nationalism, but extends to the beyond, like the future toward which it is oriented. Consequently, on a personal level, the voluntary dissolution of individuality within the supposedly 'collective Ego' symbolically incarnated in the real Ego of the Fuhrer, is also a dissolution of private temporality and individual mortality within an imaginary collective immortality. This levels the living community to a delusional petrified eternity experienced as the abandonment of every moral responsibility, except of the immoral responsibility of absolute obedience.

Myth and Ritual nurture Nazi ideology by murdering Reason. Nazis are beyond reasonable intercourse, because their worldview is immanently irrational. Their public presence appeals to primitive social instincts and their symbols echo magical and mystical references. The follower of Nazism, who wants to eliminate foreigners after he has ritually eliminated the person of his own self by absolute obedience and discipline, is beyond human morality. Having denied his freedom of will, he has denied any responsibility.

The concept of the 'Banality of Evil,' proposed by political theorist

Hannah Arendt in her report about the trial of Adolf Eichmann (Arendt 1963), is not sufficient enough to explain that instance of absolute obedience that denudes a person from any sense of morality and transforms the 'common people' to sadist murderers. It is the other side of 'Evil'—radical evil—with its unspoken and inhuman dimension, its deep irrationality that attracts deficient personalities and enslaves them in de-personalization and subjugation.

These are the specific characteristics of the Golden Dawn party as well, and these made it attractive for a desperate part of Greek society. A country that has been a protectorate for most of its history and a system that promotes glamour and celebrity instead of education can become a nest for the snake's eggs in times of self-resentment and self-pity. Behind the votes given to the Nazi party is the logic of responsibility assignment stretched to extreme limits, when the assignment of individual freedom includes the totality of existence. The pseudo-historic obsessions of official Greek nationalism provide the best fertilizers for the extreme Right.

Official xenophobic policies by recent governments have provided complementary ratification for irrational xenophobic ideas.

With its anti-historical ideology, fascism serves the re-mystification of politics that is channeled through the metaphysics of the State and the sanctification of authority as the univocal will of the nation. Fascism and Nazism emerge as extreme offshoots of State authority, when the State dominates the totality of social and political life. It is no coincidence that this monolithic State is to be governed by an equally monolithic Party. The dissolution of individuality within the totalitarian social organization is essentially the most fundamental and complete act of concession, accumulation, and defalcation of public power by the State.

Although the power of the Golden Dawn Nazis now seems to diminish, their rhetoric and the nationalistic narrative they put forth under the spotlight has been adopted by the newly elected, in July 2019, ND government and by large sections of Greek society. This nationalistic revival that has become an alarmingly strong current of contemporary Western societies is a reflex reaction to the withering of the authority of the nation-state at a time when national politics come at an end within the broader interstate coalitions of globalized capitalism.

But at the same time, the Yellow Vests, a new form of social movement, emerged, occupying streets and roundabouts of France, creating a new type of radical spatiality and temporality in the heart of European capitalism.

The Yellow Vests Against Capitalist Temporality

The past three decades have witnessed the worldwide emergence of social movements that transcend traditional political forms of organization, like the party or the syndicate and explicitly challenge the dominant capitalist temporality. Recently, the streets of France were flooded by a massive, confrontational and enduring movement, the *Gilets Jaunes* (Yellow Vests).

What are the Yellow Vests? A yellow vest is something carried in France by anyone who has a vehicle for reasons of safety, should they be forced to stop in the emergency lane during the night. The yellow vest itself symbolizes no party, that is, no part of society. Common, everyday and forgotten, the yellow vest had no symbolic value and was not something politically visible, until the spontaneous French social movement transformed it into a symbol of resistance against the State. An indifferent, petty garment suddenly gained publicity and a distinct meaning because, through the collective action of the movement, it was transformed from into something of grave historical value, a symbol of a common future. Like the people who took to the streets themselves, where each individual was re-valued from an invisible, indifferent, insignificant 'gear' of the system into an active, irreplaceable nucleus of a movement.

What do the Yellow Vests signify? In 2018 we read scattered news about barricades, tear gas, fires, plastic bullets, arrests, and thousands of protesters demonstrating on the streets for successive weekends. The significance of the weekend was transformed, from the "leisure" time of private consumption to the free temporality of collective action and creation. The weekend became a temporal 'locus' for a successive conflict of French society with the French state, a successive conflict that, despite its fluctuations, continues into 2020.

Who are the Yellow Vests? A fuel tax-propelled French society to the point of resisting not only that particular law, but also the State's jurisdiction over society. After the first protests were silenced, when the French government's propaganda bodies and the 'official,' that is to say, traditional, media outlets sounded even louder, the voice of the Yellow Vests themselves began to be heard. It began to be heard in the popular assemblies created in all parts of France, the primary institutions of collective deliberation and decision making, which gave a new form to the movement. It began to be heard in the movement's refusal to elect 'representatives' or to negotiate with Macron's government. It began to appear through the reactions of the official political parties that, with Lepen's far right party leading the way, renounced the movement, made calls for 'Law and Order' and supported the extremely strict legislation introduced by the government. They began to be heard through the 'Assembly of Assemblies' and the coordination of autonomous, local assemblies in each neighbourhood.

So, what is their ideological identity? There is none. There is no centralized leadership structure, there is no ideological manifesto. The character of the movement is recreated through the actions of the movement. Within this unprecedented and cloudy landscape, we cannot sculpt some ideological purity, but we can discern elements of the institutional activity of society. In this de-ideological movement, we see no delusions, no disorientation. We see actions with a clear political content, with a clear political sign, manifested in the proclamations and the persistent confidence of the movement. And its political content is certainly democratic, creating the conditions of freedom, equality and non-representation, proto institutions of direct democracy. One such institution is the Assembly of Assemblies, a gathering of people from local assemblies around France, where the future of the movement is debated and decided.

This collective decision is explicit enough. What more do we need to explain? It would be better to listen to the words of the movement, along with the words of French thinkers and activists, or active thinkers, like Jacques Ranciére:

> "Explain the Gilets Jaunes? What are we supposed to explain? Give reasons why things happen that we didn't expect? Such reasons, in fact, are rarely missing. [...] There are certainly many causes of suffering. But suffering is one thing, no longer suffering is quite another. It is even the opposite. Yet the aspects of suffering that are listed to explain the revolt could be equally adduced to explain its

absence: individuals subjected to such conditions of existence do not normally have the time or energy to revolt. This movement that has surprised all expectations has no other reasons than those that feed the normal order of things. The reasons behind it were also reasons for immobility."[43]

For our part, we can also discern, schematically and briefly, some of the significations that link the Yellow Vests to all social movements that successively call into question the very core of globalized neoliberal oligarchy. These are:

1. The denial of representation and the development of structures of direct democracy. While the Yellow Vests had the opportunity to behave like a traditional protest movement and enter into negotiations with the State, they consciously refused. They decided that only directly revocable individuals could be sent as delegates to other assemblies with the sole responsibility to promote coordination according to the assemblies' decisions. The inalienable right of the decision rests with the popular assemblies, which thus become the political institutions of the movement.

2. The denial of established temporality and the recreation of free social time. The gatherings continue with unprecedented consistency, transforming the meaning of social time; they occupy highways, occupy non-sites, heterotopias belonging to the circulation of commodities, and convert them into visible places and public places, where the voice of society is heard. They create a fragile, but also directly antagonistic to the system, way of collectively experiencing time, not as a time externally imposed but as a time internally created.

3. The emergence of a new type of public spatiality, that transformed what Mark Augé called 'non-places', into political spaces. According to Augé, non-places are spaces of transience where the human beings remain anonymous and that do not hold enough significance to be regarded as "places," like motorways, airports, stations, roundabouts. The difference between places and non-places is that the latter do not provide space

for individuals to meet and build common references to a group, but instead produce an experience of individual alienation and loneliness, "the inexhaustible stock of an unending history in the present."[44] The Yellow Vests movement radically transformed the character of non-places by occupying roundabouts, blocking motorways, by inhabiting them and re-organizing them as public spaces for deliberation, interaction and identification. In that way, they made them visible and invested them with a different form of temporality, the collective present of a history of emancipation.

4. Trying to overcome the State by creating political institutions, assemblies and a free public space, but also by creating horizontal information and solidarity networks, using of digital social media as a means of direct communication but also of undoing traditional forms of information mediation and interconnection. It is of particular importance that the use of digital communication does not replace tangible participation which is a prerequisite for political decision making.

5. The expanded historicity of the movement. If something concerns us are the invisible connections of the Yellow Vests with the other social movements of the 21st century. We see a shift in meaning from resistance and preservation to the occupation, defense and re-creation of free public space.

We should measure the movement as it unfolds autonomously, but within the discontinuous but common temporality created by the historical struggle for individual and social autonomy. The Yellow Vests re-appeared in the autumn of 2019, once again deregulating France's social time. In their declaration before the General Strike of November 5, 2019, the sense of community between the unprivileged and the feeling of a common present and future was apparent:

> *"Don't let them divide us! Let no branch, no trade, no sector return to work until everyone's demands have been satisfied. Let us stick together, for we all depend on one another. Leave no one behind!*

The nurses and doctors of the emergency rooms and hospitals are struggling for all of us. They are demanding more beds, more personnel, more materials and of course decent salaries and breaks. They just made a pact with the firefighters: a fine example of solidarity between respected professionals. These are the people who look after us when we are most vulnerable. Should we leave them behind?

Working women earn only 4/5 of the wages of men doing the same work, and they do 4/5 of the unpaid labour of homemaking, cooking and child-rearing. They are the true basis of civilization, yet many women are beaten, murdered, raped or trafficked in France – all too often with impunity. They are asking for justice. Should we leave them behind?

The majority of working people have long been financially insecure. Even when they work full time or do extra jobs. Although the productivity of their labour and the profits of their bosses have not stopped increasing, the men and women who create this wealth live in fear of the end of the month, in permanent worry of unemployment, anxious about their employers closing shop and moving to poor countries where labour is cheaper. The workers are fighting for decent wages and stable employment. Should we leave them behind?

Students and teachers are demanding less over-crowded classrooms, aids and assistance for handicapped and special students, the right to participate in developing curriculums that correspond to the needs of the young and not to the demands of employers. They are our children. Should we leave them behind?

Small farmers work hard to feed us and get back only 2-3% of the price their produce sells for at Carrefour. Young people who want to raise organic crops and develop permaculture are unable to find agricultural lands to buy or rent, while real-estate speculators are paving over fertile soils. On the other hand, our government is subsidizing big land-owners and agro-businesses who stuff us with chemicals and Frankenfoods. Obesity is on the rise. The French peasantry, the salt of the earth, is in crisis. Should we leave them behind?

Macron wants to privatize the French National Railways (SNCF) for the benefit of his cronies, who have already taken over the National Highway System which we had already paid for tenfold. Today, trains are more and more expensive and less and less on time. The government is closing smaller stations, isolating the people in the countryside and forcing everyone to buy cars. The railway workers are defending these public goods on which we all depend. Yet Macron calls them "privileged." The government has already reduced their rolling personnel to one (!) per train. Since September, the railway staff have been using their legal right to stop trains in case of public danger – without asking management or their union leaders for permission. Should we leave them behind?

The planet is on the brink of climate catastrophe, while the government goes on subsidizing the oil, coal and chemical companies that are raking in billions. We must immediately cut these gifts to the rich and use that money for ecological purposes, for example helping the inhabitants of Rouen who have been poisoned by industry. Should we leave them behind?

Immigrants and ethnic minorities do the most grueling work in France without enjoying the rights of citizens, while French imperialist companies are getting richer pillaging their native lands and making them unlivable. They are being discriminated, deported, brutally repressed by the police. They are demanding liberty, equality and fraternity. Should we leave them behind?

The Yellow Vests come from all these underprivileged and exploited groups. They are the glue that holds all these elements together in the struggle. For more than a year they have been brutally repressed while fighting for dignity, fiscal justice, equality and participatory democracy. They have kept Macron on the defensive at great cost. Should we leave them behind?

An Injury to One is an Injury to All!"

Let's follow their advice. Do not let them divide us. Let's think again.

Democracy is possible. If we want it. Why do we want it? To have the freedom of responsibility for our own lives. What to make of them? Certainly, this is a question we must answer ourselves. But first we must reclaim the time, the space and the right to decide.

Modern technology and digital movements

No one would deny that one of the defining characteristics of our current world is the central importance of technology. We live in the first historical period when urban population has exceeded the rural population and the megacities that emerge are also vast techno-scientific hubs that regulate and calculate social temporality.

This situation has been the source of both alienation and celebration. Technology dominates both social and individual time, invades both public and private space, and brings forth new potential horizons of annihilation or liberation.

Murray Bookchin in the 1970s argued that modern capitalist technology tends to blur the distinction between the artificial and the natural, giving rise to further illusions of technical domination over nature. He notes:

> "In our own time, the development of technology and the growth of cities has brought man's alienation from nature to the breaking point. Western man finds himself confined to a largely synthetic urban environment, far removed physically from the land, and his relationship to the natural world is mediated entirely by machines."[45]

Could technology actually replace nature, could the machines replace natural entities within the human world? Along with Bookchin, we think that this is an absurdity. Natural organisms are not artifacts but living beings. Natural organisms are ontologically autonomous and their internal logic and feeling maybe be interpreted but are radically unknown and irreducible. Interrelating natural organisms constitute self-sustainable, inter-dependent and complementary ecosystems in a flux of creation, preservation and destruction, constantly diverging and interconnecting.

On the contrary, machines and other artifacts are dependent on humanity, are extensions of human imagination and technique and are their internal logic is known, determined and reproducible. They form limited modular systems that are dependent on external factors and are designed as independent from one another. They are mathematically designed entities and obey the same set of rules based on calculation and predetermination either mechanical, or analogical or digital. What is indeterminate, creative and meaningful is not the technological artifact itself but the human social relations that it materializes and that activate it. Psychologist James Gibson proposed in 1979 a 'theory of affordances' according to which every environment affords a set of operations that is dependent on every subject's physical capabilities and intentions:

> "The affordances of the environment are what it offers the animal, what it provides or furnishes, either for good or ill. The verb to afford is found in the dictionary, the noun affordance is not. I have made it up. I mean by it something that refers to both the environment and the animal in a way that no existing term does. It implies the complementarity of the animal and the environment." [46]

If we apply this to human beings as animals within a technological, artificial, and social, environment, we can come to the conclusion that every technology is dependent on the intentions of the uses and, furthermore, the pre-existing imaginary associations with that technology. But we also should acknowledge that human beings, as animals, are not isolated within their technological artificial environment. They are also embedded in the natural world, which expands beyond and within the social-historical sphere. Moreover, humanity is dependent on the natural world, on which it leans. Whereas technology belongs to the human social-historical realm, humanity itself belongs to the natural realm in ways that are both inescapable and necessary. This co-belonging means that the ecological, technological and social issues are inextricably bonded, since our society's intentionality toward nature is integrated in its technology.

Technology is never neutral when used effectively. Castoriadis pointed out:

"Capitalism does not utilize a socially neutral technology for capitalist ends. Capitalism has created capitalist technology, which is by no means neutral. The real intention of capitalist technology is not to develop production for production's sake: it is to subordinate and dominate the producers. Capitalist technology is characterized essentially by its drive to eliminate the human element in productive labour and, in the long run, to eliminate man altogether from the production process. That here, as everywhere else, capitalism fails to fulfil its deepest tendency - and that it would fall to pieces if it achieved its purpose - does not affect the argument. On the contrary, it only highlights another aspect of the crisis of this contradictory system."[47]

We should pay attention to that contradictory aspect. Modern technology incorporates and serves capitalist significations and means, the system's mastery over nature, but it also expands humanity's knowledge of nature. Technology is never neutral but also never univocal. A tool incorporates a set of intentions, it is to be used, but also provides a horizon of potentialities, it can be used for many reasons.

This set of operations and intentions is, of course, the same for all technologies. There are technologies that are inextricably linked to the state and corporate mechanisms, because they are dependent on a highly centralized and hierarchical administrative structure. All massive-scale energy production enterprises, like fossil fuel extractions and mining operations are such technologies that presuppose and reproduce authoritarian and exploitative administrative structures and materialize the capitalist imaginary impetus for domination over nature.

A profound example is nuclear energy which, as Brian Tokar notes: "doesn't exist anywhere in the world without extremely high levels of forced public subsidy whether through the state or through private utility companies."

But, this also does not regard all technologies. It would be false to follow Martin Heidegger in denouncing modern technology pes se as enframing (Gestell) or entrapment. That would lead us to that kind or primitivism or conservatism that inspires authoritarian and irrational attitudes, as it happened with Heidegger himself, who became enchanted by Hitler after the Nazi's rise to power in 1933. We should be able to distinguish between applied technology and science and also to the manners in which technology is applied. Castoriadis writes:

> "There is no capitalist chemistry or capitalist physics as such. There is not even a specifically capitalist technique, in the general sense of the word. There certainly is, however, a capitalist technology, if by this one means that, of the 'spectrum' of techniques available at a given point in time (as determined by the development of science), a given group (or 'band') of processes actually will be selected."[48]

So, it is not a matter of technicality but a matter of imaginary rationality, a matter of the dominant values and significations of a society. Scientific knowledge can thus be appropriated in an ecological manner only in a democratic political framework and according to democratic ecological values.

Bookchin reminds us of our dependency on nature that became invisible after the Industrial Revolution and calls for a restoration of humanity's ties with the natural realm, without regressing to any sort of technophobia. Instead, he envisions a liberatory technology that would provide an alternative to the destruction of nature and society caused by the state and capitalism, an alternative where "art would assimilate technology by becoming social art."[49]

He pointed out that the capitalist industrial and quantitative approach was already beginning to become outdated in view of the new digital and cybernetic technological discoveries:

> "This quantitative approach is already lagging behind technological developments that carry a new qualitative promise-the promise of decentralized, communitarian lifestyles, or what I prefer to call ecological forms of human association."[50]

Decentralization, communication, and a different relationship with nature are the positive potentials that Bookchin saw in the informational revolution that erupted during the 1970s. Computers and cybernetic systems provided forms of technology that did not require a highly centralized hierarchical model of administration and production like the industrial technology of the 19th century. The new model of horizontal networking that would grow in prominence over the next decades could be used as the technical infrastructure for equalitarian, creative and ecological modes of production and self-management. He envisioned a use of technology that would be in accordance with the principles of social ecology and would promote small scale communitarian forms of life connected in networks based on mutual aid and solidarity:

> "Some of the most promising technological advances in agriculture made since World War II are as suitable for small-scale ecological forms of land management as they are for the immense industrial-type commercial units that have become prevalent over the past few decades."[51]

Today, technological innovation has proven that Bookchin had a point. Decentralization is a distinct feature of digital networking and the ontological revolution of the Internet[52] has provided new means for knowledge dissemination and collective innovation. But, this same technology has been used by the established authorities and centres of economic and political power as means of control, manipulation, data collection, and surveillance. The digital world has become a new plane of social reality where the collision between the forces of State and corporate power and the movements of social autonomy is multiplied and amplified.

And the established authorities have the advantage over technology, since they possess the legal and infrastructural means to control the very hubs and energy resources that make digital infrastructure possible. We should not forget that the digital plane, however distinct is deeply rooted in the social-historical reality and exists solemnly as a human communication and information system. As such, it is mainly controlled by the powers that control social temporality.

In December 2019 former US president Barack Obama placed *The Age of Surveillance Capitalism* by Shoshana Zuboff at the top of his Christmas book recommendation list in a probably deliberate gesture of sarcasm. During his presidency, Obama made full use of the surveillance and repression state apparatus and even expanded the government's surveillance powers before leaving office, issuing Executive Order 12333. This order is exactly aligned with what Zuckoff calls Surveillance Capitalism, the economic imperative of which is "the extraction imperative." This means that "raw material supplies must3be produced at an ever-expanding scale."[53] Raw materials are data and information, private details about each individual. According to Zuboff every social relation and societal process are now a "fresh terrain for rendition, calculation, modification and prediction."[54]

The mechanisms of surveillance capitalism take advantage of the digital tools available for instant communication and digital personification. Social media companies, like Facebook, have a monopoly over the data and information market that has never been seen before and would not be tolerated in other sections of economy. Facebook extracts pure value without producing any content or information, by just providing the digital platform. Information and content are freely given by its users by their own will, who thus willing become both the commodity and the consumer creating profit value for one company's stocks. The fact that many users acknowledge this relation of exploitation does not mean they stop using the medium. Such a vast amount of new social relations and personal communication has been created within the platform and is dependent by it, from professional to sexual interactions, that the platform itself has gained an almost existential significance for each individual user.

This capital is inherently profitable, as its surplus value is net worth value, generated not by the exploitation of labour, that is, the exploitation of the working part of individual time, but by the exploitation of recreation, that is, the exploitation of the "free" part of individual time. If all users decided to abstain from the medium, Facebook would collapse together with its net worth capital. The ability of the medium to generate profit equals the ability of the medium to generate communication, that is, the ability of the medium to form a community, a capacity that depends on each user individually, since Internet communities are imaginary communities of subjective identification, i.e. fragile. These imaginary communities cannot fully integrate the person. This makes every imaginary digital community fragile, but with strong penetrative dynamics, circulating from the private space to the public without the risk involved in any personal physical participation in the physical public space.

Our current situation of inhabiting both the physical and the digital world opens up before us an array of potentialities and possibilities that diverge on the essential issues of democracy, control and commodification. Against the techniques of profit, control and surveillance developed by state and corporate authorities, digital movements like the movement of Digital Commons have emerged to develop alternative, equalitarian and horizontal techniques of open source technology, knowledge sharing and free collective, non-profit production.

Peer to peer networks are organizations that freely, collectively and autonomously create digital tools of communication and envision a different production paradigm, based on commons-based peer production. It is a concept that shares Bookchin's call for decentralization and public availability of technology as well as for free individual access to technological knowledge and for collective innovation.

Vasilis Kostakis argues that the advantages provided by the digital revolution provide the blueprint for a commons-based production toward "a more inclusive and environmentally sustainable paradigm"[55] of societal organization. Kostakis, a member of the P2P network that advocates and creates digital commons, illustrates the importance of modularity in artifact design, production, usage and services, which is "a fundamental aspect of digitalness," since the binary digits represent modules of information (1,0) whose combinations create more complex structures according to a set of rules and operators. As human labour becomes more infused with digital technologies, modularity in production and consumption becomes a more apparent and significant feature. Kostakis is careful not to identify modularity with a particular political trend, showcasing how large information companies also utilize modular modes of production:

> "Modularity allows for-profit firms such as Apple, Samsung, and Amazon to outsource the manufacturing of their products and, in addition to the already stated benefits of modularity, to profit from cheap labour. [...] Further, IBM, Google, and Facebook benefit from crowdsourcing part of their value chain to freelancing or voluntary labour (e.g. the Android ecosystem, the free and open-source software, or the community-based content creation)."[56]

However, his intention is to point out the correlation and usefulness of digital modularity for commons-based, non-profit democratic collectivities. The very difference between traditional capitalist and commons-based peer production is the overthrowing of the central imaginary drive of profit and the central imaginary signification of private property in favour of the values of mutuality, equality and collective sharing. Regionalism or locality is a decisive feature of social decentralization that modern peer-to-peer networks seem to integrate in their modularity. Local units are autonomous modules that can interconnect and interact without losing their regional independence. Commons-based production in the digital world has, in this manner, produced an alternative paradigm for artifact construction based on locality and the global networking of autonomous local units. As Kostakis argues:

> "Commons-based peer production reverses the industrial logic of restrictive intellectual properties and global supply chains feeding into economies of scale. Instead, intellectual property is, as a commons, accessible to everyone, with knowledge production taking place openly on a global scale. Manufacturing takes place locally by communities or enterprises, often through shared infrastructures and with regional biophysical conditions-needs under consideration. [...] Grassroots initiatives, which are organized around shareable informational modules, can have both a local and a global orientation."[57]

Interestingly, this paradigm of commons-based production has also been implemented in agriculture, with very positive results. Chris Giotitsas studied small scale agricultural initiatives by organic farmers and ecological activists that manufacture their tools and methods collectively and in a deliberate opposition to the dominant capitalist model, like L'Atelier Paysan (France) και FarmHack (USA). Both are agricultural communities that communicate, co-ordinate and co-operate through open source digital platforms. They are collective networks of localized production based on commonly produced knowledge which he calls "open source agriculture," because the exchange of ideas and the networking utilize the digital information and communication technologies. Giotitsas argues that open source technology can be used as a tool for the democratization of technology enabling individuals to freely participate in the process of design, manufacturing and production, and "to participate effectively in a widening range of public activities." According to Giotitsas, such decenstralised productive infrastructures provide a technological framework for actual horizontal and democratic decision-making.[58]

These movements show that Bookchin was right to identify the liberatory potentials of digital technology. Digital movements like commons-based peer production and open source free software provide new ways of decentralization, global communication and local co-operation. Nevertheless, they are complementary to other, corporeal and actual forms of democratic networking and social struggle and cannot stand autonomously without a radical political content and a democratic orientation. In order for both modularity and decentralization to be combined in a common project there is also the need for a set of principles of coherency and unification of the units in open democratic networks. The network itself need to be instituted as a horizontal structure of explicit political decision-making and decision enactment that allows maximum individual participation. Modularity needs to be complemented with open connectivity and decentralization with democratic con-federalisation to avoid the enclosure of local units to themselves. This process includes the confrontation with established authorities, the struggle for the creation of an actual free public space, the collaboration with other political collectivities, the creation of another type of political and ecological 'rationality', the project of social and individual autonomy and the creation of both a new type of ecological consciousness that would re-evaluate humanity in resonance with nature and a new type of universal human citizenship based on actual equality, participation in governance and mutual autonomy.

As Alexandros Kioupkiolis points out: "[w]ithout communicating an alternative political consciousness and dream, the prevalent logics of the market—competition and private utility maximization—are bound to maintain the grip on the mind and the will of contemporary commoners."[59]

Modern digital networks have blurred the distinction between private and public and transgressed the distance between local and global. Thus, they amplify both social injustice and social struggle for emancipation. In our conversation in Athens in 2017, Jacques Ranciére described this duality of digital informational networks, while insisting that democracy requires actual individual participation and cannot be reduced to communication:

> I am always really perplexed before this twofold aspect of the Internet. On the one hand, free access to information, but at the same time, when you read comments on the Internet, you totally despair about the humankind [....] So, I think what we have is always the same thing in a way, that, of course, forms of free diffusion don't mean the increase of democracy. Democracy is not communication.[60]

What Jacques Ranciére told us was made clear during the outbreak of the Covid-19 pandemic in early 2020.

The coronavirus pandemic brought the world to an unprecedented state of global pause and restraint, in a global common temporality both interlinked and fragmented. The variety of preventive measures from country to country seemed to intensify national borders and confirm the jurisdiction of the nation-state. However, the spread of the virus effectively nullified national borders and shook the jurisdiction of the nation-state, emphasizing its weaknesses. The incapability of national governments in a globalised world was made apparent, as efforts to control human movement and regulate public life dissolved in a state of waiting and anxiety in the face of an unknown, new natural phenomenon.

From the onset of the pandemic, a philosophical dialogue developed in Europe.

"It seems that the challenge of the epidemic is everywhere dissipating the intrinsic activity of reason", Marxist philosopher Alain Badiou wrote in March 2020[61], "obliging subjects to return to those sad effects—mysticism, fabulation, prayer, prophecy and malediction—that were customary in the Middle Ages when plague swept the land."

The Italian philosopher Giorgio Agamben was the first to denounce the political measures taken in view of the virus in an article published in Italy in late February:

> "We might say that once terrorism was exhausted as a justification for exceptional measures, the invention of an epidemic could offer the ideal pretext for broadening such measures beyond any limitation."[62]

Agamben adopts a Foucauldian approach that considers any discourse a covert technique of authority and gives special emphasis to medical science as a field of preparation of disciplinary protocols that give State authorities jurisdiction over the human body. Medicine thus emerges as a pre-eminent tool of biopolitics, and the imposition of hygiene protocols on society is seen as a measure of control, surveillance and discipline, as a technique for deepening State sovereignty and jurisdiction.[63] Rationalized biopolitical discourse is therefore articulated as an injunction, and, as Agamben argues, the injunction is primarily a function of power, regardless of whether that injunction is enforced.

Agamben's position prompted responses from Roberto Esposito, who defended the Foucaldian notion of biopolitics, asserting that the pandemic was leading to the loosening of public authority rather than the tightening of a totalitarian grip and Jean Luc Nancy, who pointed out that "the viral magnifying glass enlarges the characteristics of our contradictions and our limitations."[64]

We must distinguish between law and nature, so that we do not consider nature as law, nature as something in which we can intervene freely and without exogenous resistance, neither law as nature, law as something that is imposed on us externally. Agamben is guilty of the first error in an attempt to avoid the second. There is also a romantic representation of nature as majestic and superhuman. But nature is also infinitesimal and subhuman. Distrust of rationalism must not obscure the fact that rationalism has developed primarily as a tool for interpreting non-human nature, and in this field it has made the most positive findings. It is inconceivable to abandon the rational ground for interpreting natural phenomena, just as it is equally wrong to assume that this ground covers everything.

Rational tools can be adapted to many purposes and it is there, in the realm of purpose, where human freedom seems almost absolute; because purpose is primarily an imaginary creation. The scientific knowledge that results from the "rationality of the objectively real", as Castoriadis points out, "is a creation as an arbitrary use of at the same time the rational texture of the world and its indefinite gaps."[65]

But what is ultimately important is the moral topology of society, the one that forms the boundaries of tolerance and consensus. It is formed within multiple intersecting exclusions, exclusion from information, exclusion from decision, exclusion from politics. Since society is not monolithic, the gap between the bioethics of medical treatment and the biopolitics of discipline becomes a field of conflict of broader meanings and values, of solidarity against racism, of self-restraint against innocence, of sociality versus isolation. This conflict goes beyond the pandemic, but the pandemic transformed its terms. Social time was fragmented into a multiplicity of private times and labour time placed under the supervision of State authorities. This raises the further question of social digitalness.

People saw sociality shift to the digital realm, along with modes of production and, even more, consumption. Digital sociability appeared as an alternative to a social distanced world. The Internet, a field between the familiar and the unfamiliar, the private and the public, seemed like the only non-infectious place. But the Internet is not a place, it is more of a threshold between natural and artificial places. And yet it is contagious in another, mental way. Skype coffee is a fun experiment, but for how long? The opening up of private space to digital sociality is inversely proportional to the shrinking and exclusion of public space. But digital sociability is possible precisely because there is active, physical, personal sociability, which it cannot replace, but only complement. Based on this, there can be no independent digital society without actual, real society supporting it. People suffer, desire and feel as bodies and the disease reminds us of our interdependence.

The importance of actual, not digital, individual participation in social struggles was illustrated amidst the pandemic by the riots and demonstrations that shook the U.S.A. in the months following the assassination of George Floyd by policemen on May, 25, 2020. The crowds that marched in every city demanding the defunding of the police and an end to racist policies made their voice heard around the world exactly because they assembled in the streets, they occupied actual public space, they clashed with police forces and put their bodies, not their digital avatars, in a direct confrontation with State authorities. The Black Lives Matter movement proved that, even in the digital information age, grassroots emancipatory politics require the actual presence of every individual in the collective decision-making assemblies.

And whereas digital networking technologies provide potential tools for decentralization and knowledge dissemination, we need to establish direct democracy within the real or actual public space and time in order to invest communication with an actually liberating content.

The interconnectivity and inter-complementary of the natural and the social world can be communicated digitally but can be mediated only politically. This presupposes an explicit breach with the dominant social imaginary significations and conceptual stereotypes that empower and reproduce established temporality.

NOTES

1. Lenin, *What Is to be done*, trans. Tim Delaney, The Marxist Online Archive, p.17, available at: https://www.marxists.org/archive/lenin/works/download/what-itd.pdf, last retrieved: 26/11/2019, 14:31.
2. Ibid. p.23.
3. Ibid. p. 20.
4. Lenin, *Collected Works*, Russ. ed., Vol. VI, p. 205.
5. Lenin, *The State and Revolution, Collected Works*, Volume 25, p. 381 - 492
6. Murray Bookchin, *Listen Marxist*, p. 16, note 17. Available at: https://theanarchistlibrary.org/library/murray-bookchin-listen-marxist.pdf, last retrieved on 26/11/2019, 15:59.
7. *The Rosa Luxemburg Reader*, ed. P. Hudis & K. Anderson, Monthly Review Press, 2004. p. 251.
8. Ibid. p. 256.
9. Ibid. p. 306.
10. Emma Goldman, *My disillusionment in Russia*, available at: https://autonomies.org/2017/07/the-russian-revolution-of-1917-emma-goldman/, last retrieved, 26/11/2019, 15:39.
11. Cornelius Castoriadis, *The Imaginary Institution of Society*, trans. Kathleen Blamey, New York: Polity Press, 1997, p. 11.
12. Castoriadis, Ibid. p. 381, note 10.
13. Jacques Ranciére, *A coffee with Jacques Ranciére beneath the Acropolis*, Athens: Babylonia, 2017.
14. Wilhelm Dilthey, *Auf dem Verhaltnis von Erlebnis*, in Fr. Coppleston, *A History of Philosophy*, vol. 7, New York: Bloomsbury, 2013, p . 371.
15. Ibid. p. 372.
16. *The Castoriadis Reader*, p. 270.
17. Reinhart Koselleck, *Futures Past*, New York: Columbia University Press, 2004, p. 105.
18. Cornelius Castoriadis, "The Anticipated Revolution" in the volume *Political and social writings 3*, ed. D. A. Curtis, p. 124.
19. Ibid.
20. Ibid. p. 125.
21. Ibid. p. 129.
22. Ibid. p. 148.
23. Ibid. p. 130.
24. Ibid. p. 139.

25 Paul Ricoeur, *Lectures on Ideology and Utopia*, New York: Columbia University Press, 1986.
26 Castoriadis, *Political and social writings 3*, p. 132.
27 Ibid. p. 135.
28 Ibid. p. 133.
29 Ibid. p. 132.
30 Kristin Ross, *A coffee with Kristin Ross on the continuations of May '68*, Athens: Babylonia, 2018.
31 Ibid.
32 Ibid.
33 Ibid.
34 The first anarchist ideas and collectivities in Greece emerged in the late 19th century, in the port city of Patras, where the first political collective self-defined as anarchist was founded under the name Anarchist Association of Patras (Αναρχικός Όμιλος Πατρών). The Greek State responded with repression and violence and by 1897, the year the Greek Kingdom met humiliating defeat in a war against the Ottoman Empire, most of its members were imprisoned (Fountas, 2014). However, Greek anarchist collectives where spreading across Greece, as the country was expanding and social injustice flourished alongside poverty and oppression. Anarchism was overshadowed by Leninism after 1917 and during the Second World War the Stalinist fraction of Greek resistance to German occupation led by KKE (Communist Party of Greece) eliminated all Trotskyist and Anarchist groups.

On November 17th, 1973, Polytechneio, the Polytechnic University in the centre of Athens was occupied by students protesting against the military Junta. The occupation ended when tanks invaded the building. The outlawed KKE had condemned the occupation. Among the rebelling students, a new generation of anarchists emerged, one of which wrote on the wall of the occupied building DOWN WITH AUTHORITY (ΚΑΤΩ Η ΕΞΟΥΣΙΑ). Doctor of political philosophy and participant in the events Giorgos N. Oikonomou has described Polytechneio as the first direct democratic uprising in Modern Greek history.

This social-historical phenomenon, the re-appearance of anarchist and direct democratic ideas beneath the conservative surface of Greek society is better described by the words of Protopsaltis, who was part of that movement:

"A powerful and imaginative libertarian movement, beyond the left, an independent course of action with zero roots in Greek society, with a complete lack of not only historical experience but also life experience, since the older anarchists did not exceed 23 to 25 years old. They rely on instinct and voluntarism, believe in their spontaneity, and improvise while opening the way. The two factors that favour them are, first, the echo of the subversive and creative spirit of the 1960s, which swept the planet, socially and culturally, while having in Greece as its ally the favourite wind of Metapolitefsi. And secondly, the magical interaction between Stinas and Castoriadis, Stinas being a symbol of people's struggles for emancipation, and Castoriadis being a symbol of human thinking, have come together as action and theory come together in historical praxis in a reciprocal interaction. And it is their influence that has shaped, in the years of the Junta, the first groups and gatherings, the first cells for the dissemination of anti-authoritarian ideas."

35 http://social-ecology.org/wp/2005/01/revving-it-up-the-revolutionary-potential-of-the-new-anti-globalization-movement/ , last retrieved 30/11/2019, 12:02.
36 Murray Bookchin, *The Communalist Project*, Harbinger Vol. 3 No. 1, 2002. Available at: http://social-ecology.org/wp/2002/09/harbinger-vol-3-no-1-the-communalist-project/, last retrieved 30/11/2019, 10:29.
37 https://www.bbc.com/news/world-europe-32211364, last retrieved 30/11/2019, 12:55.
38 *ContAct* maganize, issue 3, p. 36, Agrinio, December 2001.

39 *Babylonia* antiauthoritarian newspaper, no. 51, Athens, January 2009.
40 Reinhart Koselleck, *Futures Past*, New York: Columbia University Press, 2004.
41 Dimosthenis Papadatos – Anagnostopoulos, *Mavrokokkinos Decembris (Μαυροκόκκινος Δεκέμβρης)*, Athens: Topos, 2018.
42 The Castoriadis Reader, p. 56.
43 https://www.versobooks.com/blogs/4237-jacques-ranciere-on-the-gilets-jaunes-protests, last retrieved, 2/12/2019 14:31.
44 Mark Augé, *Non-Places, introduction to an Anthropology of Supermodernity*, New York: Verso, 1995, pp.104-5.
45 Murray Bookchin, *Post-scarcity Anarchism*, Montreal: Black Rose Books, 1975, p. 136.
46 James Gibson, *The Ecological Approach to Visual Perception*. Boston: Houghton Mifflin Harcourt (HMH), 1979.
47 The Castoriadis Reader, p. 61.
48 The Castoriadis Reader, p. 62.
49 Murray Bookchin, *Post-scarcity Anarchism*, Montreal: Black Rose Books, 1975, p. 151.
50 Ibid.
51 Ibid. p.115.
52 See, Alexandros Schismenos, Nikos Ioannou & Chris Spannos, *Castoriadis and Autonomy in the 21st century*, London: Bloomsbury, 2020.
53 Shoshana Zuboff, *The Age of Surveillance Capitalism*, New York: PublicAffairs, 2018, p. 87.
54 Ibid. p. 399.
55 V. Kostakis. "How to Reap the Benefits of the "Digital Revolution"? Modularity and the Commons.", 2019, available at: http://halduskultuur.eu/journal/index.php/HKAC/article/view/228/177
56 Ibid.
57 Ibid.
58 Chris Giotitsas, *Open Source Agriculture, Grassroots Technology in the Digital Era*, London: Palgrave, 2019, p. 7.
59 Alexandros Kioupkiolis, *The Common and Post-hegemonic Politics, Re-thinking social change*, Edinburgh: Edinburgh University Press, 2019, p. 65.
60 *A coffee with Jacques Ranciére beneath the Acropolis.*
61 https://www.versobooks.com/blogs/4608-on-the-epidemic-situation
62 https://www.quodlibet.it/giorgio-agamben-l-invenzione-di-un-epidemia
63 Michel Foucalt, *Discipline and Punishment*. The Birth of the Prison, New York: Vintage Books, 1995
64 http://www.journal-psychoanalysis.eu/coronavirus-and-philosophers/
65 Cornelius Castoriadis, *World in Fragments*, Stanford University Press, 1997.

IV. Conceptual Challenges

Alexandros Schismenos

The Paradoxes of Nationalistic Discourse

IS DEMOCRACY an issue of nationality? Was the British PM Boris Johnson right when he asserted in 2019 that Brexit and national sovereignty are issues of democracy? The rise of nationalistic parties in Europe and of the Alt-Right movement in the United States brings before us once again the terrifying spectre of nationalism—but this time, in contrast to the fascism of the 1930s, nationalists don't advertise their anti-democratic worldview. They rather prefer to hide it beneath the call for a retreat to 'national republics,' identifying nationalism with democracy. But can such identification stand?

It is not the first, nor the last time, that we are trying to clarify aspects of the dark mixture of nationalism. Neither is our intention to analyze or at least list the various and often contradictory interpretations of the word "Nation," from Renan, Fichte, Hegel to Anderson, Gellner, and Hobsbawm. I will only briefly examine the paradoxes found within the core of nationalistic discourse. I define nationalistic discourse as the discourse which, despite a secondary variety of forms, expressions and designs that make up the whole imaginary spectrum of the nationalist phenomenon, is constituted by the inextricable interplay of three imaginary significations:

1. The substantialization of the generic term "nation," which presents it as a compact entity, a coherent subject with a specific will and historical horizon, rather than a recent historical construct of modernity. This distinguishes nationalistic discourse from any ethnological, ethnographic, and ultimately descriptive discourse on nationality.

2. The primacy the imaginary entity "nation" over any other social institution, collectivity or entity, including individuality. This distinguishes nationalistic discourse from any historical, evolutionary, sociological discourse on community.

3. The ahistorical -temporality of the imaginary entity "nation", since the imaginary "nation", while placed within History and often based on a precisely dated foundational event is presented as an "eternal essence." This distinguishes nationalistic discourse from any theological, transcendental, metaphysical discourse on unity.

Certainly, nationalistic discourse borrows elements from other descriptive, historical, or sociological narratives, but is exclusively based on the reduction of each element to the semantic core we have just described, dominated by the metaphysical image of the nation as an originary, primordial subject.

As such, nationalistic discourse is the unifying web of the different historical derivatives of the nationalist phenomenon, whose specific aims and proclamations covers a large part of the spectrum of modern politics. Often, scholars try to classify the different aspects of nationalism by talking about the political nationalism of French origin, the romantic nationalism of German origin, the conservative nationalism of aristocratic origin and the national-liberation nationalism of anti-colonialism.

With regard to the latter, it should be noted emphatically that nationalism is a modern European creation and the emergence of national-liberation movements in colonized societies was a legacy and consequence of colonialism. Franz Fannon, for example, advocated the creation of a "national culture" as a necessary strategic weapon for unifying the resistance against colonialism and as a tool for the recognition of independence by other nation-states, but at the same time he advocated the universalism of the anti-colonial struggle and the need of the transnational solidarity of the oppressed.[1]

Some have also proposed a distinction between a first, liberation phase, when nationalists try to link themselves to social demands for self-determination, a second, centralization phase, when nationalism of an independent nation-state seeks to expand its authority on populations of the same "national" origin in other territories and a third, expansive phase, when a nation-state conquers colonies.

We could perhaps describe the fundamental contradiction between the interpretation of the nation as a political community and the interpretation of the nation as an eternal entity and unified destiny, as the contrast between a relational and a substantive conception of the nation. The relational conception interprets the nation as a set of social and political relations that evolve and adapt to the dynamics and correlations of broader, transnational, domains. The substantive conception interprets the nation as a perennial community charged with a manifest destiny, which is involved in a constant struggle for supremacy over similar entities caught in the grid of human history.

Both the substantive and the relational conceptions are imaginary schemata ridden with interpretive contradictions; both simultaneously raise a demand for historical progression, since the nation is supposed to progressively manifest itself in History, alongside a contradictory demand for historical stasis, since the nation is supposed to be determined as regards its essential attributes. Both conceptions are absorbed by the nationalistic discourse, which is constituted as a radical negation of diverging interpretations in favour of a single univocal narrative, no matter how paradoxical.

Thus, we can briefly describe three paradoxes that lie within the nationalistic discourse:

1. The contrast between the external and the internal becomes an antinomy, since nationalism seeks to isolate and homogenize its interior by closing State borders, presenting them as unchangeable, but also, at the same time, to extend and neutralize its exterior, expanding State borders and making them variable and relative. The demand for internal homogeneity corresponds to the substantive conception, while the demand for external heterogeneity, that is, the degradation of other nation-states as inferior, corresponds to the relational conception, which recognizes a hierarchy of nations. However, from another point of view, the demand for internal homogeneity implicitly addresses the problem posed by the

relational volatility it seeks to eliminate, while the demand for external heterogeneity recognizes other nations as similar substances/entities, inferior but equally eternal.

2. Secondly, however, there is a limit to the assimilation of the friend, or the elimination of the enemy raised intrinsically by the inability of the nationalistic discourse to assert universalism. Condemned to be the cause of a narrow and enclosed minority within humanity, the nationalistic discourse seeks to overcome partiality through territorial conquest and the cancerous reproduction of its internal homogeneity, but only to expose itself to external conflict and internal collapse.

3. The nation constitutes an abstract and metaphysical field between the tangible and empirical realms of locality, which is related to lived experience, and universality, which is related to mutual human recognition. As such, the nation creates its own imaginary self-justification, a closed-loop regression that renders nationalistic ideology self-referential and contradictory. While the nation is presented as the highest collective totality and unity, nationalism admits at the same time that this totality and unity is merely one among the others. The demand for national uniqueness via supremacy is by definition impossible to be fulfilled, since it is impossible for any nation to cover the entire human horizon, as empires or religions claim.

Despite appealing to a destiny inherited to the nation by a glorious past, nationalism actually fears and hates history. Ernest Renan, in his 1882 essay titled "What is a nation?" admits it explicitly: "Forgetfulness, and I would even say historical error, are essential in the creation of a nation."

Forgetfulness constitutes the base for the mythical nationalistic narrative that wants to reduce history to a genealogical linearity. Social institutions are more than means of social continuity and reproduction. They are also bridges of relative stability between the turbulences of personal time and the fluctuations of social time. The imaginary power of social belonging, traditionally provided by religion is revealed in times when the individual approaches death, their own or that of their familiars. It can also be observed in times of a social crisis, when the feeling of impending doom shakes the foundations of custom and normality, when values tremble under the feet of catastrophe, as in Europe during the Black Death plague in the 14th century.

The metaphysics of Nation became a substitute for religion after the revolutions of the 18th century corroded the metaphysical foundations of the imaginary of divine authority. Since the Church could no longer sanctify political authority and collective identity could no longer be sustained in a religious context, the substantiated generality of the Nation came to fill the void, supposedly mediating the 'General Will' of the people and providing a new foundation of legitimacy for state authority. Capitalism was developed as an international economic system of trade and communication between independent local units, namely Nation-States. Capitalism cannot be legitimized itself; it is dependent on a political structure of representation that would conceal actual social injustice caused by the system. Immanuel Wallerstein argued that the "concept of 'nation' is related to the political superstructure of this historical system [capitalist world-economy], the sovereign states that form and derive from the interstate system."[2]

So, nationalistic discourse is at the same time self-contradictory and vital to the preservation of the international status quo. The field of international politics is a field of interstate antagonisms covered by a unifying network of capitalist production, exploitation and distribution. The local units of that system, the nation-states, are the only ones that possess social justification because they construct the pastness needed for social identification. However, this identification process has been always in tension with actual social inequality created by both State hierarchy and capitalist exploitation. After the adoption of the neoliberal dogma by ruling elites, the attack on civil rights, wages, pensions, social welfare programs and public services has eroded those pillars of identification that stabilize both State authority and capitalist economy.

The revival of nationalistic discourse in the centre of mainstream political discourse can be viewed both as an instrument of population manipulation, as nationalism has always been, as a diplomatic tool to ensure the local elites' participation in world wealth distribution and as a political weapon for fringe lobbies and local authoritarians to seize power.

But it also affects the dominant representations of the social imaginary. It promotes a culture of division, isolation, xenophobia, and educational impoverishment, which is diffused through mainstream media to households, re-invigorating past monstrosities and strengthening individual complexes that arise from that very erosion of social identification.

This temporal mode of aggressive pastness, which is materialized in institutions like the Church or the army, constitutes an anti-current of conservatism, nationalism, nativism, sexism, re-opening dated social rifts that actually tighten the grip of State authority on society, excepting those that are actually created by social inequality. It is a pseudo-continuous fictitious pastness that is aggressive toward history.

While we are accustomed to correlate the past with memory, voluntary and involuntary memory, the pastness created by nationalism is based of forgetfulness. That is why it is compatible with capitalism's presentism, which values only what is presently at hand, scorns collective memory and is also based on forgetfulness. The dependence of the capitalist and interstate system on forgetfulness means that they are functions that effectively reproduce forgetfulness by attacking collective memory and public history.

Consequently, nationalistic discourse underlines the dominant social temporality of our contemporary world. A global network of presentist functions driven by the acceleration of capital growth and commodity circulation based on local nation-state units of aggressive fictitious pastness that antagonize each other for the exploitation and subjugation of both natural temporality and social historicity.

This tangled web of opposing authorities cannot, however, cover the whole magma of the social-historical plane. The temporal rifts, cracks and ruptures that social movements create, prove the fragility of the whole system and threaten to overthrow the dominant social temporality by the force of an alternative, humane, equalitarian, democratic, and ecological common future. If republican Nation-States are not forms of democracy, we should ask once again—what are they and what does democracy essential means?

Representative oligarchy and democracy

Alexis Tsipras became Prime Minister of Greece on January 2015 with the promise to get rid of austerity and the debt loans of the Troika (IMF, ECT, EU) that promoted the privatization of public wealth, leading SYRIZA, a broad coalition of left parties that were somewhat connected to recent social movements through individual participation. Soon, the Greek people discovered that the newly sworn government that consisted not only of SYRIZA but also of the far-right ANEL party, had nothing to oppose to the plans of the EU and the IMF. After a semester of negotiations, which led to the Europeans exerting their authority by closing Greek banks, Tsipras declared a referendum on July 5, 2015. Was that a turn toward a more inclusive form of democracy? Well, the events that unfolded provide us with a definitive answer—no.

"No" was also the result of the referendum with a staggering 63% of the votes, but no one actually knew what that 'no' meant. The question put forth by the government was obscure, technical and in essence regarded only a bailout draft plan suggested by European Commision's President Jean-Claude Juncker. Wikipedia gives an accurate description of the obscurity of the referendum question. Greek citizens were asked whether they approve of the proposal made to Greece by the Juncker Commision, the IMF and the ECB during the Eurogroup meeting on 25 June, titled "Reforms For The Completion Of The Current Program And Beyond" and "Preliminary Debt Sustainability Analysis." The possible answers were stated as "Not approved/ No" and "Approved/Yes."

The obscurity of the question helped Tsipras overturn the result, interpreting it in the narrowest way and signing a new bailout program, a third MoU that mortgaged Greece's natural resources and public wealth for 99 years.

So, what did the referendum show us?

The referendum was only a momentary process, during which the people had to answer Greece's political problems with a single 'yes' or a 'no'; it was a process politically designed by the government and not society. It felt more like an interrogation than any form of democracy. Accordingly, despite its density, the mainstream political time before the referendum moved slowly, and felt suffocating, due to the exclusion of society from actual decision-making processes. On the contrary, the dense political time of any direct democratic process is fast, public, liberating, creative, and diverse.

After the referendum, the coalition of SYRIZA, which had by now become a traditional centralized party, and ANEL was elected into government for a second term. The government policies of that second term were perfectly aligned with the demands of the bailout agreement and promoted further privatization of public services and exploitation of natural resources.

On July 2019 they lost the elections, which brought the traditional right-wing party of New Democracy (ND) to power.

Alexis Tsipras, addressing SYRIZA's Central Committee before the elections of 2019, summed up the meaning of parliamentary elections in one phrase: "We must never forget who we are, who we represent and for whom we fight." To answer these three questions, we have to interpret them literally:

1. Who were they? The Central Commitee of SYRIZA.
2. Who did they represent? The SYRIZA party.
3. Who were they fighting for? For the interests of their party.

Of course, Tsipras would prefer a difference answer. He would like, for example, to say that they represent the middle and lower classes of society and that they fight for the interests of the 'people' or the 'country.' But, this would mean that we are already implicitly transferred to a second level of representation, symbolic or metaphorical, beyond the first, literal or empirical representation. But we cannot move on to the second representation level, by abandoning the first, the party, which is the actual political authority unit.

The first level must be attached to the second, first arbitrarily and then formally, through the electoral process. That is necessary, because in the electoral process of representative oligarchy the party precedes the individual or rather the individual is always mediated by the party. Of course, the electoral process always brings forward a minority of voters who legitimize or are 'affiliated' with the party. But the party assumes State governance in the name of the abstract totality of the 'people/nation.'

This intermediate level of representation, which alternates between the empirically representative (the actual members of the party) and the symbolically representative (the 'people/nation' which is an abstract source of authority's legitimacy) is the electoral, which combines a specific empirical calibration (it is measurable) with an abstract general reference (in the name of the people).

But the interpretation we have given so far of Tsipras' words does not take into account who is speaking. If our answer includes the speaker, we can add an extra dimension. Let's take that into consideration and answer his questions, again literally:

1. Who was talking to whom? He is the Prime Minister of the Greek State, who addresses the Central Committee of the party supporting his government.
2. Who did they represent? The Greek government.
3. Who were they fighting for? For the interests of the Greek State.

There is certainly an institutional difference between the State and the party. How is the institutional distance between the President of a Party and the Prime Minister of a State bridged in the same person? Through the same reference to the abstract generality of the 'people,' the second, symbolic, level of representation, mediated by the intermediary, the electorate.

So far, we have discovered three levels of representation, starting from the actual members of the party mechanism. At each level, representation becomes more abstract, while a greater degree of authority is assigned to a lesser number of individuals. At each level representation becomes more indirect, as the authoritarian structure narrows toward the summit. Each higher level contains more power and fewer obligations. This is logical, since both the party and the State are hierarchical structures. As Castoriadis has pointed out:

> "In a society where the people have been robbed of political power, and where this power is in the hands of a centralizing authority, the essential relationship between this authority and its subordinate organs (and, ultimately, the people) can be summed up as follows: Channels of communication from the base to the summit transmit only information, whereas channels from the summit to the base transmit decisions (plus, perhaps, that minimum of information deemed necessary for the understanding and execution of the decisions made at the summit). The whole setup expresses not only a monopoly of power by the summit - a monopoly of decision-making authority - but also a monopoly of

the conditions necessary for the exercise of power. The summit alone has the 'sum total' of information needed to evaluate and decide."[3]

Control of communication flows and selective transmission of information is essential to the preservation of hierarchical State authority. This was apparent during the 2015 referendum, and it also becomes apparent whenever general elections are held, and people vote to choose between parties whose inner workings and real aspirations are hidden from the public.

As we change levels, however, representation becomes more indirect, more volatile, more general, and tends to conceal the divergences and conflicts that lie in between, the horizontal tensions between the lower and upper levels of representation, but also the vertical tensions, between the temporarily governing party mechanism and the permanent State bureaucratic apparatus. Representative mechanisms tend to normalize the conflicts between party and government, party and state, government and society, by concealing or suppressing them.

According to political theorist Panayiotis Kondylis (1988), there is a dependence of military operations on the objective political conditions (the social-political dynamic of a society) and a subjugation of subjective politics (meaning actual political personalities) to the specifics of war. That means that there is primacy of objective political conditions over personal ambitions. Therefore, politicians do not, by definition, serve peace more than generals, nor is any pacifist political strategy capable of handling the objective amount of violence accumulated within a society. Politics resorts to warfare when politics is founded on warfare, when politics expresses the objectivity of a society subjugated to an oligarchic elite with no access to the monopoly of power.

The State as a mechanism of power stands on the frontline between the real source of political power and the circles that peculate it. This dynamic antithesis is not initially generated by wealth inequality, but from the monopolization of political power, the limitation of political decision making to the elite few. Wealth inequalities follow, hierarchical state institutions precede them, historically and logically. What Kondylis calls "objective politics" is, nevertheless, interwoven with "subjective politics." Dominant social imaginary significations define the legitimacy of public and private behaviour. Moreover, they inform personal emotions and psychic urges and regulate them in accordance to social norms. The actual point of divergence between objectivity and subjectivity is utterly indefinable.

Apart from violence, the mechanism for the elimination of social conflicts is political representation. Social conflicts spring from social exploitation, oppression and alienation, which are, at the same time, the conditions of oligarchy. The various political parties cannot claim central State power in the name of their own interests alone, nor can State authority be exercised in the name of the State per se. Since authority aims at general representation, authority tends to expand, and the State apparatus occupies all internal political decision-making space within the external boundaries imposed on it by other States.

The need for representation is maintained in all modern nation-state forms, at least as a ritual. In totalitarian states and one-party dictatorships, representation is absolute and unequivocal, the state and party coincide, and elections are rigged. Dissenters are persecuted and declared 'enemies of the People/Nation.' And yet, elections are still being held. Only in traditional hereditary monarchies and theocracies are there no elections. This happens because in traditional monarchies and theocracies power, authority and legitimacy come explicitly from above—God. Elections are held in constitutional monarchies where power stems explicitly from below, the people.

In all cases, the election result legitimizes and activates the symbolic identification of the three levels of representation, the electorate, the party and the State, with one political elite group, the cabinet.

Of course, the election results elect a Parliament, not a government. The government will be elected by an even smallest number of people, the leaders of the elected parliamentary parties. So, by adding another level of representation, a fourth, the parliamentary, we get to the real body of political authority, the cabinet and the prime minister. These are the actual people who will make effective political decisions and set the laws that will determine social life.

We can consider elections as a mechanism legitimating and unifying two distinct but complementary hierarchical structures—the State and the Party. They are not the only hierarchical mechanisms in modern society. Private capitalist enterprises, individual government agencies, educational institutions, financial banking mechanisms have a similar structure and their interrelations, common or opposing interests and hidden affiliations create the 'national' authority-power complex.

But the State and the Party are the mechanisms that monopolize explicit political power. As they complement each other, the State's monopoly of power is legitimized by the parties' oligopoly of representation. They are also parasitic mechanisms that reproduce themselves. Finally, they are expansive mechanisms, whose jurisdiction and function extend beyond their formal limits, until they meet an external boundary.

Where is democracy? Can it actually be reduced to the instance of vote casting of each voter, a motion that already represents not only himself but also the generality of the 'people/Nation'? Or was Jean Jacques Rousseau justified when he wrote the famous following passage from *The Social Contract*: "The people of England regard itself as free; but it is grossly mistaken; it is free only during the election of members of parliament. As soon as they are elected, slavery overtakes it, and it is nothing."

England never became a democracy and neither did the rest nation-States of the world. Formally, most liberal oligarchies are called 'Republics.' The most powerful republic in the world, the United States of America, was not founded as a democracy, as Yascha Mounk reminds us:

> "The United States was founded as a republic, not a democracy. As Alexander Hamilton and James Madison made clear in the Federalist Papers, the essence of this republic would consist—their emphasis—'In the total exclusion of the people, in their collective capacity, from any share' in the government. Instead, popular views would be translated into public policy through the election of representatives 'whose wisdom may' in Madison's words, 'best discern the true interest of their country.' That this radically curtailed the degree to which the people could directly influence the government was no accident."[4]

We must be able to distinguish democracy, which originated in ancient Greek autonomous cities from the republic, which originated from the Roman oligarchic administrative compromise between the patricians and the plebeians as regards res publica, the public thing.

In his *Politics* Aristotle, who was not a fervent supporter of direct democracy, associates democracy with the participation of the poor and the working classes in government, "a privilege which they only required under the extreme democracy."[5]

Extreme democracy for Aristotle was the direct democracy of the Athenian institution, the rule of the many, which he distinguished from oligarchy not by the number of the rulers but by the difference of principle between freedom and wealth:

> "Therefore, we should rather say that democracy is the form of government in which the free are rulers, and oligarchy in which the rich; it is only an accident that the free are the many and the rich are the few."

But Aristotle acknowledges that this criterion is not sufficient for a complete distinction between the two forms of government and he adds the principle of equality:

> "Democracy, for example, arises out of the notion that those who are equal in any respect are equal in all respects; because men are equally free, they claim to be absolutely equal. Oligarchy is based on the notion that those who are unequal in one respect are, in all respects, unequal; being unequal, that is, in property, they suppose themselves unequal absolutely. The democrats think that as they are equal they ought to be equal in all things, while the oligarchs, under the idea that they are unequal, claim too much, which is a form of inequality."[6]

So here we have the first radical difference between democracy and oligarchy. In democracy, equality is a condition of freedom, whereas in oligarchy, inequality of wealth justifies social inequality. Democracy, for Aristotle, has this founding principle, the combination and unbreakable interrelation between freedom and equality. Political freedom, liberty, is based on equality, and so is private and personal freedom. In contrast to modern thinkers that oppose freedom and equality, Aristotle knew all too well that, for personal freedom equality of all is necessary:

> "Every citizen, it is said, must have equality and therefore in a democracy the poor have more power than the rich, because there are more of them, and the will of the majority is supreme. This, then, is one note of liberty which all democrats affirm to be the principle of their state. Another is that a man should live as he likes. This, they say, is the privilege of a freeman, since, on the other hand, to not live as a man likes is the mark of a slave. This is the second characteristic of democracy, whence has arisen the claim of men to be ruled by none, if possible, or, if this is impossible, to rule and be ruled in turns; and so, it contributes to the freedom based upon equality."[7]

This was not just Aristotle's opinion. Similarly, the Attic orators, whose words were heard in the general assembly, the *ekklesia* and directly influenced political decisions or in courts and determined legal decisions, warn against the evils of inequality. Lysias considers equality an essential characteristic of democracy, which is "equal to all," while Aeschines identifies the inequality with injustice. Isocrates renounces inequality as well as the favourability toward the rich or the contempt toward the poor in front of the public court, while he stresses the importance of the fact that the citizens are also the judges, selected by lot, which interconnects the political and judicial aspects of equality:

> "Besides, it would be a most shocking state of affairs if in a democratic state we should not all enjoy equal rights; and if, while judging ourselves worthy of holding office, yet we should deprive ourselves of our legal rights; and if in battle we should all be willing to die for our democratic form of government and yet, in our votes as judges, especially favour men of property."[8]

Aristotle also correlated judicial and political power in his definition of the citizen, who is "whoever is able to participate in political and judicial power, we say that he is a citizen of that city, and a city on the other is, so to speak, the whole of such people who are enough to ensure self-sufficiency in their lives."⁹ And, later on, he added: "And a citizen is one who shares in governing and being governed." This is the essence of communal self-governance, since communal un-governance is impossible.

Consequently, in democracy there is no concealment of social conflict, but social control of wealth and the economy. Even in antiquity, when the question of economic competition did not put private property or wealth inheritance into question, democratic equality was also a countermeasure to the power of the rich.

Of course, ancient democracy suffered from other inequalities that remained unchallenged until the revolutions of modernity. Castoriadis highlights the limits and failures of ancient democracy:

> "Nevertheless, explicit self-institution never became for them the principle of political activity encompassing the social institution in its totality. Property was never really challenged, any more than was the status of women, not to mention slavery. Ancient democracy aimed at achieving, and it did achieve, the effective self-government of the community of free adult males, and it touched to the least extent possible the received social and economic structures. Only the philosophers (a few Sophists in the fifth century, Plato in the fourth) went any further."[10]

Modern direct democratic forms, the Communes, the Workers' Councils, the free communities, have deepened the issue of political equality by calling for the social equality of all people. Ancient democracy imploded because of its refusal to universalize the rights of the citizen.

But after the 1871 Commune in Paris, the emancipatory horizon of the project of direct democracy was opened up both in depth and width, encompassing the whole of society. That means everybody that was not a member of the State apparatus that delimits society. Kristin Ross, who wrote an excellent book regarding the Parisian Commune, entitled *Communal Luxury*, told us:

"The workers' movement represents a very narrow kind of perspective, compared to something like the commune form, which is very socially inclusive. It includes all people. It includes unemployed people, it includes babies, it includes animals, it includes all the parameters of social life. For that reason, I think it is more politically rich as a recurrent vernacular form whose history we can trace."[11]

So, we can conclude that contemporary republican regimes do not fall under the classic definitions of democracy, but under those of oligarchy. But why they are also called Representative/Parliamentary "democracies," which forces us to adopt the opposite designation, i.e. Direct Democracy?

The legitimacy of contemporary oligarchic regimes cannot be explicitly based on wealth distinctions, since their power is nominally derived from the people. The regime itself is not the offspring of ancient democracy, not even the Roman oligarchy that spawned the theoretical models of republicanism. It is the offspring of the autocratic monarchical State and the Church hierarchy of the late Middle Ages. Duplicity, ideology, the distinction between discourse and action are already an element of the Christian imaginary. But it is also a result of the great revolutions that forced the State to cover its mechanisms behind expanded representational structures. Since the imaginary of God-derived authority collapsed and power was nominally attributed to the people, the State had to re-establish its authority in terms of the 'Will of the people,' without however the people gaining power—consequently, this had to be done indirectly by reducing living society to the abstract historical generality of the "Nation."

Let's look at some of the structural anti-democratic features of the modern liberal oligarchy:

1. The separation of Power from Society through the identification of Power with the State. This is standardized by the election of non-revocable representatives, the State monopoly on violence and taxation, and the separation between public and private, with the public attributed to the State and the private attributed not to the individual, but to the capitalist mechanisms that infiltrate and organize private life.

2. The separation of Equality and Freedom, which is a remnant of the medieval imaginary. In the Middle Ages there were 'freedoms,' which meant privileges of different guilds and groups that belonged to specific social strata in the dominant hierarchy, but not freedom.

3. The interplay of various interest groups, lobbies and authorities, either formal or informal that promotes secrecy, manipulation of information and the complete opacity of decision making.

4. he pursuit of sovereignty over nature and the destruction of the natural and social environment driven by the imaginary of capital growth.

And yet, this regime insists on being called a "democracy." Why? Because, if something threatens it, this is direct democracy. Which is not a utopia, but a feasible system of political institutions that allow for everyone's participation, self-government and autonomy.

This is the horizon of a common future opened up by contemporary social movements, a horizon, whatsoever, that cannot be sustained by the movements themselves, but involves the broader participation of society beyond resistance, toward direct—democratic institution building.

The Temporality of Autonomy

In 1781, in his newly published magnum opus, *The Critique of pure Reason*, German philosopher Immanuel Kant proposed three questions that define "all the interest of my reason": "What can I know?", "What must I do?" and "What may I hope?"[12] His attempt to an answer constituted his system of transcendental idealism, which however, did not resolve the practical question of ethics, besides delimiting human reason to a priori anthropic epistemological boundaries beyond which lies the utterly unknowable realm of the thing in itself, Ding-an-sich. The Kantian system was, however, delimiting itself within the limited boundaries of individual consciousness, perception and reason, obscuring the empirical facts that no person is born isolated, no infant possesses actually the faculties of a grown human, that every adult individual has passed through a process of socialization that has transmitted certain values and that ethics is a matter of collective life.

To resolve the practical issues of ethics, Kant resorted to the concept of a necessary categorical imperative, inherited a priori to each individual human being:

> "If I think of a hypothetical imperative in general, then I do not know beforehand what it will contain until the condition is given to me. But if I think of a categorical imperative, then I know directly what it contains. For since besides the law, the imperative contains only the necessity of the maxim, that it should accord with this law, but the law contains no condition to which it is limited, there remains nothing left over with which the maxim of the action is to be in accord, and this accordance alone is what the imperative really represents necessarily. The categorical imperative is thus only a single one, and specifically this: Act only in accordance with that maxim through which you can at the same time will that it become a universal law."[13]

This conception, however, re-inserts deity into the system, under the guise of transcendental moral reason, because Kant acknowledges that people are not purely reasonable creatures. If they were, his Critiques would not be necessary. The a priori synthetic proposition of the categorical imperative and the moral law gives rise to a posteriori emergence of God and religion on the grounds of inherent morality.

> "But if, now, the strictest obedience to moral laws is to be considered the cause of the ushering in of the highest good (as end), then, since human capacity does not suffice for bringing about happiness in the world proportionate to worthiness to be happy, an omnipotent moral Being must be postulated as ruler of the world, under whose care this [balance] occurs. That is, morality leads inevitably to religion."[14]

Hence Kant, who reintroduced and advocated the value of human autonomy by proclaiming: "[a]utonomy then is the basis of the dignity of human and of every rational nature,"[15] feels the need to return to the idea of God in order to ground justice. His individual-centred philosophy loses sight of the broader horizon of the social-historical, whence all human beings construct their perceptions of the world and themselves, individuality itself being a social-historical creation.

We turn to Cornelius Castoriadis, who introduced the concept of a social-historical ontological field, distinguished from both the psychical and the physical realms, where "existence is signification."[16] However distinct, these ontological fields are intermingled within the magma of time, since "being is time—and not in the horizon of time."[17] This means that we should turn our attention to temporality and the temporal modes of human co-existence and social becoming in order to clarify the questions of knowledge, morals and aspiration.

According to Castoriadis, the three Kantian questions and philosophical questioning, per se, can only appear in the social-historical field, the particular historical temporality of every society, both in its historiographical and political dimension. The emergence of philosophical inquiry has specific social-historical preconditions and is closely linked to the emergence of the project of direct democracy in ancient Greek cities. The precondition of philosophy is the breaking down of social imaginary closure by the democratic creation of a free public space, where the questioning of tradition can aspire the conscious and collective transformation of social time.

For Castoriadis, every society creates an identitary, repetitive representation of social time. This deals with the measurable, quantifiable dimensions of time, the time of clocks. But this identitary dimension of quantity does not include the multiple dimensions of time that are beyond measurability. It fails to take into consideration the quality of time, the significant content of every temporal instant. So, there is also an implicit imaginary dimension of social time, which gives particular meaning or value to quantifiable partitions of time. Castoriadis argues that there are many categories of time, such as the physical, the social-historical, the inner psychical, that intersect and converge between the individual and society, but are mutually irreducible.

The unconscious human psyche—the constant current of representations, images, urges, which Castoriadis calls "radical imagination"—creates its own primal psychical temporality, that differs from natural time because it does not share the temporal attributes of irreversibility and succession. However, the psychical monad, the unconscious core of subjectivity, must conform to the structures and norms of the dominant social time, the time created by the collective social imaginary, in order for the individual to survive, both physically and mentally. Individual radical imagination and the social imaginary are the two distinct, though interdependent, creative matrices of the social-historical. Every conscious individual is already a social institution, and conscious subjective time is located at the interface between psychical and social time. Language and education impress on individual imagination the predominant social significations that constitute the meanings and values of social reality.

Social institution determines the content of the distinction between meaning and validity, the distinction between the meaning of a proposition (whether it states something meaningful, either true or false) and the validity a proposition (whether it is true or false). That is, for the individual, reality exists only with the meaning that society invests on it.

As everyone knows, the natural daylight, the natural duration of each day, varies from season to season and from place to place. But the regular common hours of our clocks, sharing the exact same duration and repetition, which were conceived by the medieval monastic congregation and later dominated the social temporality of modernity, signify the imaginary autonomy from the natural flow of time and the modern human desire for sovereignty over nature. The clock (first mechanical and later digital) stands between the medieval feudal and the modern capitalist worlds like a bridge and a form of realization of new imaginary significations.

Georg Simmel complained in 1902 that "the mechanism of life in the metropolis is therefore not understood without classifying all activities and reciprocal relations, in the strictest sense, into a stable, supra-subjective form of time."[18] This supra-subjective time-frame is the divided labour-hours of the productive industrial processes.

Political time is the time of decision-making and decision-enactment as regards public issues. It seems to be dependent on the degree of separation of power from society by the structures of authority. The issue of political time is therefore inextricably linked to the issue of power. The control over social temporality by the dominant capitalist mechanisms, the subordination of politics to the economy, is based on the deeper separation of power and society, manifested as the identification of social power and State authority. This identification is expressed by the alienation of society within its own institutions that become separate authorities which perpetuate social inequality.

The conceptual identification of Power/State from the socialist perspective led to the interpretation of the revolution as a coup, as a seizure of state power.

From the point of view of political republicanism, this identification led to the distinction between two forms of liberty, one negative and the other positive.

Isaiah Berlin, in 1958 clearly distinguished between the positive and negative aspects of liberty. Negative liberty "involves an answer to the question: What is the area within which the subject—a person or group of persons—is or should be left to do or be what he is able to do or be, without interference by other persons."[19]

That is to say, the extent of individual freedom over state power. Positive liberty "is involved in the answer to the question: What, or who, is the source of control or interference that can determine someone to do, or be, this rather than that? The two questions are clearly different, even though the answers to them may overlap."[20]

Namely, it identifies the source of authority and determines participation in the institutions of authority. We could attribute positive liberty to the apparatus of the State and negative liberty to society. The separation and mutual opposition of the two forms, entail the separation of society from power, that is, the identification of the State and the power, while their complementarities indicate that they constitute a common political sphere of influence, where the primacy of positive liberty reproduces social division, since it constitutes the authority of State-power.

Castoriadis explicitly disagrees with the position of Berlin. For Castoriadis, "negative liberties" are not at all negative, although they are partial and defensive: Even Isaiah Berlin's qualification that they are "negative" is inadequate. The right to assemble, to seek redress of grievances, to publish a newspaper or a book is not 'negative': the exercise of such rights comprises one component of social and political life and can have, and even necessarily does have, important effects on the latter.[21]

As regards "positive liberty," Castoriadis replaces it with the notion of an "effective liberty" dependent on the participation of all citizens in power. However, he acknowledges that Berlin would consider such democratic participation "potentially totalitarian," due to his confusion between the common good and happiness. This confusion that is deeply rooted in the republican political imaginary obscures the limits between private and public, elevating the State to the summit of the guardian of "social happiness." However, happiness is not a public matter, but a personal affair. If I love someone who does not love me back, no political regime can force me to be happy. This promise of happiness is actually a veil of heteronomy, an undemocratic aspiration that negates autonomy.

> "The end of politics is not happiness, which can only be a private matter; it is freedom, or individual and collective autonomy. [...] Happiness belongs to the private sphere and to the private/public sphere. It does not belong to the public/public sphere as such. Democracy, as regime of freedom, certainly excludes any sort of 'happiness' that could be rendered, in itself or in its 'means', politically obligatory. Yet, even more than this can be said: No philosophy can define at any moment a substantive 'common good'—and no politics can wait for philosophy to define such a common good before acting."[22]

Contrary to happiness which belongs to the private/private (domestic) sphere and the private/public (social) sphere, the common good belongs to the public/public (political) sphere, the political dimension of public space and public time. On the one hand, the question of what is good for the public can only be raised within public space and time, in the space and time of political decisions concerning the common good. On the other hand, all issues concerning public space and time, and in particular the political dimension of public space and time, that is, power, cannot be raised unless there is an understanding of the common good that goes beyond individual happiness:

"Ontological analysis shows that no society can exist without a more or less certain definition of shared substantive values, common social goods (the "public goods" of economists constitute only a portion thereof). These values make up an essential part of the social imaginary significations as they are each time instituted. They define the push of each society."[23]

Consequently, the sense of the common good constitutes the common future dimension of social time, the common horizon of expectations and its relation to a common past, a common space of experience. In that way, we can understand that if we define individual and social autonomy, freedom, as the common good, we project a different future horizon of expectations, rooted in a different past space of experiences, a different tradition that if we define the common good as 'national glory' or 'capitalist development.' Whereas any formal identification of the common good with private happiness is a trait of heteronomy, which pragmatically leads to the dominant elites identifying the common good to their private happiness at society's cost.

The emergence of democracy, as direct democracy, is tantamount to the emergence of politics as actual common politics, politics aimed at individual and social autonomy. Indeed, the concept of autonomy is linked to the emergence of democratic cities as autonomous political entities vis-à-vis the great empires and authoritarian states. Democracy places politics in the epicentre of public space, via the potential participation of all individuals in power. Doing so, it raises questions that cannot be resolved by appealing to traditional representations of the common good. It opens up a public space for philosophy.

But it is not only that common lineage that links philosophy and democracy; there is a more important connection. It is the connection and coherence of theory and action within the political praxis. It makes the participation in direct democratic rule at the same time an education in direct democratic ethos.

This does not mean that politics can be reduced to a philosophy or that a philosophy can dictate a policy, since political practice changes reality and so transforms the objects of theory. But it means that politics and philosophy share the same social-historical preconditions, that is, the institution of an effective, common liberty to radically challenge accepted norms and established laws.

Jean Luc Nancy has argued that a community is a relation among a plurality of singularities that constitutes a form of ethos and praxis.[24] However, there is also an important temporal element that defines both the ethos and the praxis, an element of historicity, which needs to be made public and explicit in order to prevent the formation of implicit inequalities based on experience. This stresses the need for archive and education institutions that solidify the limited common time created by social movements into a public time for the collective representation of the past. Without it, the basic features of direct democracy, self-reflection and self-limitation, are excluded.

Democratic institution presupposes the creation of a truly common public/public space, a place for political decision-making and bridging the public-private opposition with the active involvement of citizens in decision-making and implementation.

The creation of a public space implies the creation of a free public time, which Castoriadis defines as "the emergence of a dimension where the collectivity can inspect its own past as the result of its own actions, and where an indeterminate future opens up as domain for its activities."[25]

In this sense, the creation of free public time implies the transformation of society's relation with tradition. In a traditional heteronomous society, as Marx and Engels famously proclaimed, "the past dominates the present";[26] on the contrary, in an autonomous society tradition is a source of inspiration and reinvention, open to critique and transformation.

Therefore, an autonomous society creates the demand for a new kind of de jure validity of power against the de facto validity of authority. Direct democracy presupposes a common education on the responsibility of collective self-government and the actualization of the potentialities of public space and time. Since there is no guiding authority, actual co-existence within the free public sphere, is at the same time an education in autonomy that constitutes a common ethos.

Modern society is a fragmented world, where local enclosed societies are overwhelmed by a potentially global cultural, political and economic power network. Where, under a dominant and incomplete global temporality defined by the multinational ruling elite, radically different local social temporalities coexist, violently disturbed by the seismic vibrations of the global economy and pressurized by the neoliberal destruction of the plant.

On the one hand, we are witnessing a homogenization of the dominant social time on a global level, along with the globalization of financial transactions, the internationalization of State policies and the exhaustive exploitation of natural resources. However, this homogenization does not cover the local aspects of imaginary time, holidays and symbols, although it erodes and incorporates them. Individual subjective time is also being colonized by the forces of production, consumption and entertainment.

On the other hand, social movements, rebellions and autonomous communities that have appeared in the 21st century around the globe, create other forms of public time, both on the periphery, and within the centres of the dominant social temporality. That is, different forms of education, coexistence, assembly, production and political life, which combine equality with democratic participation in the form of horizontal social networks.

The contradictory coexistence of these currents explodes in social conflicts and political tensions; while the internet creates a new form of global digital time. We live in an era of deep societal crisis, a crisis of significations, a crisis of representation, a crisis of identification, but also a crisis of survival, an ecological crisis, under the unprecedented specter of extinction.

Should we attempt an abstract classification of the strata of contemporary global social temporality, we might come up with a rough diagram of an ever-changing becoming, like a cross-section of a planet.

On the surface lie the international networks of established social temporality; that is the time of international transactions and formal external State relations, characterized by the continuity of transnational institutions and the acceleration of capitalist markets in an ever-expanding multi-procedural Present. Externally it appears continuous, interconnected, unlimited and unified. It is based on the quantifiable, commonly measurable temporal dimension. Its main temporal feature is the expanding continuity of capitalist expansion.

If we examine it closely, however, we will discover that internally it is fragmented in differentiated and conflicting national temporal units or hubs. Every hub of the global network comprises a semi-closed local temporality, formulated by the tradition of authority that determines the relations between the State and the people. Formal local temporality is structured along formal processes of social identification and political representation and is characterized by repetitiveness (like national holidays, annual celebrations, elections) and the virtual linearity of an imaginary common (national) history pointing to the Past. It is the temporality of national myths that obscure the origins of the nation-State, producing a kind of imaginary, alternate history in order to justify State authority. It is also the temporality of social procedures controlled by State authority, like taxation, education, and military service. Its main temporal feature is the repetitive duration, the repetition and conservation of the status quo. It creates the continuous univocal historicity of the dominant national narrative.

Against that, we can see the temporality created by the social movements. Externally, it seems discontinuous and fragmented, marked by local political events and uprisings that constitute a temporal field divided by instant ruptures of the dominant local temporality. However, if we look closely, we find the situation reversed, since it is unified by multiple associative connections that transcend borders and constitutes a different network of solidarity, commonality and resistance.

This disrupts local social temporality, upends its repetitiveness and breaks down its continuity. It is the indeterminate temporality of innovation.

As such, its temporal specificity is the event (or kairos), which however singular, is not isolated. A succession of similar events produces a different kind of non-linear disruptive duration, which is the history of the project of social liberation alongside currents of solidarity and mutual recognition. It is within this imaginary temporal dimension that we feel connected with the revolutions and social movements that are distant from us, in time or space, but also seem to concern our present situation. Within this disruptive duration we find the common causes and common aspirations that unify particular social movements to the historical project of autonomy, like steps toward a common future.

The main temporal features of social temporality per se are continuity, repetition, conservation, against the event, rupture, innovation, that produce two different kind of temporal durations. The repetitive duration of instituted authority imposed against the disruptive duration of instituting society.

Regardless that the first is oriented toward the Past and the other toward the Future, it is only in the Present that potentialities become realities. The present is the ontological locus of co-existence, action and consequence, the present is our actual common temporal plane, and the present is the link between the imaginary representations of the past and the imaginary aspirations of the future. But which present is more real? The one formulated by the dominant temporal systemic processes or the one determined by the radical political events created by social movements? We should be wary that none of them is exclusively real. It is rather their conjunction, collision and confrontation that give our present its real wholeness, like a crossroads that simultaneously divides and unifies diverging and opposite paths that lead to completely contrasting directions or future timelines. It creates the discontinuous multivocal historicity of social struggles.

Democratic ecological collectivities, which explicitly combine the project of social ecology with the project of direct democracy, must move beyond the collegial and create institutions of education and communication marked by cohesive political activity across a wider social-historical field.

We may, perhaps, schematically designate four moments of political time to autonomous collectivities. They all involve and presuppose a public conflict with established authorities.

The first moment, when the collectivity first opens up to society, involves the initial creation of a broader social environment. The creation of free social spaces seems to be the limit of this moment. If this limit is not exceeded through connection with broader society, free social spaces can become self-referential and, sooner or later, collapse internally.

If this limit is exceeded, then we proceed to the next moment, which can only occur within society—that is, beyond the collective since the activity of the collectivity exceeds the collectivity itself. It involves the co-creation of networks of solidarity, communication and action on local, regional and global scales. It involves the creation of free open public spaces. It means creating a limited public space-time for communication and a limited public space-time for political decisions.

Opening a free public space presupposes a break with state and capitalist mechanisms. It is an initial step. The second step is explicit self-determination to enact institution-building through direct democracy and public deliberation, in order to realize autonomy in terms of social functions and a complete rupture with the State.

We can imagine explicit self-determination if we consider a self-sufficient local network that is not subject to state or capitalist taxation or oversight. It constitutes a fundamental division between free communities and the State. However, it is not yet an autonomous society until a complete public space is established along with a public time for free communication, yet with limited public space-time for political decision-making.

The experience of the revolution of Rojava shows us that second and third-order institutions are necessary for the self-administration of a territory in terms of direct democracy and gender equality.[27] The horizontality of decision-making and political power distribution can be combined with institutions that facilitate the co-ordination of decisions and enable their enactment on larger social scales than local units.

The democratic character of a con-federation can only be ensured by the effective control of second-order institutions (councils) by the horizontal base collectivities (assemblies) and the exercise of the power of political decision-making exclusively from the base, according to the principles of individual autonomy and equality. Between the horizontal base network and the vertical second-order institutions a set of functions and rules should be explicitly established that can ensure direct democracy and the autonomy of local units:

1. All "delegates" of the base assemblies to the second-order councils should be directly revocable by the assemblies themselves and with a clear mandate by them. As Castoriadis has argued, direct democracy implies "the maximum amount of autonomy and self administration for the local units."[28]
2. Transparency and critique of political decisions and subsequent collective actions should be guaranteed by public deliberation and the promotion of free speech within the public space of decision-making.
3. The dominant hierarchical flow of information, which consists of a double one-way manner, where information flows upwards, from the base to the summit, and decisions are transmitted downwards, from the summit to the base, must be reversed. Direct democracy demands an open leveled, horizontal field of both information and decision and

an established two-way open channel of communication between the base and second-order institutions. Castoriadis writes accordingly: "Two-way communications will be instaurated between the 'base' and the 'summit.' One of the essential tasks of central bodies, including the council government, will be to collect, transmit, and disseminate information conveyed to them by local groups." [29]

In order for social autonomy to be realized, society must have the power to explicitly re-create its central institutions, namely politics, justice, and education, in a democratic and equalitarian manner. The people, as free individuals, must be able to establish laws by means of open public deliberation and through the establishment of direct democracy. This would presuppose abolishment of the State and subordination of the economy to democratic politics. But it also presupposes the psychical transformation of the individual to an autonomous, reflective and deliberative subjectivity. It presupposes a democratic education that cannot be separated from the experience of direct democracy in practice, via the praxis of autonomy. It also means establishing a complete public space and time for free communication, and a complete public space and time for political decision and action.

Back in 1969, Ecology Action East—a collective that included Murray Bookchin—published a statement that called for a revolutioned, "which will produce politically independent communities whose boundaries and populations will be defined by a new ecological consciousness." It is now evident that this ecological consciousness is also a political consciousness that demands a self-reflecting direct democracy against hierarchy and economic growth—one that combines ecological and social struggles within the project of building a democratic ecological society.

However, there is an additional temporal feature that pressurizes our present situation, which has never been apparent in the past. It is the feature of urgency, and urgency imposed by the destruction of our natural habitat and the planetary ecosystem, which brings humanity to the brink of self-destruction and pushes innumerable forms of life beyond the edge of extinction. This urgency, a unique feature of the era that is now called "Anthropocene," corrodes every form of social temporality, presenting us with an unthinkable horizon of no-future.

In November 2019, the UN warned that the chances to halt global warming are narrowing down each moment. According to UN's assessments carbon emissions should be decreased by 7.6% annually, whereas in reality they keep increasing, by 1.5% in 2018.[30] Before this urgency, all other systemic temporal features of duration, repetition, and reproduction collapse.

This is the time when the project of social ecology becomes a necessary supplement of the project of social autonomy and burdens social movement with the responsibility of appealing to the universal and global, besides the particular and local. No local victory over systemic authorities is now nearly enough, even for the victors; a complete overthrow of the capitalist and nation-state system seems like the necessary condition for the survival of humanity in terms of equality, dignity, freedom, and common good.

NOTES

1. Franz Fannon, *The Wretched of the Earth*, New York: Grove Press, 1961.
2. Immanuel Wallerstein – Etienne Balibar, *Ambiguous Identities: Race, Nation, Class*, London: Verso Books, 1991.
3. The Castoriadis Reader, p. 58.
4. https://www.theatlantic.com/magazine/archive/2018/03/america-is-not-a-democracy/, last retrieved 2/12/2019, 15:38.
5. Aristotle, *Politics*.
6. Aristotle, *Politics*, 1301a.
7. Aristotle, *Politics*.
8. Isocrates, *Against Lochites*, 20.
9. Aristotle, *Politics* C '1, 3-4 / 6/12.
10. Cornelius Castoriadis, "The Idea of the Revolution", interview, *Thesis Eleven*, 26, 1990.
11. *A coffee with Kristin Ross on the continuations of May '68*, Athens: Babylonia, 2018.
12. Immanuel Kant, *Critique of pure Reason*, trans. Marcus Weigelt, London: Penguin Classics, 2007.
13. Immanuel Kant, *Groundwork for the Metaphysics of Morals*, trans. Allen W. Wood, Yale University Press, 2002, p. 37 [Ak 4: 421]
14. Immanuel Kant, *Religion within the limits of Reason alone*, Harper One, 2008, Preface to the 1st edition, note 2
15. Immanuel Kant, *Fundamental Principles of the Metaphysics of Morals*, Dover Philosophical Classics, 2005.
16. Castoriadis, *World in Fragments*, p. 11.
17. Cornelius Castoriadis, *Fait e a faire*, Paris: Points.
18. Georg Simmel, «The metropolis and mental life», in *The Sociology of Georg Simmel*, New York: Free Press 1976.

19 Isaiah Berlin, *Two concepts of liberty*, lecture on October 31, 1958. Published in the volume *Four Essays on Liberty*, Oxford: Clarendon Press 1969.
20 Ibid.
21 Cornelius Castoriadis, "Democracy as Procedure, Democracy as Regime", in the volume *The Rising Tide of Insignificancy*, trans. and published anonymously, available at: http://www.notbored.org/RTI.html, last retrieved 26/11/2019, 21: 08.
22 Ibid.
23 Ibid.
24 Jean -Luc Nancy, *Being Singular-Plural*, Stanford: Stanford University Press, 2000.
25 *The Castoriadis Reader*, p. 281.
26 Karl Marx – Friedrich Engels, *The Communist Manifesto*.
27 Michael Knapp, Anja Flach & Ercan Ayboğa, *Revolution in Rojava. Democratic Autonomy and Women's Liberation in Syrian Kurdistan*, London: Pluto Books, 2016.
28 The Castoriadis Reader, p.56.
29 The Castoriadis Reader, p. 58.
30 https://www.independent.co.uk/environment/climate-change-global-warming-carbon-emissions-neutral-targets-un-report-a9218181.html , last retrieved 27/11/2019, 14:28.

BIBLIOGRAPHY

I. Political Ecology and Social Change

Biehl, Janer. *Ecology or Catastrophe: The Life of Murray Bookchin*, Oxford: Oxford University Press, 2015

Biehl, Janet & Staudenmaier, Peter, *Ecofascism Revisited: Lessons from the German Experience*, Porsgrunn: New Compass Press, 2011

Boehm, Christopher. Hierarchy in the Forest: The Evolution of Egalitarian Behavior, London: Harvard University Press, 1999

Bookchin, Murray. *Our Synthetic Environment*, Eastford: Martino Fine Books, 2018

Bookchin, Murray. *Post-Scarcity Anarchism* (Second Edition), Montreal: Black Rose Books, 1986

Bookchin, Murray. *Re-enchanting Humanity*, New York: Cassell, 1995

Bookchin, Murray. *Social Ecology and Communalism*, Oakland: AK Press, 2006

Bookchin, Murray. *The Limits of the City*, Montreal: Black Rose Books, 1985

Bookchin, Murray. *The Murray Bookchin Reader* (Edited by Janet Biehl), Montreal: Black Rose Books, 1999

Bookchin, Murray. *The Next Revolution: Popular Assemblies and the Promise of Direct Democracy*, London: Verso, 2015

Bookchin, Murray. *The Philosophy of Social Ecology: Essays on Dialectical Naturalism*, Montreal: Black Rose Books, 1996

Bookchin, Murray. *Urbanization without Cities,* Montreal: Black Rose Books, 1992

Clastres, Pierre. *Society Against the State: Essays in Political Anthropology*, New York: Zone Books, 1989

Castoriadis, Cornelius. *A Society Adrift*. unauthorized translation, 2010 (Available online at http://www.notbored.org/ASA.pdf)

Castoriadis, Cornelius. *The Castoriadis Reader*, Oxford: Blackwell Publishers, 1997

Castoriadis, Cornelius. *The Rising Tide of Insignificancy: The Big Sleep.* unauthorized translation, 2003 (Available online at http://www.notbored.org/RTI.pdf)

Eiglad, Eirik. *Communalism as Alternative*, Porsgrunn: New Compass Press, 2014

Eiglad, Eirik (Editor). *Social Ecology and Social Change*, Porsgrunn: New Compass Press, 2015

ENTITLE Fellows. *Political Ecology for Civil Society*, ENTITLE Network, 2016

Gorz, Andre. *Capitalism, Socialism, Ecology,* London: Verso, 2013

Gorz, Andre. *Dear motorist: The social ideology of the motor car*, London: Loin Cloth Press, 1998

Graeber, David. *The Utopia of Rules*, London: Melville House, 2015

Harvey, David. *Rebel Cities: From the Right to the City to the Urban Revolution*, London: Verso, 2012

Hawley, Joshua & Roussopoulos, Dimitri. *Villages in Cities: Community Land Ownership, Cooperative Housing, and the Milton Parc Story*, Montreal: Black Rose Books, 2019

Heller, Chaia. *Ecology of Everyday Life: Rethinking the Desire for Nature*, Montreal: Black Rose Books, 1999

Internationalist Commune of Rojava. *Make Rojava Green Again: Building an Ecological Society*, London: Dog Section Press, 2018

Jacobs, Jane. *The Death and Life of Great American Cities*, London: Vintage Press, 1992

Jacobs, Jane. *The Nature of Economics*, London: Vintage Press, 2001

Kadalie, Modibo (Editor). *Pan-African Social EcologySpeeches, Conversations, and Essays*, Atlanta: On Our Own Authority! Press, 2019

Klein, Naomi. *This Changes Everything: Capitalism vs. the Climate*, New York: Simon & Schuster, 2014

Lefebvre, Henri. *The Urban Revolution*, Minnesota: University of Minnesota Press, 2003

Montgomery, Charles. *Happy City: Transforming our Lives Through Urban Design*, London: Penguin Books, 2015

Morris, Brian. *Anthropology, Ecology, and Anarchism: A Brian Morris Reader*, Oakland: PM Press, 2015

Morris, Brian. *Pioneers of Ecological Humanism: Mumford, Dubos and Bookchin*, Montreal: Black Rose Books, 2017

Ocalan, Abdullah. *Democratic Confederalism*, London: International Initiative Edition, 2011

Ostrom, Elinor. *Governing the Commons: The Evolution of Institutions for Collective Action (Political Economy of Institutions and Decisions)*, Cambridge: Cambridge University Press, 1990

Price, Andy. *Recovering Bookchin: Social Ecology and the Crises of our Time*, Porsgrunn: New Compass Press, 2012

Robinson, Eric W. *The First Democracies: Early Popular Government Outside Athens*, Stuttgart: Franz Steiner Verlag, 1997

Roussopoulos, Dimitri. *Political Ecology: System Change not Climate Change*, Montreal: Black Rose Books, 2018

Roussopoulos, Dimitri. *The Rise and Fall of Cities: Montreal, Toronto, Vancouver and other Cities*, Montreal: Black Rose Books, 2017

Tokar, Brian. *Earth for Sale: Reclaiming Ecology in the Age of Corporate Greenwash*, Boston: South End Press, 1999

Tokar, Brian. *Redesigning Life?: The Worldwide Challenge to Genetic Engineering*, London: Zed Books, 2001

Tokar, Brian. *The Green Alternative: Creating An Ecological Future*, Gabriola: New Society Publishers, 1994

Tokar, Brian. *Toward Climate Justice: Perspectives on the Climate Crisis and Social Change* (Second Edition), Porsgrunn: New Compass Press, 2014

Venturini Federico & Degirmenci, Emet & Morales, Inés (Editors). *Social Ecology and the Right to the City: Toward Ecological and Democratic Cities*, Montreal: Black Rose Books, 2019

Weil, Simone. *The Need for Roots*, London: Routledge, 2002

Wright, Erik Olin. *Envisioning Real Utopias*, London: Verso, 2010

II. Theoretical Outlines of Direct Democracy

A "Socialisme ou Barbarie" Anthology: Autonomy, Critique and Revolution in the Age of Bureaucratic Capitalism. unauthorized translation, 2017. (Available online on http://www.notbored.org/SouBA.pdf)

Adams, Suzi. *Cornelius Castoriadis: Key Concepts*. Sydney: Bloomsbury, 2014.

Arendt, Hannah. *The Origins of Totalitarianism.* San Diego: A Harvest Book, 1979.

Cardan, Paul (Castoriadis). *History and Revolution: a revolutionary critique of historical materialism.* Solidarity Pamphlet No38, 1971.

Castoriadis, Cornelius. *Window on the Chaos, Including "How I Didn't Become a Musician" (Beta Version).* unauthorized translation, 2015. (Available online on http://www.notbored.org/WoC.pdf)

Castoriadis, Cornelius. *Democracy and Relativism: Discussion with the "MAUSS" Group.* unauthorized translation, 2013. (Available online on http://www.notbored.org/DR.pdf)

Castoriadis, Cornelius. *Postscript on Insignificancy.* unauthorized translation, 2017. (Available online on http://www.notbored.org/PSRTI.pdf)

Castoriadis, Cornelius. *A Society Adrift.* unauthorized translation, 2010. (Available online on http://www.notbored.org/ASA.pdf)

Castoriadis, Cornelius. *Figures of the Thinkable (including "Passion and Knowledge").* unauthorized translation, 2005. (Available online on http://www.notbored.org/FTPK.pdf)

Castoriadis, Cornelius. *The Rising Tide of Insignificancy: The Big Sleep.* unauthorized translation, 2003. (Available online on http://www.notbored.org/RTI.pdf)

Castoriadis, Cornelius. *History as Creation.* Solidarity Pamphlet No.54, 1978.

Castoriadis, Cornelius. *Political and Social Writings Volume 1.* Minneapolis: University of Minnesota Press, 1988.

Castoriadis, Cornelius. *Political and Social Writings Volume 2.* Minneapolis: University of Minnesota Press, 1988.

Castoriadis, Cornelius. *Political and Social Writings Volume 3.* Minneapolis: University of Minnesota Press, 1993.

Castoriadis, Cornelius. *The Imaginary Institution of Society.* Cambridge: The MIT Press, 1998.

Castoriadis, Cornelius. *Workers' Councils and the Economics of a Self-Managed Society.* Fordsburg: Zabalaza Books, 2007.

Curtis, David Ames (Editor). *The Castoriadis Reader.* Oxford: Blackwell Publishers, 1997.

Eriksen, Erik Oddvar & Weigard, Jarle: *Understanding Habermas: Communicative Action and Deliberative Democracy.* Oslo: Bloomsbury, 2004.

Karalis, Vrasridis(Editor). *Cornelius Castoriadis and Radical Democracy.* Leiden: Brill, 2014.

Klooger, Jeff. *Psyche, Society, Autonomy.* Leiden: Brill, 2009.

Latouche, Serge. *Farewell to Growth.* Oxford: Polity, 2009.

Lefort, Claude. *Democracy and Political Theory.* Cambridge: Polity Press, 1988.

Mouffe, Chantal(Editor). *Dimensions of Radical Democracy.* London: Verso, 1992.

Rousseau, Jean-Jacques. *The Social Contract.* Ware: Wordsworth Editions, 1998.

Roussopoulos, Dimitrios. *Political Ecology: Beyond Environmentalism.* Porsgrunn: New Compass Press, 2015.

Weil, Simone. *On the Abolition of all Political Party.* New York: New York Review of Books, 2013.

III. The Temporality of Social Movements

Augé, Mark. *Non-Places, introduction to an Anthropology of Supermodernity,* N. York: Verso, 1995

Bookchin, Murray. *Post-scarcity Anarchism,* Montreal: Black Rose Books, 1975

Bookchin, Murray. *Listen Marxist.* Available at: https://theanarchistlibrary.org/library/murray-bookchin-listen-marxist.pdf, last retrieved on 26/11/2019, 15:59

Bookchin, Murray. *The Communalist Project,* Harbinger Vol. 3 No. 1 2002. Available at: http://social-ecology.org/wp/2002/09/harbinger-vol-3-no-1-the-communalist-project/, last retrieved 30/11/2019, 10:29.

Castoriadis, Cornelius. *The Imaginary Institution of Society.* Cambridge: The MIT Press, 1998.

Castoriadis, Cornelius. *Political and social writings 3, 1961-1979,* ed. D. A. Curtis, Minneapolis: Minnesota Archive Editions, 1992.

Coppleston, Fredric. *A History of Philosophy,* vol. 7, N. York: Bloomsbury, 2013.

Curtis, David Ames(Editor). *The Castoriadis Reader.* Oxford: Blackwell Publishers, 1997.

Gibson, James. *The Ecological Approach to Visual Perception.* Boston: Houghton Mifflin Harcourt (HMH), 1979.

Giotitsas, Chris. *Open Source Agriculture, Grassroots Technology in the Digital Era,* Palgrave, 2019.

Goldman, Emma. *My disillusionment in Russia*, available at: https://autonomies.org/2017/07/the-russian-revolution-of-1917-emma-goldman/, last retrieved, 26/11/2019, 15:39.

Kioupkiolis, Alexandros. *The Common and Post-hegemonic Politics, Re-thinking social change*, Edinburgh: Edinburgh University Press, 2019.

Koselleck, Reinhart. *Futures Past*, New York: Columbia University Press, 2004.

Kostakis. Vasilis, "How to Reap the Benefits of the "Digital Revolution"? Modularity and the Commons" in *Halduskultuur* journal, 2019, available at: http://halduskultuur.eu/journal/index.php/HKAC/article/view/228/177

Lenin, V.I. Collected Works, Russ. ed., Vol. 7.

Lenin, V.I. *The State and Revolution, Collected Works*, Volume 25.

Lenin, V.I. *What Is to be done*, trans. Tim Delaney, The Marxist Online Archive, available at: https://www.marxists.org/archive/lenin/works/download/what-itd.pdf, last retrieved: 26/11/2019, 14:31

Luxemburg, Rosa. *The Rosa Luxemburg Reader*, ed. P. Hudis & K. Anderson, Monthly Review Press, 2004.

Papadatos – Anagnostopoulos, Dimosthenis. *Mavrokokkinos Decembris (Μαυροκόκκινος Δεκέμβρης)*, Athens: Topos, 2018.

Ranciére, Jacques. *A coffee with Jacques Ranciére beneath the Acropolis*, Athens: Babylonia, 2017.

Ricoeur, Paul. *Lectures on Ideology and Utopia*, New York: Columbia University Press, 1986.

Ross, Kristin. *A coffee with Kristin Ross on the continuations of May '68*, Athens: Babylonia, 2018.

Zuboff, Shoshana. *The Age of Surveillance Capitalism*, N. York: PublicAffairs, 2018.

IV. Conceptual Challenges

Aristotle, *Politics*, trans. Tr.J. Saunders, Penguin Classics, 1981.

Berlin, Isaiah. *Four Essays on Liberty*, Oxford: Clarendon Press, 1969.

Castoriadis, Cornelius, "The Idea of the Revolution", interview, *Thesis Eleven*, 26, 1990.

Castoriadis, Cornelius. *The Castoriadis Reader*, trans. D. A. Curtis, London: Wiley-Blackwell, 1997.

Castoriadis, Cornelius. *World in Fragments*, Stanford University Press, 1997.

Castoriadis, Cornelius, *The Rising Tide of Insignificancy*, translated and published anonymously, available at: http://www.notbored.org/RTI.html, last retrieved 26/11/2019, 21:08

Fannon, Franz, *The Wretched of the Earth*, Grove Press, 1961.

Isocrates, *Against Lochites,* Loeb Classical Library.

Kant, Immanuel. *Critique of pure Reason*, trans. Marcus Weigelt, London: Penguin Classics, 2007.

Kant, Immanuel. *Groundwork for the Metaphysics of Morals*, trans. Allen W. Wood, Yale University Press, 2002.

Kant, Immanuel. *Fundamental Principles of the Metaphysics of Morals*, Dover Philosophical Classics, 2005.

Kant, Immanuel. *Religion within the limits of Reason alone*, HarperOne, 2008.

Knapp, M., Flach, A., & Ayboğa, E., *Revolution in Rojava Democratic Autonomy and Women's Liberation in Syrian Kurdistan*, London: Pluto Books, 2016.

Nancy, Jean Luc. *Being Singular-Plural*, Stanford: Stanford University Press, 2000.

Simmel, Georg. *The Sociology of Georg Simmel*, New York: Free Press, 1976.

Wallerstein Immanuel – Balibar Etienne, *Race, Nation, Class, Ambiguous Identities,* London: Verso, 1988.

ALSO AVAILABLE FROM **BLACK ROSE BOOKS**

**Participatory Democracy:
Prospects for Democratizing Democracy**
D.I. Roussopoulos, C. George Benello, eds.
978-1-55164-225-3 cloth
978-1-55164-224-6 paper
978-1-55164-568-1 ebook

**Take the City:
Voices of Radical Municipalism**
Jason Toney, ed.
978-1-55164-729-6 cloth
978-1-55164-727-2 paper
978-1-55164-731-9 ebook

**Enlightenment and Ecology:
The Legacy of Murray Bookchin in the 21st Century**
Yavor Tarinski, ed.
978-1-55164-711-1 cloth
978-1-55164-709-8 paper
978-1-55164-713-5 ebook

**Villages in Cities: Community Land Ownership,
Cooperative Housing, and the Milton Parc Story**
Josh Hawley, D.I. Roussopoulos, eds.
978-1-55164-688-6 cloth
978-1-55164-687-9 paper
978-1-55164-689-3 ebook

Lightning Source UK Ltd.
Milton Keynes UK
UKHW021123160221
378867UK00006B/90